FAITH ENCOUNTERS OF THE THIRD KIND

Faith Encounters of the Third Kind

Humility and Hospitality in Interfaith Dialogue

David J. Brewer

FOREWORD BY
Veli-Matti Kärkkäinen

CASCADE *Books* · Eugene, Oregon

FAITH ENCOUNTERS OF THE THIRD KIND
Humility and Hospitality in Interfaith Dialogue

Copyright © 2021 David J. Brewer. All rights reserved. Except for brief quotations in critical publications or reviews, no part of this book may be reproduced in any manner without prior written permission from the publisher. Write: Permissions, Wipf and Stock Publishers, 199 W. 8th Ave., Suite 3, Eugene, OR 97401

Cascade Books
An Imprint of Wipf and Stock Publishers
199 W. 8th Ave., Suite 3
Eugene, OR 97401

www.wipfandstock.com

PAPERBACK ISBN: 978-1-7252-5846-4
HARDCOVER ISBN: 978-1-7252-5847-1
EBOOK ISBN: 978-1-7252-5848-8

Cataloguing-in-Publication data:

Names: Brewer, David J., author | Kärkkäinen, Veli-Matti, foreword writer

Title: Faith encounters of the third kind : humility and hospitality in interfaith dialogue / by David J. Brewer, foreword by Veli-Matti Kärkkäinen.

Description: Eugene, OR : Cascade Books, 2021 | Includes bibliographical references and index.

Identifiers: ISBN 978-1-7252-5846-4 (paperback) | ISBN 978-1-7252-5847-1 (hardcover) | ISBN 978-1-7252-5848-8 (ebook)

Subjects: LCSH: Dialogue—Religious aspects. | Religions—Relations. | Christianity and other religions. | Peace—Religious aspects. | Religious pluralism.

Classification: LCC BL410 B74 2021 (print) | LCC BL410 (ebook)

Scripture quotations, unless otherwise noted, are from New Revised Standard Version Bible, copyright (c) 1989 Division of Christian Education of the National Council of the Churches of Christ in the United States of America. Used by permission. All rights reserved worldwide.

To My Wife, Judy Y. Chung

Contents

Foreword by Veli-Matti Kärkkäinen ix
Preface xi
Acknowledgments xii

Introduction 1

Part I. A Philosophical and Theological Approach to Interreligious Dialogue
1. The Bible and Hospitality 13
2. Deep Pluralism and the Need for Humility 28
3. Dialogue and Practical Hospitality 46
4. Humility, Hospitality, and Missions 62

Part II. Abrahamic Faiths in Mutual Constructive Engagement
Overview of Part II 81
5. Christianity and Providence 84
6. Islam and Providence 101
7. Judaism and Providence 122

Part III. Eastern Faiths in Mutual Constructive Engagement
Overview of Part III 141
8. Buddhism, Metaphysics, and Science 144
9. Hinduism, Metaphysics, and Science 161
10. Conclusion: Honesty, Truth, and Humility 181

Works Cited 189
Index 199

Foreword

SUSPICION AND RESISTANCE; MISUNDERSTANDING and misjudgment; hatred and enmity; even violence and war. These are the kinds of reactions and attitudes that in recent times too often have come to characterize encounters between followers of different faiths. Religious plurality is considered to be a problem in principle and the diversity of faith commitments a liability for conflict *per se*.

Humility and hospitality speak another language. They display a desire for connection, embrace, acceptance, and welcoming. Yet, at the same time—and this is the main argument of this profound enquiry—humility and hospitality also bespeak *commitment* and *conviction*. To be humble in relation to the religious other does not have to mean the lack of one's own deeply held faith commitments. Nor does hospitality mean that everything goes, or that every faith and religious opinion is necessarily equally right.

To live humbly and in a hospitable manner in the utterly complex and complicated world of religious pluralisms—as well as deepening secularisms—means a happy struggle between affirming one's own religious identity and, at the same time, making room for the religious others' otherness. A sincere sharing of one's own faith commitment with an opportunity to give a witness for what one considers the truth and a willingness to listen carefully to the others' testimonies is a key to a peaceful living together.

This is called "tolerance." Or is it? Many voices, particularly in the secular media, but also among the experts in interfaith encounters, define tolerance in a radically different manner. For them, tolerance means blocking one's own faith commitment with the hope of building bridges and expecting the religious other to act similarly. In other words: at the table of the interfaith dialogue "neutral" non-commitments will politely talk to each other. Respectfully and strongly I disagree. There is no need for tolerance if differences are not allowed. Everybody agrees with each other! Tolerance, etymologically from the Latin term "to bear [a burden]," rather is badly needed when Christians, Muslims, Jews, Buddhists, Hindus, and others are not only "tolerated" for their faith but even encouraged to express their deepest convictions as long as it is done peacefully and with respect for others. This is where true tolerance is tested! That kind of posture also prepares the way for a truly pluralistic society where all religious and secular views have a safe space to flourish, talk to each other, and even attempt to persuade the other—as long as it is done peacefully and with respect for others!

This is what I am reading in this inspiring and exciting work. As Dr. Brewer puts it succinctly in his preface: the main goal is "to offer an approach to interreligious dialogue predicated on humility and hospitality that also strives for honest discussion of difference." I couldn't agree more with this noble aim!

What is particularly useful about this enquiry is that rather than staying at the abstract level of philosophical and theological negotiation of similarities and differences among religions, it also goes into some specifics. The latter part of the study considers carefully a central theme in all living faiths, namely how to understand (divine) providence. That approach provides an excellent platform for testing the general principles of interfaith engagement (theology of religions) by delving into a detailed study of a particular topic (comparative theology). This is, I believe, a highly fruitful methodology for the third millennium!

Veli-Matti Kärkkäinen, Dr. Theol. Habil.
Professor of Systematic Theology, Fuller Theological Seminary
Docent of Ecumenics, Faculty of Theology, University of Helsinki

Preface

THE BOOK YOU HOLD in your hand will hopefully be of great interest to many. It seeks a middle way between two poles of a discussion on interfaith dialogue, and by virtue of doing so, will interest those on either end of the spectrum. The goal is a sincere one: to offer an approach to interreligious dialogue predicated on humility and hospitality that also strives for honest discussion of difference. The root concern of this book is philosophical more than theological—can all our various descriptions of God and the world, with all their attendant differences, be true? Or is it possible to be mistaken in some of our beliefs and thus be open to learning from those of other faith traditions? These are the sorts of questions this book is designed to answer. If these are your questions too, then the invitation is open to close encounters of the third kind, opportunities for mutual constructive engagement with those of other faith traditions.

Acknowledgments

THIS BOOK GROWS, IN part, out of a series conducted at Johns Creek United Methodist Church in July 2017, as well as out of my own doctoral work. My sincerest thanks to Rev. Sandra Jones for her encouragement in writing this book; to Nancey Murphy for all that she has taught me over the years; to Dr. Brian Austin for the foundation he provided me in philosophy, especially on issues of science and religion; Rev. Brian Tillman, for his meticulous feedback on many of these chapters; my good friend Tareef Saeb and his encouragement; my colleague Sabrina D. MisirHiralall for her meticulous feedback; and of course, my wife, the Rev. Dr. Judy Y. Chung, for her love and forbearance. I am particularly indebted to her contribution; much of chapter 4 comes from her Doctor of Ministry dissertation and the research she has done in missiology. Thank you, Judy, for your years of service to missions in the United Methodist Church.

Introduction

I COULD NOT WRITE a book on interreligious dialogue without mentioning Sumi Bose. Sumi was a close friend of mine in middle school, and one of the first upper-level students to make me feel welcome. It goes without saying that the transition to middle school can be difficult. This transition was made all the more challenging for me as a result of my band schedule. In my first year, I was the only 6th grader placed in the 7th and 8th grade wind ensemble. While this was certainly an honor—an indication of my teacher's estimation of my abilities—it also meant that my lunch period was not with other 6th graders. I still remember walking into the cafeteria during the 7th and 8th grade lunch period not knowing who I would sit with or who would want anything to do with me. The thought of eating alone around older students did little to allay my fears about entering middle school. In the midst of this, Sumi was a friendly face. She was one of a small group of 7th grade band members who welcomed me to their table. Sumi was soft-spoken and gentle; she radiated kindness. On our first meeting, she gave me a clip-on shoelace trinket that was small and insignificant, but which meant the world to me at the time. In that gift I heard Sumi saying, "You are welcome here. You are one of us," and I didn't feel so alone.

Sadly, I later wound up hurting Sumi very deeply in a misguided attempt to convert her. One evening, several years later, as we were talking on the phone, she began sharing with me some of her family's Hindu beliefs and practices. At the time, these sounded strange to me. Driven by a need to correct her "wrong" beliefs and convert her to the "right" ones, I began pointing out to her the "absurdity" of her family's religious practices. I then proceeded to tell her my own conviction, at the time, that a person needed to profess personal belief in Jesus Christ in order to be forgiven of her sins, be saved from hell, and go to heaven. She then asked me very pointedly if I believed that she was going to hell. After a moment's hesitation, I told her, "Yes, if you don't believe in Jesus." She then asked to be excused for a moment. I remember praying for her while she was away from the phone, hoping that she had been convicted by our conversation, that perhaps I had gotten through to her and that she was off to tell her mother what she had come to believe. But when she came back to the phone, it was clear that this was not the case. Sumi was in tears, devastated that I would belittle her family's beliefs and that I could insinuate that she was destined for hell.

Our friendship was never the same afterward. In truth, it was over. How can you mend a relationship when you have consigned the other person to the worst possible fate, when you have implied that someone is so beneath you and your beliefs that they are worthy of little better than eternal damnation? Of course, this was not what I intended to imply. My conviction, at the time, was that *everyone*, myself included, was destined for hell save for God's grace. My intent, misguided though it might have been, was not to proclaim her condemnation, but to offer her a means of salvation, not realizing how presumptuous and hurtful this thinking was. More regrettable still, I not only lost a good friend that day, I lost any chance to be a part of her life in any capacity moving forward. I wonder if it would not have been better to refrain from such a blatant attempt at proselytization and, instead, continued a friendship that could have produced other opportunities for spiritually edifying conversations. Might this have been a better way to allow God's grace to work in its own time and on its own terms? My actions had the opposite of their intended effect. Instead of leading her to a transforming experience of God in Jesus Christ, I turned her away, perhaps forever.

My sense is that many mainline Protestant and evangelical Christians can identify with this story. There is a tension, especially within American evangelicalism, between recognizing the centrality of Christ for faith and salvation, on the one hand, and wanting to tread lightly when engaging people of other faiths, on the other. This is especially true in our current context where those of other faith traditions are no longer distant, exotic peoples who can be dismissed out of hand, but rather our neighbors, colleagues, and friends. These are people who are close to us and who seem as devout and as spiritual as we are, sometimes more so. Given this dilemma, how do we as Christians approach interfaith dialogue? It seems to me that there are two extremes that need to be avoided. On the one hand, there is overt, aggressive proselytizing, which usually views the other person as a target, a potential convert, not an equal worthy of interreligious conversation. On the other hand, there is the extreme of avoidance, where we refrain from having interreligious dialogue at all, particularly dialogue over real difference, out of fear of hurting the other person. Is there no middle ground? Is there no way to have meaningful, constructive interreligious dialogue that allows for honest discussion of difference and even disagreement, but that does not necessarily result in or aim at conversion? I believe that there is, and it is my hope in this book to explore this possibility.

It is important to recognize that the Christian tradition has had varied responses to the issue of interreligious dialogue throughout its history. The earliest Christian theologians of the third and fourth centuries—the church fathers—tended to have a much more open view of God's presence in other religions.[1] There was by no means universal agreement among the church fathers, and there were certain religious beliefs and practices that they explicitly opposed, such as polytheism, mystery religions, pagan mythologies, astrology, and Eastern cults such as Manichaeism. Nevertheless, they tended to interpret certain biblical material dealing with other religions more openly, leading them to a more accepting view. This was due, in part, to the fact that the church fathers were faced with the challenge of showing not only the distinctiveness of Christianity as a new religion, but also its compatibility to the existing religions around them.

It was St. Augustine of Hippo who solidified a more exclusive attitude. By the end of the fourth century, as Christianity became the official state religion in Rome, the majority position was summarized in the Latin phrase, *extra ecclesiam nulla salus*, no salvation outside of the church. For most of Catholic Church history in the West, this exclusivism primarily took the form of *ecclesiocentrism*, the belief that salvation is connected to the church itself. Anyone outside the church could not have the guarantee of salvation. This is to be contrasted with later Protestants who tended to maintain a form of *Christocentrism*, whereby salvation is to be found principally in Christ.

These exclusivist attitudes, however, which characterized much of Christian history since Augustine and, for Protestants, since the Reformation, began to shift following World War II with concerns over colonization and anti-Semitism, both of which contributed to the atrocities of the Holocaust. The Second Vatican Council, in particular, constituted a first step in the Catholic Church toward improved attitudes toward other

---

1. Käkäinen, *Introduction to the Theology of Religions*, 55–56.

religious traditions in the hope of building better relationships with them. The general stance of the council on this issue is succinctly stated in the *Nostra Aetate*, a papal encyclical admonishing Christians to "recognize, preserve and promote the good things, spiritual and moral," found in other religious traditions, and to engage those traditions respectfully.[2]

Protestants have faced a similar challenge. While Protestants do not constitute a unified body in the same way that Catholics do, they have created inter-denominational contexts for discussing this and similar issues. One of the primary contexts has been the World Council of Churches (WCC), an international, inter-church organization that grew out of the ecumenical movement. It was founded in 1948 with the purpose of working toward greater unity among Christian denominations worldwide. In keeping with its global and ecumenical focus, the WCC has given considerable attention to the church's theological responsibility toward other religions. While the council's position has changed over time, it has tended to seek a balance between recognizing the importance of dialogue, on the one hand, while preserving the uniqueness of Christ, on the other. In 1968, the General Assembly of the WCC convened in Uppsala, Sweden to discuss the possibility of interreligious dialogue as opposed to the traditional approach of missionary evangelism. The Assembly, however, made it clear that such dialogue should not detract from either the Christian commitment to Christ's uniqueness or the need for proclamation and evangelism.[3]

This dual commitment to evangelism and dialogue remains the basic stance of the WCC. Its official statement today is a document drafted in 2000 called "Mission and Evangelism in Unity Today," revised with little change from an earlier document adopted in 1982 called "Mission and Evangelism: An Ecumenical Affirmation." The document emphasizes the role of the Trinity in missions. The belief in God's triune nature allows the WCC to uphold its commitment both to the presence of God in other religions, principally through the presence of the Holy Spirit, and the fact that it is specifically *Christ's presence* that is being recognized. As "Mission and Evangelism in Unity Today" states:

> A trinitarian approach to the *missio Dei* [mission of God] is therefore important. On the one hand, this promotes a more inclusive understanding of God's presence and work in the

---

2. Vatican II Council, *Nostra Aetate*.
3. Goodal, *The Uppsala Report*, 28.

whole world and among all people, implying that signs of God's presence can and should be identified, affirmed, and worked with even in the most unexpected places. On the other hand, by clearly affirming that the Father and the Spirit are always and in all circumstances present and at work together with the Word, the temptation to separate the presence of God or the Spirit from the Son of God, Jesus Christ, will be avoided.[4]

In the wake of these monumental shifts within the Catholic and Protestant Churches following World War II, there have been several waves of theologians contributing to an ongoing discussion concerning the relationship of Christianity to other religions. Broadly speaking, there have been three basic responses to the problem of religious diversity: *exclusivism*, *inclusivism*, and *pluralism*.[5] Exclusivism, as already noted, has characterized much of Christian history. This is the belief that only one tradition offers the fullest and most complete revelation of God, that truth and salvation are to be found in the Christian tradition alone. Inclusivism is a mitigating position, one that seeks to preserve the uniqueness of God's revelation in Christ, while allowing for the possibility that those outside of the Christian tradition can experience or participate in the salvation afforded by Christ. This is the belief that while Christianity may offer the most complete revelation of God, it does not preclude those of other traditions from discovering many of the same truths or from participating in God's salvation. For inclusivists, this usually means that members of other religions are unknowingly participating in the salvation offered specifically through Christ. It is an attempt to broaden the salvation message to *include* others. Thus, the term "inclusivism."

Pluralism is a relatively new position. In its short time, however, it has produced several waves. First-wave pluralists not only acknowledge the intrinsic truth, beauty, and goodness of other religions, but hold that "salvation" is available, in one way or another, in all the major religious traditions. One of the most influential forms of this position is found in John Hick's *An Interpretation of Religions*. Hick maintains that the great religious traditions are all different ways of "experiencing, conceiving,

---

4. Goodal, *The Uppsala Report*, 3.

5. These three basic options—exclusivism, inclusivism, and pluralism—originated with the nineteenth-century European Christian missionary John Farquhar, but were put into widespread use by Alan Race. See Race, *Christians and Religious Pluralism*. Other typologies have been proposed as well. See Käkäinen, *Introduction to the Theology of Religions*; Knitter, *Introducing Theologies of Religion*; and Küng, "What Is True Religion?"

and living in relation to" the same divine reality.⁶ That is, there is one underlying divine reality and all the major world religions are various ways of describing and relating to it, and none is any more "right" or "correct" than any other. Hick's position, however, has a way of flattening the distinctiveness of the major religious traditions, suggesting that every tradition is essentially saying the same thing. This form of pluralism has been labeled *identist*, because it maintains that all religions share a similar identity as equally valid expressions of the same ultimate reality. If the Catholic Church was defined, historically, by *ecclesiocentrism* (the centrality of the church), and the Protestant Church by *Christocentrism* (the centrality of Christ), this form of pluralism is characterized by *reality-centrism*, the primacy of the Real.

Identist pluralism, however, needs to be distinguished from *differential*, *deep*, or *dialogical* pluralism, a form of second-wave pluralism, which holds that all religions are really quite different from one another and must seek some common ground for meaningful dialogue. This book holds a form of deep pluralism. That is, I take it that there is real difference between religious traditions. While it may be true that there is only one God and that the various traditions are endeavoring, in their own ways, to describe that divine reality and to participate in it, the conclusions that each tradition reaches and the implications of those convictions for belief and practice are fundamentally different. They cannot be glossed over or ignored, and the various traditions cannot be conflated without doing a disservice to the traditions themselves.

This does not mean that interaction between traditions is impossible or undesirable. Quite the contrary, it is because of our differences that dialogue is so important. Learning how to live together peaceably and to cooperate on shared concerns is an increasingly important need. Dialogue, then, needs to take place along several lines. First, it should entail a proactive effort to understand each other better so that we can live alongside each other respectfully. The world is shrinking, and if we do not seek to understand each other, we will be motivated by baser instincts of fear and distrust, which will continue to sow seeds of enmity and conflict. Second, it should entail a search for common ground and

---

6. Hick, *An Interpretation of Religion*, 236–37. Hick identifies "post-axial" religions as those that developed after the life and work of individuals like Buddha, Confucius, Lao-Tze, Socrates, and Jesus, where the purpose of religion shifted from the "preservation of cosmic and social order" of the pre-axial age, to a "quest for salvation or liberation" (23).

meaningful interaction on shared concerns. There are enough social and human rights concerns that most religious traditions hold in common to warrant interreligious dialogue and cooperation. Third, however, it should entail an honest discussion of difference as a means of aiding each other to better understand the nature of God and the world. This is a philosophical point. If it is true that each religious tradition is seeking, in its own way, to describe God and the world as accurately as possible, then there should be some possibility of discussion that helps adherents of differing religious traditions come to some common conclusions about the way things are. This means that dialogue will also necessarily include discussion of difference.

It is important to note that discussion of religious difference need not be antagonistic. Rather, it can and should be hospitable. This is one of the underlying concerns about any form of interreligious dialogue that broaches discussion of difference. The fear is that we will inevitably slip into sectarianism or, worse, bigotry, hatred, and violence. Tragically, these sorts of responses have been all too common in the history of relations between religions. However, this has not always been the case, nor need it be. There are plenty of examples of religious traditions coexisting peaceably and, in many instances, they were able to engage one another's differences with civility and hospitality. I am reminded, here, of Corrie ten Boom's account in *The Hiding Place*. The ten Booms were a Dutch Christian family who helped hide and protect Jews from the Nazi regime during World War II. They freely opened their home, at their own risk, to house Jews and to conceal them from the Gestapo. Their purpose in doing so, quite simply, was to show hospitality—to save as many Jews as they could from the ravages of the Nazi regime. While the ten Boom's continued their own Christian practices and even had lively theological debates with their Jewish guests, they never tried to convert them.[7] They even began observing certain Jewish rituals and holidays in an attempt to make their Jewish guests feel more comfortable. Conversion was not the goal. Hospitality, itself, was a way of extending God's grace to those who were different.

Note that hospitality does not require us to gloss over genuine difference. The ten Booms were not timid about engaging in theological debate with their guests. However, their disagreements always remained hospitable. One story from Corrie ten Boom's account captures this well.

---

7. Atwood, *Women Heroes of World War II*, 119.

Prior to the war, Corrie's father, Casper, often traveled to Amsterdam to conduct business with wholesalers, many of whom were Jewish. Corrie recounts how her father, after a brief discussion of business, would take out his small Bible, while the wholesaler would take out a book or scroll, put on a prayer cap, and the two would "be off, arguing, comparing, interrupting, contradicting—reveling in each other's company."[8] On one occasion, the wholesaler stopped mid-argument, suddenly remembering Corrie, who as a small child had accompanied her father, and cried out:

> "A guest! A guest in my gates and I have offered her no refreshment!" And springing up he would rummage under shelves and into cupboards and before long I would be holding on my lap a plate of the most delicious treats in the world—honey cakes and date cakes and a kind of confection of nuts, fruits, and sugar.[9]

Neither Casper ten Boom nor the Jewish wholesalers were afraid to engage in vigorous debate over important differences of biblical interpretation and application, but they also never forgot the importance of hospitality.

In the pages that follow, I want to propose an approach to interreligious dialogue that honors the real differences between religious traditions, one that encourages discussion and even debate over those differences, but one that is rooted in hospitality. How can we conduct interreligious dialogue in a way that seeks a meaningful exchange of ideas, not mere platitudes, but that does not seek outright conversion or proselytization? Earlier I suggested that there is a middle way between these two extremes. This book is an attempt at that middle way—faith encounters of the third kind, as it were. Drawing on Hynek's scale for alien encounters, a faith encounter of the first kind would entail mere awareness of religious others, second-kind encounters some sort of basic interaction. Faith encounters of the third-kind, however, go beyond mere awareness or simple interaction and seek mutual constructive engagement. The position outlined here, then, seeks points at which traditions have encountered problems that expose vulnerabilities in their own beliefs and practices, placing the participants in a position of genuine humility where they are open to learning from those of another tradition.

The book is divided into three parts. In Part I, I outline my approach to interreligious dialogue. Chapter 1 begins by providing a biblical and

---

8. Ten Boom, *The Hiding Place*, 40.
9. Ten Boom, *The Hiding Place*, 41.

theological rationale for interreligious dialogue, in the first place. Chapters 2 and 3 explain in detail the philosophical underpinnings of this approach. Since the goal of this book is to find ways in which religious traditions can learn from each other in their descriptions of God and the world, the approach presented here is more sweeping than one-on-one, interpersonal dialogue. It requires understanding how traditions arrive at their beliefs and practices, more broadly, as well as how traditions can be mistaken in their beliefs and practices, for it is only when we recognize this as a genuine possibility that we become humble enough to learn from those of other traditions, thus making interreligious dialogue truly possible. Chapter 4 concludes Part I by looking at the role of missions in light of this approach to interreligious dialogue. I contend that while there is still a need for missions, the focus needs to shift from one of conversion, only, to helping religious others better describe the religious experiences of God that they have already had. This is in keeping not only with the philosophical approach outlined here, but also with trends already present in missions today.

In the other two parts of the book, I apply the philosophical approach outlined in Part I. In Part II, I bring the three Abrahamic traditions—Judaism, Christianity, and Islam—into conversation over a crisis that threatens all three. Specifically, the rise of modern, Newtonian science has made discussion of God's providence problematic, for if the causal order of the universe is entirely fixed and law-governed, then what room is there for God to act in the world without either becoming one cause among many or, else, a tiresome tinkerer, who is constantly intervening in the world to bring about changes? More importantly, if modern science precludes God's action in the world, then it also eliminates the possibility of special divine revelation, upon which all particular theological knowledge is derived. It is this deeper concern that poses a threat not only to the three Abrahamic traditions, but any metaphysical tradition that is predicated on revelatory knowledge.

While the problem of modern science has presented itself most acutely for the Christian tradition, all three Abrahamic traditions faced a similar problem during the medieval period, with the adoption of ancient Greek philosophy. Neoplatonism, in particular, brought with it the doctrine of emanation, which constrained certain shared theological commitments to God's action in the world, and raised similar concerns about the possibility of revelation and theological knowledge. What I will show in Part II, then, is that all three traditions relied on each other during the medieval period to resolve this problem, in a form of mutual constructive engagement, and that they stand to benefit from each other again, today, in response to the challenge of modern science. I will consider each tradition in turn and examine how each has dealt with its own problem of divine providence. Along the way, I will point out places where each has stood to benefit from the others.

In Part III, I attempt to do something similar with the Eastern traditions, particularly Buddhism and Hinduism. While the Eastern traditions differ from the Abrahamic traditions in their concepts of God and the ultimate, the problem, I contend, is not fundamentally different. Any tradition that relies on special revelation for its theological or metaphysical knowledge is in danger of experiencing the problem posed by modern science, which seemingly rules out the possibility of special revelation in the first place. This is as true for Buddhism and Hinduism as it is for any other religious tradition. I will endeavor to show that the fundamental beliefs and practices of both traditions are irreducibly metaphysical and, as such, stand to face the challenge posed by modern science. Again, I will consider each tradition in turn, looking at how each is susceptible to this crisis, the resources that each has for addressing it, and the ways in which Buddhism, Hinduism, and Christianity stand to benefit from each other in mutual constructive engagement.

While the book has been written to be read in order from start to finish, the reader need not feel locked into this approach. If, for example, you need no convincing of the importance of interreligious dialogue from a Christian perspective, and if you are chiefly interested in the approach this book offers for such dialogue, you may skip chapter 1 and proceed to chapters 2 and 3. If, however, you are unconvinced of the importance of such dialogue and would like to know how the role of interreligious dialogue comports with evangelism and missions, be sure to read chapters 1 and 4. Parts II and III of this book provide case studies for how the major religious traditions can engage in mutual constructive engagement over the issue of science and providence. So these chapters may be approached in a number of different ways. They may be treated as an extension of chapters 2 and 3, providing in-depth examples of how this model of interreligious dialogue works, or they can be treated individually for those who are interested in how each tradition has dealt with questions of science, providence, and interfaith dialogue.

Part I

A Philosophical and Theological Approach to Interreligious Dialogue

Chapter 1

The Bible and Hospitality

Let us renounce that bigotry and party zeal which would contract our hearts into an insensibility for all the human race. . . . With an honest openness of mind let us always remember that kindred between man and man, and cultivate that happy instinct whereby, in the original constitution of our nature, God has strongly bound us to each other.[1]

—JOHN WESLEY, *NOTES ON THE BIBLE*

Introduction

BEFORE DISCUSSING *HOW TO* have interreligious dialogue, some will want to know *why* we should have it in the first place. Shouldn't we as Christians focus either on evangelizing people of other faiths, or else respecting their right to worship in their own way as they see fit? What benefit is there to interfaith dialogue, much less dialogue that does not seek conversion? Several responses to this question immediately present themselves. First, we are living in an increasingly globalized and pluralistic world. The advances of technology, travel, and education have resulted in contracting the space between people of diverse cultural and religious backgrounds. In a practical sense, then, we must learn to live alongside

---

1. Wesley, "Notes on the Gospel according to St. Luke," 207, note on v. 37.

one another peaceably. This will likely require more than merely tolerating one another, but rather building bridges of trust and collaboration that are more sustainable. While fear of the other and of difference is a powerful deterrent, we no longer have the luxury of cloistering ourselves from those of other religions and cultures. We are interconnected, if not in our own neighborhoods, communities, and workplaces, then online and in innumerable global interdependencies—political, economic, and so on. Understanding those who are different from us is a first step in overcoming fear and distrust and paving the way for peaceful coexistence.

A second reason that presents itself for this kind of dialogue is the very urgency of global concerns themselves. There are enough social, ecological, and geopolitical issues that matter to people of various backgrounds—religious or otherwise—to provide sufficient reason for engaging one another across cultural and religious lines. There will, of course, be vast disagreement both within and between religious communities about what those issues are and how to remedy them, but this simply means that dialogue is all the more important. Differences cannot be overcome without dialogue, and progress on these sorts of global issues is difficult when differences cannot be addressed in any meaningful way.

These sorts of considerations should be enough to suggest the importance of interreligious dialogue on its own merit. However, neither reason offers an explicitly *Christian* rationale. The reasons offered so far are pragmatic and come down to the singular concern for peaceful coexistence among people of diverse religious backgrounds. However, is there a distinctly biblical or theological justification for Christians to engage in interreligious dialogue that does not depend on or result in evangelism? I believe there is. While I do not deny that evangelism or conversion may continue to play a role in these kinds of conversations, I hope to show that this does not have to be the *only* motivation, or the *primary* one. In this chapter, I will explore the biblical and theological grounds for this position. In particular, I will look at two specific biblical accounts—one from the Old Testament, one from the New—that I take to be paradigmatic for Christian approaches not only to interreligious dialogue, but to hospitality in general and how we should treat those who are different from us.

I begin by looking at the story of the Levite and his concubine at the end of the book of Judges, a gruesome story that ends in the haunting rape and murder of an unnamed concubine. The brutality of the narrative, however, serves as a cautionary tale against the inhospitable treatment of foreigners—we can justify any behavior, no matter how heinous, when we begin to overlook the God-ordained dignity of others and fail to welcome them with hospitality. I then look at the Parable of the Good Samaritan in the Gospel of Luke, where Jesus subverts the very distinction between neighbor and enemy, and makes it clear that there is no one who is beyond the scope of God's love and compassion.

Blessed to Be a Blessing: Judges 19:1–30

At first glance, the Old Testament may seem an odd place to look for support for interreligious dialogue. A popular belief is that the God of the Old Testament is wrathful and narrowly nationalistic, one that uses Israel at almost every turn to destroy and conquer other nations. This picture is a far cry from the sort of interreligious dialogue under consideration here. Indeed, as early as the second century, a position developed known as Marcionism, named for its originator, Marcion of Sinope, which claimed that the two testaments describe two different gods—one who is a demiurge responsible for the evil in the world, the other the God of love and compassion revealed in Jesus Christ. Marcion went as far as to develop his own canon (Bible), one that excluded the entire Old Testament and removed any references to Judaism in the New. While this dualistic position was rejected by the early church, it is hard to ignore the lingering influence in popular readings of the Old Testament today. These readings, however, are cursory at best and do not do justice to the scope of God's compassion in the Hebrew Bible.

While it is true that the Old Testament focuses almost exclusively on the Israelites as the chosen people, its scope extends far beyond them. The initial covenant that God makes with Abraham promises that through him "*all the families of the earth* shall be blessed." (Gen 12:3b; see also Gen 22:18; my emphasis). The idea from the start was that the Israelites were blessed *to be a blessing*. They were chosen so that through them the other nations could come to know YHWH. In the covenant that God makes with Moses, YHWH declares, "*the whole earth is mine*, but you shall be for me a priestly kingdom and a holy nation" (Exod 19:6; my emphasis).

The implication is not that Israel was intrinsically more important than the rest of the world; but rather that they had been called to a special function, a priestly one that was designed to mediate YHWH's blessings *to the rest of the world*. Within the Israelite community, itself, the function of the priests was to mediate God's presence to the rest of the Israelites. The comparison then is that the relationship of Israel to the rest of the nations is to be like that of the Israelite priests to the rest of Israel. Just as the priests were called to a higher degree of holiness so that through them the rest of Israel could experience God's presence, the Israelite community as a whole was called to serve as priests to the rest of the nations—mediators of God's justice and mercy to the world.

This responsibility was an extension of the Israelites' exodus experience. In Egypt the Israelites were foreigners in a foreign land; they were maltreated, used as slave labor for the building of an empire. It was YHWH who observed their misery and showed them mercy by delivering them from their bondage (Exod 3:7–8). In turn, the Israelites were to show this same mercy to the rest of the nations. They were to remember their captivity in Egypt and avoid re-creating the same kind of oppression for others that had been created for them. Walter Brueggemann describes this as a "countercommunity with a counter-consciousness,"[2] one that ran against the prevailing powers and kingdoms of this world—kingdoms like Egypt that sought to advance their own geopolitical ends at the expense of those like the Israelites who were easy to exploit. It was in this counter-consciousness that Israelite holiness consisted. The term *holy* literally means "set apart." Thus, the Israelites were called to be a holy nation in that they were to be different from the other nations, identifying themselves completely with YHWH's compassion, mercy, and justice so that through them, other nations could come to know the nature and character of God.

A central theme of the Old Testament, then, is the ongoing commitment to justice for the poor, the widow, the outcast, and the foreigner. Exhortations throughout the Old Testament enjoin the Israelites to avoid wronging or oppressing the resident alien precisely because they had been aliens in Egypt and YHWH had delivered them (see: Exod 22:21; 23:9; Lev 19:33–34). In Deuteronomy 10:12–22, YHWH reminds the people of their covenant responsibility, which entails both devotion to YHWH (Deut 10:12–13) and care for the defenseless (10:17–19), which turn out to be one and the same, for, as YHWH states:

> the Lord your God is God of gods and Lord of lords, the great God, mighty and awesome, who is not partial and takes no

---

2. Brueggemann, *The Prophetic Imagination*, 21.

bribe, who executes justice for the orphan and the widow, and who loves the strangers, providing them food and clothing. You shall also love the stranger, for you were strangers in the land of Egypt. (Deut 10:17–19)

By showing compassion to the defenseless—the orphan, the widow, and the stranger—we demonstrate our devotion to YHWH precisely because YHWH is a God of the defenseless. In saving the Israelites from slavery, God's character was revealed as one that sides with the oppressed over the oppressor. The hope, then, was that the Israelites, having been oppressed and having experienced the compassion of YHWH, would then be sympathetic to others who were similarly oppressed and would share God's compassion with them. It is in regard to this covenant responsibility toward the defenseless that the prophets repeatedly admonish the Israelites, whereby Micah declares: "He has told you, O mortal, what is good; and what does the LORD require of you but to do justice, and to love kindness, and to walk humbly with your God?" (Mic 6:8); and Isaiah cries: "cease to do evil, learn to do good; seek justice, rescue the oppressed, defend the orphan, plead for the widow" (Isa 1:17).

This concern for justice, then, was no passing consideration. It was central to the covenant. The extent to which YHWH would continue to uphold Israel as the chosen people and use them for divine purposes was dependent on the degree to which they were willing to show God's mercy and justice to others. The covenant that God made with the Israelites at Mt. Sinai was conditional: *If you obey my voice and keep my covenant—*read here, acting in accordance with God's nature as one who shows mercy to the poor, the widow, the outcast, and the alien—*then, you will be my treasured possession out of all the peoples* (Exod 19:5). The evidence of this condition is in the consequences, both large and small, that the Israelites experience each time they stray from obedience, leading ultimately to the destruction of the northern kingdom by the Assyrians and the exile of the southern kingdom in Babylon.

The book of Judges is one of the clearest examples of Israel's struggle with this covenant responsibility. The temptation for the Israelites throughout Judges is to adopt the customs of the surrounding nations, where the poor, the widow, and the foreigner were maltreated. These customs were antithetical to YHWH's covenant and, in adopting them, the Israelites were posturing themselves against God and forgetting the mercy and justice that YHWH had shown them while they were foreigners in Egypt. Throughout Judges, there is a recurring cycle of obedience and disobedience, where the Israelites enjoy periods of faithfulness to the covenant accompanied by prosperity, followed by periods of extreme disobedience, where they are lured into adopting the inhospitable practices of these foreign nations. Their disobedience always results in divine punishment, usually in the form of some kind of military defeat, which in turn, necessitates divine deliverance in the form of a judge—a warrior-ruler, who rises up to save Israel from their suffering. This pattern is a downward spiral, such that each successive episode is worse than the last. The cycle reaches its climax in Judges 19:1–30 with the story of the Levite and his concubine. Here it becomes clear that the Israelites have not only become like the surrounding nations, they have become *worse*, exceeding them in their abuse of the defenseless.

The story begins with a Levite who goes to retrieve his concubine (a wife of secondary status), who has returned to her father's house because she "became angry with him [the Levite]" (Judg 19:2a). The context of the story is grim from the beginning, suggesting that there may have been some domestic abuse that caused this separation in the first place.[3] The Hebrew verb used to describe the reason for the concubine's leaving is zānâ, which literally means "to commit adultery" or "to prostitute oneself." In this context, since the concubine had no right to divorce the Levite, the very act of leaving him to return to her father's household was, itself, considered to be an act of unfaithfulness.[4] However, the implication is that the Levite gave her reason to leave. This is reinforced by the fact that the Levite pursues her "to speak tenderly to her and bring her back" (Judg 19:3), indicating that he is complicit in the situation. That is, if he shared no blame, he would have no reason to be so overly kind to her, sweet-talking her to return. The Levite, then, is an abusive husband pleading with his wife to come home.

When the Levite arrives at the father's house, he is greeted with excessive hospitality. The father-in-law lavishes the Levite with food and rest, and encourages him to stay well beyond the intended length of time. The hospitality is gratuitous and over-exaggerated. It is a reminder to the reader of the sort of kindness Israelites were to show the foreigner. While the Levite was not a foreigner in a technical sense, he was a guest in the father-in-law's home and a visitor to the region. Moreover, Levites, not unlike foreigners, depended on the tithes and generosity of the Israelites

---

3. Olson, "The Book of Judges" 876.
4. Green, *The Wesley Study Bible*, 323. Note on Judges 19:2–3.

because they were prohibited from owning their own property (Deut 10:9; 18:1). This exaggerated hospitality, then, serves as a sharp contrast to the inhospitable treatment the Levite and his concubine later receive.

The father's excessive hospitality keeps the Levite and his concubine until late afternoon on the fifth day. Since they leave so late, they are forced to find a place to stay the night *en route*. Two options are available to them. The closer of the two is a Jebusite city that the Levite explicitly avoids because it is not an Israelite town. His primary concern is that they will not receive the same kind of hospitality that his own people would provide. Instead, they travel a bit farther to the city of Gibeah, an Israelite city of the tribe of Benjamin. However, as the Levite and his concubine enter the town square, they find no one to welcome them or to take them in, as was the custom in Israelite hospitality. It is not until late in the evening that an old man coming back from working in the field greets them and welcomes them into his home (Judg 19:20). This old man is, himself, a foreigner in Gibeah, originally from the city of Ephraim. The irony, then, is that a resident alien extends greater hospitality to a native Israelite than the rest of the Israelites show to one of their own. It is an indication of the greater irony to come.

As the Levite and his concubine are settling into the old man's home, the men of the city surround the house. They pound on the door and demand that the old man bring the Levite out so that they "may have intercourse with him" (Judg 19:22b). This scene echoes the story of Sodom and Gomorrah, where the men of the city demand to have sex with the disguised angels who are visiting Abraham's nephew, Lot (Gen 19:5). This version, however, more so than the one in Genesis, makes it clear what the real issue is. It is not one of homosexuality, but rather one of hospitality. If hospitality is a benchmark for the covenant relationship with YHWH, the Israelites have fallen far short of it. Not only have they failed to show hospitality by neglecting the Levite and his concubine in the town square, they have gone so far as to subject the foreigner to one of the most humiliating forms of violence—public sexual assault. The Israelites of Gibeah have not only become inhospitable, they have become hostile and barbarous, the antithesis of the sort of community YHWH had called them to be.

The story ends in an even more disturbing twist. In an act as brutal and vile as the actions of the men outside the door, the Levite, himself, seizes his concubine and thrusts her outside the house for the men to ravage. This unnamed woman, who has been a victim of domestic violence from the beginning of this narrative, having been abused by her husband to the point that she was forced to flee to her father's house, then having been an object of barter between her father and her husband, is now callously cast out to be raped and left for dead (Judg 19:26). The horrific treatment of the concubine not only by the men of Gibeah, but also by the Levite, himself, is an indication of how far the Israelites have come from the radical countercommunity that YHWH had called them to be. Joel B. Green notes that one indication of Israel's declining condition in the book of Judges is "the deteriorating treatment of women."[5] While the story of the rape, death, and eventual dismemberment (Judg 19:29–30) of the concubine is one of the most disturbing depictions of violence against women in the Old Testament, appropriately deemed a text of terror,[6] it must not be read as sanctioning this sort of behavior, but as a critique and condemnation of it. This chapter serves as the crescendo of the downward spiral of Israel's disobedience throughout the book of Judges. It falls like a thunderclap against our sensibilities, jarring us from our complacency to help us see how far the Israelites have come in their covenant responsibility. The Israelites were delivered from Egypt in order to be holy, set apart, a contrast to this very kind of behavior; they were set apart to show God's radical justice and mercy to the other nations. Now they stand diametrically opposed to everything that God is and has called them to be. Not only have they matched the surrounding nations in their maltreatment of women, the poor, the outcast, and the foreigner, they have surpassed it. The true irony of this story, then, is that it would have been better for the Levite and his concubine to stay in the Jebusite city with non-Israelites than in Gibeah with their own people.

    The implication is clear. A telling indication of a community's relationship with God is its treatment of the defenseless and the marginalized, including the foreigner. When a society reaches the point where foreigners and other minorities are overlooked or, worse, mistreated, it has come a far way from the character of God. Consequently, we should be wary of public attitudes and policies that marginalize those who are racially, culturally, and religiously different, for once we start down the path of fear and distrust, hostility and violence are not far to follow. As people of God, we are called to show hospitality to the foreigner, so that through our hospitality others may come to see God. This is the heart

---

5. Green, *The Wesley Study Bible*, 322. Note on Judges 19:1–30.
6. See Trible, *Texts of Terror*.

of the biblical mandate for interreligious dialogue. While the Bible does not explicitly address the question of interfaith dialogue in the way that the issue is framed today, it does provide a mandate for how we are to treat others who are different from us. In this respect, interreligious dialogue begins with hospitality to the other, to the foreigner, not for the purposes of conversion, *per se*, but because we are called to extend God's love and grace to others so that, in doing so, others may come to know God. Conversion is the result of an authentic encounter with God. We merely provide the context, through hospitality, where others may have that encounter.

Love Your Neighbor: Luke 10:25-36

If the story of the Levite and his concubine reinforces the notion that we are to welcome the foreigner, the Parable of the Good Samaritan makes it clear that even this is not enough—we are also to love our *enemies*. Overfamiliarity with the parable often obscures this deeper message. The story is typically introduced to children (and adults) as an object lesson in kindness—help others in need! Do-gooders are often referred to as good Samaritans. Hospitals, charities, and laws bear the namesake. However, as important as the message of kindness and helpfulness is, it misses the larger point. The Parable of the Good Samaritan is much more radical than this. It is not merely about extravagant kindness, it is about loving those who hate us.

The passage begins with an expert in Torah testing Jesus by asking him about the requirements for entering the kingdom of God: "what must I do to inherit eternal life?" (Luke 10:25) Here, the expert in the law is putting Jesus to the test. He is challenging Jesus' authority and his understanding of the law. Jesus, however, evades the challenge by turning the question back on him, asking, "What is written in the law? What do you read there?" (Luke 10:26). The expert responds with a well-known prayer from the Torah, the *Shema*, that Jews recited twice daily: "Love the Lord your God with all your heart, and with all your soul, and with all your strength, and with all your mind; and your neighbor as yourself" (Luke 10:27). Jesus affirms his answer, stating, "You have given the right answer; do this, and you will live" (Luke 10:28). Dissatisfied with this response, the expert redoubles his efforts. If his initial question is designed to challenge Jesus, the second is intended to trap him.[7] Seeking to justify himself, the expert asks: "And who is my neighbor?" (Luke 10:29). Again, Jesus evades the trap. Instead, of providing a direct answer, Jesus answers the expert's question with a parable.

If told today, the parable might run something like this: A woman was driving from Washington DC to New York City, when her car ran out of gas. By the side of the road, she fell into the hands of robbers, who stripped her of everything; they beat her, and went away, leaving her for dead. A bishop of the United Methodist Church happened to be driving down the same road, and when she saw the woman, kept driving. So too, a professor at Wesleyan University, when he drove near the place and saw the woman, kept driving. But then an *illegal immigrant*,[8] as she was traveling, came near, and when she saw her, she was moved with pity. She went to her and bandaged her wounds. Then she put the woman in her truck, drove her to a hotel and took care of her. The next day she put her credit card on file with the hotel management to pay for the room and any incidentals, and said, "Take care of her; and when I come back, I will repay you whatever more you spend" (Luke 10:35).

What is often overlooked in teaching this parable is the historical context, which moves the story beyond the realm of mere helpfulness to radical and surprising love for our enemies. In Jesus' day, Samaritans would have been treated in much the same way undocumented immigrants are treated today. They would have been considered foreigners and outcasts, hated and despised. Jews used to travel well out of their way to avoid taking a more direct route through Samaritan territory, just to avoid them, not unlike the treatment of blacks during the antebellum South or apartheid in South Africa. The division between Jews and Samaritans was both racial and religious. Racially, Samaritans were descendants of mixed marriages between Israelites and gentiles from various regions who had been brought into Samaria by the Assyrians following the destruction of the northern kingdom in 722 BCE (2 Kgs 17:24).[9] Samaritans, then,

---

7. Culpepper, "The Gospel of Luke," 229.

8. It should be noted that the term "illegal immigrant" is a misnomer. Immigrants who are in the United States without proper documentation are technically "undocumented" and have committed no punishable crime merely by virtue of being here. Only if they attempt reentry after having been deported are they, then, in commission of a crime. I use the former term to capture the force of the stigma in this parable, the name Samaritan carrying a similar connotation to that of illegal immigrant.

9. Culpepper, "Gospel of Luke," 229.

were considered a mixed race, and thus inferior. Religiously, Samaritans diverged radically from Jews in their "view of scripture, of messianic expectation, and, most importantly, of what constitutes authentic faith before God."[10] These racial and religious differences were sources of enmity between Jews and Samaritans, just as they continue to be in our own context between peoples of different racial and religious backgrounds. One need only think of ongoing mistrust between Jews and Palestinians today, or Christians and Muslims.

In making the Samaritan the protagonist of this story, then, Jesus is making the enemy the exemplar. The idea is that we are to view this story from the perspective of the person lying in the ditch. Jesus and those first hearing this parable were Jewish, and they would have assumed that the principal character in this story—the unfortunate traveler—was Jewish as well. Placing ourselves in this person's shoes, we are dismayed as members of our own community—religious leaders, no less—pass us by and refuse to offer help. Then, when we awake in a hotel room and discover that we have been rescued by our sworn enemy we are astonished! Our entire perspective is thrown into relief, and we are forced to reevaluate the divisions that we have always assumed. We can no longer see *them* the same. In fact, we can no longer distinguish between us and them, friend and enemy, because the one we thought was our enemy has saved our lives.

An actual instance of this kind of radical hospitality occurred in 2017 at the Unite the Right Rally in Charlottesville, VA. There, Ken Parker, a grand dragon of the Ku Klux Klan, became severely dehydrated from the heat and lack of water. Surprisingly, he was cared for by Deeyah Khan, a person of color who was filming a documentary called "White Right: Meeting the Enemy." As a result of her kindness, which she extended to Parker's wife as well, Ken Parker began to reconsider his animosity toward Jews, gays, and people of color. Over the course of the following months, Ken Parker continued to have unexpected interactions with people of color that undermined his long-standing prejudices. Eventually, he attended the church of one of these acquaintances, who turned out to be an African-American pastor. There Parker confessed his bigotry, repented of it, and eventually received baptism from this pastor, a man, who only months prior, would have been viewed as the enemy. This transformation

---

10. Green, *The New International Commentary*, 405.

was the result of the radical hospitality that was shown on the part of the ones he despised.[11]

The Parable of the Good Samaritan, then, is not simply a story about a good person doing something nice for someone in need. It is about a *despised* person going above and beyond what is asked of her to help someone who, otherwise, hates her. In the parable, when those who were supposed to be "neighbors" kept driving down the road, neglecting to help one of their own, it was the Samaritan, the illegal immigrant, the member of the Black Lives Matters movement, the member of the LGBQT+ community, the Muslim, the Jew, the democrat, the republican—choose your enemy—who showed loving kindness. In going out of his way to help one who hated him, this Samaritan teaches us what it means to love your neighbor as yourself. When we love those who hate us, when we bless those who curse us, when we give freely to those who take from us, *then* we, like the good Samaritan, love our neighbor as ourselves.

Who is our neighbor? Who is our enemy? Jesus removes these comfortable distinctions. In Christ's conception of the kingdom of God, the demarcation between *us* and *them* is removed. The question that initiated this parable—"who is my neighbor?"—becomes irrelevant. The better question is: Who is *not* my neighbor?[12] In the Sermon on the Mount, Jesus goes even further in obliterating this distinction between neighbor and enemy. There he states:

> You have heard that it was said, "You shall love your neighbor and hate your enemy." But I say to you, Love your enemies and pray for those who persecute you, so that you may be children of your Father in heaven; for he makes his sun to rise on the evil and on the good, and sends rain on the righteous and on the unrighteous. For if you love those who love you, what reward do you have? Do not even the tax collectors do the same? And if you greet only your brothers and sisters, what more are you doing than others? Do not even the Gentiles do the same? Be perfect, therefore, as your heavenly Father is perfect. (Matt 5:43–48)

The implication is clear, we are not merely to love those who are like us. We are also to love our enemies, for our enemies are also children of God, people deserving of God's compassion and love.

---

11. Franco and Radford, "Ex-KKK member denounces hate groups."
12. Green, *The Wesley Study Bible*, 1257. Note on Luke 10:25–37.

In the Old Testament, there was a gradation of distinction between several categories of outsider—alien (*ger*), foreigner (*neker, nokri*), and stranger (*zar*). Aliens were those who had left their own social context to live with another, foreign community. In ancient tribal cultures, one could not survive long without the support of a larger clan or tribe. So if a family or an individual left the protection of their own community, they would have to find protection from another group or else face the nearly impossible task of surviving on their own. As a result, aliens were dependent on the "goodwill of those with full status as citizens."[13] Moreover, aliens were often economically disadvantaged, meaning they often fell into the larger litany of disenfranchised: the poor, the widowed, the outcast. It was precisely these sorts of people that Israel was called to protect, not for purposes of conversion, necessarily, but simply because they themselves had once been destitute in Egypt and YHWH had shown them mercy. The act of protecting the foreigner was, itself, an act of sharing God's blessings with others. Consequently, the Israelite law granted aliens wide-ranging protections. They were permitted to participate in Sabbath rest (Exod 20:10; 23:12; Lev 16:29); to observe the festival of unleavened bread (Exod 12:19) and the Day of Atonement (Lev 16:29); and because of their economic status, they were granted the right to glean from the fields of Israelite landowners (Lev 19:10; 23:22).[14]

The term "foreigner," though closely related to "alien," had a slightly different connotation. These were the ones who were considered to be not of the Israelite people, and thus not privy to the same rights and privileges, though no less dependent on the hospitality of the Israelites. The stranger, however, was the one who posed a potential danger, the one who was a possible enemy. Israelite hospitality did not necessarily extend to this last category. The stranger was the one "who is likely to be suspected and even feared."[15] Thus, Israelite law only extended to the alien and the foreigner. However, Jesus calls us to go beyond the Old Testament injunction, extending the sphere of hospitality beyond the

---

13. Dempsey, "Alien, Foreigner, Stranger, Orphan, Widow," 5.

14. Notably, this latter provision plays a central role in the book of Ruth. There, Naomi returns with her the Moabite daughter-in-law to Israel. Since Naomi is a widow and Ruth is a foreigner, they are poor and have little means of providing for themselves. Consequently, Naomi sends Ruth to the fields of Boaz, a wealthy landowner and relative of Naomi's late husband, to take advantage of the provision in the law that foreigners may glean from the fields of Israelite citizens.

15. Dempsey, "Alien, Foreigner, Stranger, Orphan, Widow," 6.

neighbor, the foreigner, and even the stranger to the enemy. In doing so, Jesus removes the distinction between those who are our neighbors and those who are not. Our enemies are also children of God, people deserving of our hospitality, compassion, and concern.

The mandate to love our enemies is a limiting principle. If we are called to love our enemies, then there is no one that we are *not* called to love, including those who are religiously and culturally different from us. It is for this reason that Jesus, at the conclusion of this parable, reframes the expert's question. Instead of answering the question, "who is my neighbor?" Jesus asks: "which of these ... *was a neighbor* ... ?" (Luke 10:36; my emphasis). The expert's question is searching for a boundary, a limit to how far we have to go in showing God's compassion and mercy. Jesus' question dismisses those boundaries and calls us *to be* the neighbor to anyone, up to and including our enemies. There is no limit, no boundary to how far our neighborliness should go. The true neighbor, then, is the one who *acts* in accordance with God's mercy and compassion toward others, regardless of religion, race, or culture.

Moreover, it should be noted that this radical love of enemy is a prerequisite for participation in the kingdom of God. Recall that this entire conversation between Jesus and the expert begins with the question: "What must I do *to inherit eternal life*?" The Parable of the Good Samaritan is designed to clarify one of those requirements—love of neighbor—making this a *central*, not peripheral, theological issue. If I am not willing to love my neighbor, which now includes my enemy, then I have no place in God's kingdom. Again, the implication for interreligious dialogue is clear. If God's love extends to the enemy, then surely it extends to the religious other. There is no one that we should not be willing to welcome to the table to engage with in conversation. The biblical mandate calls us beyond provincial neighborliness and enjoins us to engage with those who are different from us, up to and including those who would be our enemies. Nowhere is the biblical rationale for interreligious dialogue clearer.

Conclusion

In this chapter, I have considered two biblical accounts—the story of the Levite and his concubine and the Parable of the Good Samaritan. Neither account deals explicitly with the question of interreligious dialogue, yet both make it clear how we are to treat others who are different from us, and thus provide an implicit rationale for interfaith dialogue. The Bible calls us beyond our own parochial communities and narrow nationalistic ties to a broader horizon that encompasses our neighbors, foreigners, and even those who are our enemies. Jesus, in particular, eliminates the distinction between these categories so that we are to treat our enemies as our neighbors.

What does this mean for interreligious dialogue? First, it begins with hospitality to the foreigner and extends to our enemies. By definition, the foreigner is one who is different from us, whose practices and customs are alien to our own. The biblical call to welcome the foreigner, then, means that we cannot avoid engaging with others who are culturally and religiously different. This is not always easy and it will require work on our part to learn more about others' practices and customs.

Second, hospitality is an extension of God's grace. Hospitality is a way of providing a context in which others may have an authentic encounter with God through our own loving-kindness. The hope is that, in doing so, others may catch a glimpse of God in a way that is life-changing. However, we must always be careful to guard against the ulterior motive of conversion for its own sake. If we are not careful, this can often be a subtle attempt on our part to change others into our own image and likeness, to make them conform to our ways. True conversion is an authentic response to God's transforming presence, not to our attempts at manipulation—intentional or not.

As I noted at the start of this chapter, we no longer have the privilege of secluding ourselves from people of other religions and cultures. This is true, pragmatically, given our current global context. However, it is also true biblically and theologically. There is no stronger biblical rationale for interreligious dialogue than the mandate to welcome the foreigner and to love our enemies.

Chapter 2

Deep Pluralism and the Need for Humility

Beware you are not a fiery, persecuting enthusiast. Do not imagine that God has called you (just contrary to the spirit of Him you style your Master) to destroy men's lives, and not to save them. Never dream of forcing men into the ways of God. Think yourself, and let think. Use no constraint in matters of religion. Even those who are farthest out of the way never compel to come in by any other means than reason, truth, and love.[1]

—JOHN WESLEY, *THE NATURE OF ENTHUSIASM*

Introduction

IF THE PURPOSE OF interfaith dialogue is not necessarily conversion, then what is its goal? In this chapter I want to suggest that one aim, though certainly not the only one, is truth, or at least an attempt to work together across religious lines toward a truer description of the way things are. If the participants of religious communities are interested in accurately describing their religious experiences of God and the world, then, at least in theory, there should be a shared interest across religious traditions to work toward a truer account of those experiences. Insofar as there is a God independent of all our varied understandings, and insofar as that

---

1. Wesley, "Sermon 37" 478, par. 36.

God has been divinely revealed to the various traditions to one degree or another, then the question is not so much about whether or not others have had authentic spiritual experiences of God, as it is about how well we have described those experiences and, correspondingly, how well we have described the nature of God and the ultimate. It then becomes a matter of ascertaining, together, across religious traditions, the truth of the way things are.

Here it is important to distinguish between two aspects of religious experience that are often conflated: spiritual experiences, themselves, and the language that we use for describing them. The fact that these can be differentiated is indicated by the fact that it is always possible to *misdescribe* our religious experiences. That is, it is possible to have an authentic spiritual experience, perhaps even an authentic *saving* experience of the divine, and still fail to describe it accurately. This happens even for those of us who remain within one faith tradition all of our lives. As we grow and mature, our language for describing our religious experiences often evolves over time. Does this mean that our earlier experiences of faith are negated simply because we misunderstood or misdescribed them? I should think not.[2]

I am suggesting, then, that interreligious dialogue should take place primarily along the line of description—of the language that we give to our religious experiences—and should avoid challenging the authenticity of other people's religious experiences. If these kinds of experiences are discounted outright, then true dialogue is negated; it is merely a thinly veiled attempt at proselytization. By the same token, if real difference is discounted, dialogue becomes mere platitude. Instead, interreligious dialogue requires a balance. On the one hand, it must proceed with the recognition that each participant in the discussion has had an authentic experience of God; on the other hand, it must recognize that the descriptions of those experiences are going to differ, often dramatically. Both sides of this equation require a great deal of humility, a willingness, on the one hand, to acknowledge the presence of God in others and the willingness, on the other hand, to acknowledge the possibility of error in our own beliefs. Only by approaching interreligious dialogue in this spirit of humility, can we hope to achieve the goal of helping each other sharpen

---

2. This is one of the reasons that the early church fathers rejected *Gnosticism*, the belief that salvation is based on knowledge. It is not our own understanding that saves us; it is solely the saving work of God in Jesus Christ.

our descriptions of God and ultimate reality, for it is humility that truly allows us to listen to others.

In this chapter I hope to provide some philosophical tools for approaching this kind of dialogue. This chapter proposes a form of deep pluralism, which holds that every tradition has had a unique history of development resulting in radically different conceptions of the world and of ultimate reality.[3] While this may seem to exacerbate the problem of interreligious dialogue by accentuating the differences between religious traditions, I suggest that this is the only way to preserve the balance noted above between acknowledging the authenticity of other religious experiences and honoring the profound differences. I begin by offering a general philosophical overview of traditions—how they tend to develop, the sorts of rational resources that emerge from them, and how they shape our various conceptions of God. I go on to argue, however, that this sort of pluralism does not have to result in relativism, for it is always possible that a tradition's rational resources can falter in such a way that it calls into question closely held beliefs and practices. In these circumstances, humility is the touchstone, for only when we are able to admit that we are wrong do we become genuinely open to learning from religious others.

Deep Pluralism

Traditions emerge from the hustle and bustle of life. They originate with particular beliefs, institutions, and practices already in place as the givens of a particular community. Regrettably, the Western popular imagination on this matter has been shaped by Thomas Hobbes' social contract theory, which implies a sharp demarcation between a simple state of nature and a complex sociopolitical arrangement, and where the choice between the two options is equally sharp, such that an individual knowingly and deliberately makes the choice to be a part of one or the other. Closer scrutiny does not bear this out. Historians, sociologists, and even some philosophers now recognize that communities and traditions emerge with particular beliefs, institutions, and practices already in place as givens.

Alasdair MacIntyre, a philosophical ethicist who has written extensively on the nature of moral and rational traditions, argues that it is precisely this notion of historical traditions that has been missing in Western philosophy. René Descartes is the paradigmatic example of this.

---

3. There are other forms of deep pluralism. I will be focusing on my own approach.

In seeking to set aside all previously held beliefs, Descartes fails to realize the tradition-constituted nature of his own reasoning, that even the languages he uses interchangeably, French and Latin, are comprised of words whose meanings are tradition-laden. By contrast, MacIntyre argues that rational behavior is only intelligible in light of shared cultural *schemata*—ways of ordering our lives that make our actions intelligible to others and *vice versa*.[4] This leads MacIntyre to the conclusion that all rationality is ultimately tradition-dependent. All our modes of reasoning emerge from some tradition of enquiry and, in turn, help to shape and guide the participants of that tradition. There is no tradition-neutral context. As MacIntyre states:

> Every such form of enquiry begins in and from some condition of pure historical contingency, from beliefs, institutions, and practices of some particular community which constitute a given. Within such a community authority will have been conferred upon certain texts and certain voices. Bards, priests, prophets, kings, and, on occasion, fools and jesters will all be heard.[5]

This is what Ludwig Wittgenstein calls the hurly-burly of life, that for which there is no firmer bedrock. Instead, we find ourselves already immersed in some tradition of enquiry. Early on, then, and until participants have reason to do otherwise, members of a tradition tend to place their full confidence in these ways of life without much question; they take them to be a matter of course. These various forms of life will necessarily be different from one community to another since each tradition develops in response to different historical conditions. Thus, every tradition cannot help but be unique.

It is MacIntyre's understanding of traditions that underlies my own use of the term deep pluralism. Indeed, a more accurate name for this approach would be historically-contingent, tradition-dependent pluralism, were it not such a mouthful. By deep pluralism, then, I mean that religious traditions are fundamentally different due to their unique histories of development. Every tradition experiences a different process of formation, shaped by unique historical conditions—geographical, sociopolitical, economic, linguistic, and all the various points of conflict and debate that challenge a community's ways of engaging each other and the world.

4. MacIntyre, "Epistemological Crises," 59–60.
5. MacIntyre, *Whose Justice?* 354.

While some traditions may develop in proximity to one another and, thus, may bear some family resemblance, each tradition tends to develop in response to its own unique historical circumstances, commitments, and concerns, as well as its own formative texts and authoritative voices.

Among the many historical conditions that define a tradition will be ongoing experiences of God. This is especially true for religious traditions, which will have distinct revelatory experiences that shape their understanding of the world and of ultimate reality. The problem is that because each tradition has developed so distinctively in respect to its unique history of formation, each tradition will interpret those experiences differently and will describe them in light of their own respective languages and conceptual categories. The Hindu and Buddhist conception of *karma*, for example, has no conceptual equivalent in the Christian tradition. It can be translated into other languages, such as English, but only by means of longer definitions such as, "*karma* is the law of moral causation that determines the outcome of *saṃsāra*, the cycle of reincarnation and rebirth, resulting in *mokṣa* or *nirvāṇa*, the state of perfect happiness and freedom from *saṃsāra*." Notice, however, that conceptual categories are not reducible to a single term; but rather entail a myriad of interconnected terms—*karma, saṃsāra, mokṣa, nirvāṇa*—that cannot be divorced from each other or from the particular, historical questions and concerns that gave rise to them. One may find similar concepts such as fate or destiny in other traditions, but these will be embedded in entirely different sets of belief, arising from different historical particularities, and will certainly not be tied to the specific Hindu or Buddhist conceptions of reincarnation and rebirth.

In this way, as each tradition progresses it develops its own methods for describing the world and the various experiences that the participants have, including experiences of God. These methods that a tradition develops are its *rational resources*—the various tools that members of a tradition draw on to make rational choices and to make sense of world. Not unlike the coping mechanisms that children develop for navigating the world, these resources will be unique to every tradition and will result in unique ways of understanding and living into reality.

Rational resources

The rational resources of a tradition will be numerous, but they will include, among other things, the languages that traditions develop and the conceptual categories that participants use to describe God and the world. Terms such as sin, grace, forgiveness, and kingdom of God are substantially and irreducibly different from those of *karma*, *saṃsāra*, *mokṣa*, and *nirvāṇa*. They constitute not only two fundamentally different sets of descriptive language about God and the world, but two entirely different conceptual schemes with significant implications for the kinds of choices that people make—spiritually, morally, politically, socially, etc. The Hindu caste system, for example, is predicated on the theory of *karma*, which explains a person's present circumstances in terms of choices made in a former life. The social hierarchy corresponds to this metaphysical theory. A person occupies a higher or lower status in the caste system depending on how many good or bad deeds they committed in a previous life. The important point, here, is that conceptual categories are not merely abstract. They have concrete ramifications not only for the individual choices that people make in the world, but for entire ways of organizing culture and society. Similar examples can be found in all traditions.

Rational resources will also include a tradition's primary and secondary authoritative texts and voices. For religious traditions, primary texts and voices are those that are formational in the development of the tradition. These will include sacred scriptures such as the Torah, the Qur'ān, the Bible, the Vedas, and the Tripitaka, as well as religious founders, such as Moses, Muḥammad, Christ, Buddha, and so on. Secondary texts and voices are those that may not have been formational in starting the tradition, but that have augmented it substantially. In the Christian tradition, for example, these may include Athanasius, Gregory Nazianzen, Augustine, Maximus the Confessor, Aquinas, Martin Luther, John Calvin, John Wesley, and so on.

It should also be noted that these sorts of authorities are not unique to religious traditions. While it is widely believed that the great achievement of the Western Enlightenment was that we cast off the tyranny of authority, this is woefully inaccurate. Consider the ways in which ethical and political traditions continue to be indebted to their own formative texts and voices, such as Western democracy's ongoing engagement with the Auguste Comte, John Stuart Mill, and John Rawls, not to mention, in

America, the Constitution and the founding fathers; or consider the ways in which, even the scientific tradition—that great pinnacle of Enlightenment freedom from the shackles of tradition—remains in ongoing engagement with Copernicus, Galileo, Newton, Darwin, and Einstein, over against, say, Democritus, Aristotle, Epicurus, or Ptolemy. Every tradition is defined by its authoritative texts and voices. Religious traditions are no exception.

The rational resources of a tradition, in all their varied forms, then, constitute the very criteria that participants of a tradition appeal to in making rational choices, defining for them what is acceptable and what is not. They are designed to answer the question: "What makes it rational to act one way rather than another?" The answer to this question will govern how the members of a given tradition address subsequent questions of ethics, morality, spirituality, theology, philosophy, jurisprudence, and so on. In this way, the rational resources of a tradition serve as the *standards of rationality*. They are the benchmark by which we determine what is rational and what is not. This is the reason why certain practices and beliefs of other traditions not only appear foreign to members of another tradition, but sometimes irrational. They do not coincide with that tradition's own standards of rationality.

All of us, then, are members of some tradition. Our beliefs and practices, our customs and rituals, our ethical and moral choices are all deeply rooted in our respective traditions and their rational resources. None of us can escape being part of some tradition, religious or otherwise. One may choose to adopt a new tradition through conversion or dissatisfaction with their current tradition and its rational resources, but once a person adopts a new tradition, their choices are then governed largely by the rational resources of that tradition, though perhaps informed by their previous one. In either case, rationality always takes place within the confines of some tradition. We are never able to stand outside of any and all traditions in a place of neutrality. Its traditions all the way down.

As the basic criteria of rational choice in a tradition, rational resources also serve to define one tradition from another. MacIntyre's fuller definition of tradition makes this clear. According to MacIntyre, a tradition is

> an argument extended through time in which certain fundamental agreements are defined and redefined in terms of two kinds of conflict: those with critics and enemies external to the tradition who reject all or at least key parts of those fundamental

agreements, and those internal, interpretative debates through which the meaning and rationale of the fundamental agreements come to be expressed and by whose progress a tradition is constituted.[6]

A tradition, then, is defined in large measure by its ongoing *debates*—both those among members of a shared tradition and those with members of other traditions. In terms of the first, as long as communities continue to discuss and engage the *same* authoritative texts and voices and the same standards of rationality, they constitute the same historical tradition, regardless of culture, geography, or historical context. Notice that agreement is not required. Some have argued that identifying a cohesive historical tradition is impossible since there is so much disagreement among beliefs over vast historical, cultural, and geographical contexts.[7] MacIntyre resolves this problem by noting that it is not agreement that is required, only acceptance of shared rational resources. As long as individuals continue to engage in debate over the interpretation and application of the same primary texts and voices, they constitute the same ongoing tradition regardless of historical, geographical, or cultural context. In this way, theologians as diverse as St. Augustine, Thomas Aquinas, John Calvin, Friedrich Schleiermacher, Karl Barth, Paul Tillich, and Wolfhart Pannenberg constitute the same, ongoing religious tradition.

By contrast, insofar as communities reject certain authoritative texts and voices in favor of others, they constitute entirely different traditions. The fact that Christians deny Muḥammad as God's prophet and the Qur'ān as God's primary text in favor of Jesus of Nazareth and the Christian scriptures, while Muslims, in turn, reject the latter in favor of the former, indicates that these are two distinct traditions. In short, these are debates precisely over what it means to be a particular tradition, both in respect to a given tradition's own standards of rationality (e.g., orthodox vs. heterodox, or even heresy) and in contradistinction to those of other traditions (e.g., Islam over Christianity, Christianity over Judaism, etc.).

Of course, traditions are rarely, if ever, entirely monolithic. Every tradition tends to have its own sub-traditions, as well. Sub-traditions are communities that tend to remain in some measure of debate with the adherents of the larger tradition regarding some of the initial formative

---

6. MacIntyre, *Whose Justice?* 12.

7. As one example, see Demitri Gutas' arguments against Islam as a reified tradition in Gutas, "Islam and Science," 215–20.

texts and voices, but diverge over the application and interpretation of those sources. This is often the result of later authoritative texts and voices that serve as sources for interpretation on the earlier, formative sources. In this sense, sub-traditions tend to be derivative of and deferential to the larger tradition's primary texts and voices, continuing to give them a place of primacy, while diverging in how to understand and apply them. Examples of these are not hard to find. Within Protestantism, alone—itself a major sub-tradition of the Christian tradition—there is, to name but a few, the Lutheran tradition, relying as it does on Luther and the Ninety-Five Theses; the Reformed tradition, looking to Zwingli and the sermons and spiritual writings of Calvin and the Canons of Dort; the Wesleyan tradition, which follows the sermons, theological treatises, letters, and journals of John Wesley and his brother Charles, as well as the work of contemporaries such as John William Fletcher, Thomas Coke, and Francis Asbury. Despite their divergences, these sub-traditions continue to take as authoritative the Bible, Jesus the Messiah, and, in some cases, even some of the same councils and early church fathers; the divergences are principally over interpretation and application of those primary authorities.

Deep pluralism, then, recognizes that each tradition, religious or otherwise, develops from unique historical forces, including influences of the divine, and cultivates its own distinct ways of describing those experiences of God and the world in response to these conditions. The result is fundamentally different conceptions of reality and different prescriptions for engaging it. This means that religious traditions are not essentially the same, nor are they saying the same thing. They are historically different with different understandings of reality, and these differences have significant ramifications for how members of different traditions act in the world in all their various forms of social engagement. In this sense, rationality is more than the claims or doctrines that a tradition makes. It is the entire array of social expression—rituals and customs, practices, moral choices, forms of jurisprudence, forms of government and polity, names and modes of naming, ways of dressing, and even the ways "in which houses are structured and villages and towns are laid out."[8] All of our various ways of acting and being in the world constitute rational choice and behavior, and they are all governed by the rational resources of our respective traditions.

---

8. MacIntyre, *Whose Justice? Which Rationality?* 355.

Conceptions of God

One of the benefits of deep pluralism is that it accounts for the differences in conceptions of God that vary from one tradition to another. As I have already noted, one of the influences in the formation of a religious tradition will be its experiences of the divine. Recall that I do not discount the authenticity of any tradition's revelatory experiences. In fact, the main point that I am making is that interfaith dialogue should proceed from the presumption of other tradition's revelatory experiences and focus on the level of description—how well have we understood those revelatory experiences and how well have we described them? The distinction that I am making has to do with the nature of revelation itself. Revelation straddles a fence between *the way things are* (ontology) and *what we as humans can know about the way things are* (epistemology).

On the one hand, God may be eternal, timeless, and unchanging (ontologically speaking), independent of what we know about God. That is, God's nature transcends our explanations of who God is; God's nature is not constrained by history or by our various descriptions. On the other hand, God's revelation is always a disclosure of the divine *in the world* and *in history*. Revelation always occurs to particular people at particular times in the particular languages and conceptual categories available to those who receive it in their historical circumstances. It is this historically-conditioned aspect of revelation that remains open to differing descriptions of God. There will be similarities, but there will always be vast discrepancies as well, since our historical traditions and rational resources will always color and shape our interpretations of those experiences.

In simplistic terms, one might argue that each tradition is striving in its own way with its own conceptual categories to describe the same divine phenomena. There is a parallel, in this respect, to be found between religious and scientific traditions. Gravity—or the propensity for objects to move downward—for example, was described differently by Aristotle and Ptolemy than it was by Newton's laws of thermodynamics, which, in turn, differs from Einstein's general laws of relativity. These various scientific accounts are all attempting, in their own ways, with their own conceptual schemes, to explain the same basic phenomenon. The limitations of language and conceptual categories, however, means that the accounts vary significantly. There are similar debates raging presently over the interpretation of quantum theory, string theory, and so on.

Unfortunately, even this description is a bit too simplistic. It is far more complicated both for religious and scientific traditions alike. It is not simply the case that each tradition is describing the same phenomena using different conceptual schemes. In many cases, the experiences themselves will be vastly different. Again, we can look to science for a parallel. Philosopher of science, Thomas Kuhn, argues that different scientific paradigms are not always simply accounting for the same phenomena in different ways, but rather dealing with vastly different phenomena. The unique conceptual categories of each scientific paradigm conditions its scientists to look for certain kinds of data and not others. In fact, scientists often discount anomalous data because the conceptual categories of their paradigm do not anticipate them and cannot account for them. (Think about those high school science experiments and the line graphs you created. Whenever there was a data point that was off the line, what did you do? Ignored it, of course, and chalked it up to a fluke accident.) This is one reason for paradigm shifts. When enough of the same kind of anomalous data is observed, new technologies, vocabularies, and skill sets have to be developed to account for it, resulting in a new paradigm of scientific enquiry.[9] Religious traditions are similar. It is not simply the case that each religious tradition is accounting for the same religious data. Our conceptual categories and rational resources guide us to focus on certain religious experiences and discount others as anomalous.

This is why it is not simply the case that each religious tradition is describing the same basic experiences of God. Some theologians have offered the analogy of a jigsaw puzzle, arguing that every religious tradition is working on different aspects of the same puzzle; if we could zoom out the camera lens, we would see that all our various pieces make up a whole. It is a variation on the analogy of the elephant, where the members of each religious tradition are unknowingly describing different sections of the same animal; their descriptions seem so vastly different because they are focusing on different aspects—the ears, the tusk, the tail, the leg. The form of deep pluralism I am proposing, however, suggests that these are false analogies. It is more the case that each tradition is working with fundamentally different puzzle pieces, putting together radically different pictures of the world that cannot be harmonized. One must choose among the different pictures *in toto*.

---

9. See Kuhn, *The Structure of Scientific Revolutions*.

Indeed, one of the problems that has been raised by philosophers on this topic is the issue of incommensurability—the possibility that traditions understand things so differently that they are rarely if ever addressing the same concerns. Incommensurability suggests that the claims of different traditions do not correspond in any meaningful way to allow for agreement or disagreement. Rather, they are saying entirely different things—apples and oranges—two ships passing in the night. If this were the case, interreligious dialogue would be impossible, for a prerequisite of two or more traditions engaging one another is that, at some level, they understand each other *and* that they understand each other as agreeing or disagreeing on the same issue. If all interreligious dialogue were incommensurate, not only would there be no grounds for disagreement, there would be none for agreement either.

Happily, I do not think this is the case, certainly not to the extent that it prevents dialogue. Points of incommensurability may present themselves, but they are not insurmountable. Understanding the claims of another tradition and locating those points of logical incompatibility merely require careful translations of the languages-in-use, the everyday vernacular of the participants of each tradition. Once there are reliable translations that seek to understand the other tradition's language sympathetically on its own terms, it is entirely possible to identify points of agreement and disagreement. This may require lengthy translations that use longer descriptions to convey concepts that are otherwise commonplace in the other tradition. As I noted above, using terms such as *karma* requires lengthy explanations not only of their meanings but also of their connection to other terms, their histories, interpretations, and so on. Nevertheless, once the terms are translated and defined clearly, understanding is entirely possible, and so is agreement or disagreement.

Furthermore, I do not mean to suggest that there will be no similarities between religious traditions whatsoever in their descriptions of God and the ultimate. There will certainly be instances where traditions have arrived at common beliefs and practices and will seek to describe similar kinds of experiences. In fact, this is one of the goals of interreligious dialogue that I am proposing, to help each other across religious lines to a closer account of God and reality. The more we find in common, the more confirmation we have that we are on the right track in our descriptions of God and the world. Nevertheless, these similarities will be the result of historical contingencies such as: (1) proximity: where members of two or more traditions live near enough to remain in ongoing dialogue with each other; (2) fragmentation: where one cohesive tradition splits into two or more subsequent traditions (e.g., Judaism and Christianity; Catholicism and Orthodoxy); (3) mergers and assimilations: where either, (a) two traditions merge into one, or (b) one tradition adopts and assimilates certain terms and conceptual categories from another tradition; and (4) shared humanity: similarities based on commonalities that we share by virtue of being human, concerns over the preservation of life, the protection of the earth, the raising of children, etc. However, even in this last case, such concerns will be substantially shaped by the broader commitments of a given tradition—commitments on what constitutes life and its preservation, what constitutes a child and the appropriate forms of love and discipline, etc.

Epistemological Crises and the Need for Humility

All in all, traditions tend to be fairly insulated. Although they may remain in dialogue with other surrounding traditions, they tend to be shaped principally by their own rational resources and conceptual categories, and remain resistant to sweeping, large-scale changes in their beliefs and practices. This is so for at least two reasons. First, excessive change is destabilizing. If we tried to change all our beliefs all the time—aside from being impossible—we would never be able to make coherent sense of the world. We would be in a constant state of confusion and bewilderment. The second reason is pragmatic. Insofar as our beliefs are working, we have little reason to change them. In this sense, conservatism is a virtue. If our rational resources have not failed us, if they seem to be working, we have little reason to question them and even less reason to consider alternatives. It is only when our own rational resources seem to fail us that we find ourselves genuinely open to new perspectives and alternative descriptions of reality. When we experience this sort of crisis—a crisis concerning the reliability of our own rational resources—we find ourselves in a position of intellectual humility, where we recognize that perhaps our own description of reality is not as adequate as we had assumed. It is this humility that opens us up to the possibility of truly learning from another tradition and its rational resources.

The sort of crisis I have just described happens at both the personal and the communal level. Personal examples are not far to find. Consider the housewife who discovers after thirty years of marriage that her husband has been unfaithful, making a sham of everything she had ever thought or believed about her husband, their marriage, their family, God, and even their place in the community. Or consider the college student whose beliefs about the world are challenged and overturned in her first-year philosophy class. Or consider the father who discovers that his son is gay, upending longstanding beliefs about human sexuality, what it means to be a man, what it means to be in relationship. All of these are examples of what MacIntyre calls an *epistemological crisis*—a crisis that throws into question everything we thought we knew about the world. Epistemological crises are more than just existential—that is they are not simply questions about the meaning of life. Epistemological crises call into question the very reliability of our rational resources, the conceptual categories that help us make sense of the world. They undermine our very ability to make reliable *truth* claims and rational choices. These kinds of crises force us to reconsider most or all of our closely held beliefs.

The example that MacIntyre uses for an epistemological crisis at a personal level is that of Hamlet. Upon returning to Elsinore, Hamlet is confronted with the dilemma of too many schemata—too many conceptual schemes for making sense of reality. As MacIntyre states:

> There is the revenge schema of the Norse sagas; there is the renaissance courtier's schema; there is a Machiavellian schema about competition for power. But he not only has the problem of which schema to apply, he also has the other ordinary agents' problem: whom now to believe? His mother? Rosencrantz and Guildenstern? His father's ghost?[10]

Until Hamlet can decide which conceptual scheme to apply, he does not know how to act rationally, nor does he know how to interpret the behavior of those around him. The madness he displays is due precisely to his inability to make rational sense out of his or others' behavior. This sort of crisis is possible for any of us. Once the meaning-making structures we come to rely on are called into question, we find ourselves without a reliable means of making rational choices.

Epistemological crises are not only possible for individuals, but for communities and traditions as well. It is always possible for an entire tradition to encounter a problem that its rational resources are not equipped to resolve. When this happens, it will be an indication to the participants of that tradition that something about their rational resources is not quite

---

10. MacIntyre, *Whose Justice? Which Rationality?* 55–56.

right, that they do not square with the way things are. In this respect, traditions are not unlike submarines. The captain and crew of a submarine are never able to see obstacles directly; rather they rely on sonar as an indirect means of navigating the ocean depths. If the sonar is functioning properly, it will navigate the crew away from potential dangers, and that information can be trusted as a reliable description of the way things are, albeit indirect and incomplete. It is only when we encounter some obstacle that our "sonar" is not equipped to anticipate that we are in a position to reconsider our equipment—our rational resources.

One of the clearest historical examples of this was the failure of the pre-Copernican scientific tradition. From the time of Aristotle through the late medieval period, the predominant scientific understanding of the universe was one based on Platonic astronomy and Aristotelian physics, culminating in the work of the second-century astronomer Ptolemy. Ptolemaic astronomy was the prevailing cosmology up to the modern period. Commonly known as the geocentric worldview, it held that the earth is the center of the universe with the sun and planets revolving around it in concentric circles. However, even before Copernicus, the state of the Ptolemaic system was inconsistent and unable to account for certain sorts of phenomena, such as retrograde motion.[11] While the new science of Copernicus, Galileo and, eventually, Newton, proved itself superior in the sense that it was able to account for these inadequacies, it was ultimately the rational resources of Ptolemaic system that failed on their own terms.

Another example of this kind of crisis within the Christian tradition is the Reformation disputes of the fifteenth and sixteenth centuries (ca. 1450–1710) over the "rule of faith" or the "proper standard of religious knowledge." Up until the mid-fifteenth century, the standard by which one measured the truth of a religious claim in the Christian tradition was based on *authority*—that of Church tradition, the councils, or the pope. However, individuals such as Girolamo Savonarola in his dispute with papal authority in 1497 and 1498, and Martin Luther in his *Ninety-Five Theses*, his letter to Pope Leo X, and his writings of 1520—*The Appeal to the German Nobility* and *The Babylonian Captivity of the Church*—began to call such standards of religious knowledge into question. At the heart

---

11. Kuhn, *The Structure of Scientific Revolutions*, 67.

of these disputes was a dilemma anticipated by the ancient Greek Pyrrhonists, appropriately called "the problem of the criterion of truth."[12]

Stated simply, the problem of the criterion of truth recognizes that insofar as there is a *shared standard of knowledge*, a common criterion to which everyone can unanimously appeal, e.g., scripture, tradition, the pope, etc., there is little or no difficulty in settling disputes. However, once the very standard of rationality itself is called into question, not only is there no commonly agreed upon means for settling disputes that may arise, but, more importantly, there is no means for judging the competing standards of rationality themselves. As such, how does one secure scripture as *the* foundation of all truth-claims over against tradition, or tradition over the pope, and so on? The problem of the criterion of truth, then, as it developed within the Christian tradition, is, at root, a debate over the reliability of a tradition's own standards of rationality. The vexing concern cuts to the heart of a tradition's truth-making abilities: How does a tradition determine its own claims to truth when the very standard by which those claims are typically evaluated has been called into question?

The possibility of these sorts of epistemological crises exposes the central problem with relativism, namely, it is always possible to be wrong, to misdescribe one's own experience. The relativist assumes that every position will always be able to justify itself; but this is not the case. There is always the possibility that our ways of describing reality will mislead us. When this happens, it is cause for reevaluating the reliability of our rational resources, not because we have been argued into doing so, but because we recognize the inadequacy ourselves. The crisis makes it apparent that long-standing prescriptions for navigating the world no longer work.

While it may seem presumptuous in the context of interreligious dialogue to insinuate that faith traditions may be wrong in their descriptions of reality, it is actually the starting point for humility. Only when we recognize the possibility that we could be wrong do we find ourselves genuinely open to new possibilities. When the adherents of a tradition encounter this sort of crisis, it requires a great deal of humility, first, to admit to themselves that their own resources have failed them and, second, to admit that they may have to reconsider their ways of understanding the world. Indeed, if a tradition is to recover from this kind of crisis, humility will be essential.

12. Popkin, *The History of Scepticism*, 3.

When the participants of a tradition encounter an epistemological crisis, they may find themselves more willing to listen to members of a different tradition. They may find that the very resources that were lacking in their own tradition are present in another. It is in this context that members of religious traditions find themselves genuinely open to learning from each other. As I have already mentioned, insofar as our rational resources are working, we have little reason to question or to change them. However, once we encounter an epistemological crisis that calls into question most or all of our trusted beliefs, we find ourselves surprisingly open to hearing something new, even from unexpected places, such as a different religious tradition.

It is this sort of humility that is required for genuine interreligious dialogue. Prior to this point, interfaith dialogue may provide for interesting discussions of comparison and contrast, and we may be open to gleaning certain insights or truths about the world. But it is not until we are in a position of destitution that we are entirely willing to reconsider longstanding, closely held beliefs and practices.

Conclusion

In this chapter, I have argued that interreligious dialogue should take place, primarily, at the level of descriptive language, that is, at the level of assessing how well our respective traditions have described our various experiences of the divine. The fact that all traditions develop out of unique historical forces, resulting in different forms of rationality that provide distinct ways of understanding reality and living into it, leads to my current proposal of deep pluralism. Only this sort of historical perspective can account for the rich plurality of religious beliefs and practices, including the variety of conceptions of God. Furthermore, it is this historical approach that allows us to preserve both the authenticity of other people's religious experiences, while at the same time addressing the descriptive accounts of those experiences, for it recognizes that all experiences—religious or otherwise—are always shaped and molded by some tradition-dependent lens. Thus, we can address the rational resources of a tradition and evaluate their adequacy without calling into question the authenticity of those resources or the sincerity of those who hold to them.

I also argued, however, that this sort of deep pluralism does not have to result in relativism. Relativism fails precisely because it is always possible for the rational resources of a tradition to misdescribe some experience and, thus, to misdirect its adherents. Epistemological crises play a pivotal role in this, exposing points at which our own rational resources may be inadequate. Far from being a threat to interreligious dialogue, however, I have argued that these sorts of epistemological crises are actually the starting point for genuine engagement between traditions, for only when we are humble enough to admit where our own resources may be failing us are we then open to hearing from those of another tradition. In this approach, then, humility is key. If we are humble enough to admit when we are wrong, and if we are humble enough to learn from those of another tradition, then we may find ourselves genuinely willing to engage in mutual constructive dialogue, dialogue that moves toward shared understandings of God and the world.

Chapter 3

Dialogue and Practical Hospitality

Thou shalt love thy neighbour as thyself. Neither is love content with barely working no evil to our neighbour. It continually incites us to do good: as we have time, and opportunity, to do good in every possible kind, and in every possible degree to all men.[1]

—JOHN WESLEY

Introduction

IN THE PREVIOUS CHAPTER I argued that interreligious dialogue requires a great deal of humility. First, it requires the humility to acknowledge that people of other religious traditions have had authentic revelatory experiences. If this is discounted outright, then there is little reason for reciprocal interreligious dialogue, only unilateral proselytization. Second, interreligious dialogue requires the humility to admit where our own ways of understanding the world may be inadequate. Only when we find our own descriptions of reality to be lacking do we find ourselves in a place of genuine openness to learn from those who are different from us. Prior to this point, we may remain open to helpful insights, but we are seldom ready to make significant changes to our fundamental convictions until we find that our own beliefs are somehow insufficient. This

---

1. Wesley, "Sermon 36," 465, sec. III, par. 3.

usually happens not because someone argues us out of our beliefs, but because we find our own beliefs have failed us in some way. We tend to reconsider our beliefs when we find that they are not working, when they are not squaring with reality in some way. Only then, do we find ourselves open to something truly novel.

This suggests that the way forward in interreligious dialogue is not simply debate and discussion, though these may continue to play a role. Instead, what is ultimately required is a form of empathy, the ability of members of one tradition to come alongside those of another in order to understand their tradition as sympathetically as possible—to learn their histories, customs, beliefs, even their languages to such an extent as to be an "insider" to it. Only then is one able to see the strengths and weaknesses of a foreign tradition as the members of that tradition would see it. Suggestions for change, then, become congruent with the internal pursuits of the members of that tradition, not as challenges from the outside. This, of course, requires humility on both sides. Humility to relinquish the safety of one's own tradition and to venture into another; and the humility to allow a foreigner to become intimately acquainted with one's own tradition. Inevitably, this will lead to the mutually humbling prospect that both sides have something to learn from the other.

In this chapter, I will provide several approaches for accomplishing this kind of dialogue. First, I will consider dialogue at the interpersonal level, where individuals have opportunities to discuss their beliefs and practices intimately one on one. Second, I will outline ways that traditions, more broadly, can work together toward what I call mutual constructive engagement, where entire traditions look for ways to aid one another in striving toward clearer descriptions of reality. Finally, I will outline some practical ways in which communities of faith can incorporate the methods outlined in these proposals.

Interpersonal Dialogue

One approach to interreligious dialogue is at the interpersonal level. This is the point of contact for most people. It is in our daily lives—at work, in our neighborhoods, in our school systems, and in our online social media outlets—where we are most likely to encounter people of other faith traditions. It is in these contexts that individuals have the greatest opportunities for discussing their differing beliefs and identifying points of commonality and contrast. One form of one-on-one, interpersonal dialogue is known as the *ad hoc* apologetic approach, whereby members of various traditions engage in dialogue over specific issues as occasions arise. Two proponents of this approach are William Werpehowski and William Placher, respectively.[2]

Werpehowski and Placher each encourage Christians to "seek common ground" with people outside the Christian faith to allow for personal discussion and debate.[3] Werpehowski, for his part, uses an example from medical ethics to illustrate his point. He contends that both Christians and non-Christians agree on three critiques of the medical profession: 1. It is paternalistic, restricting how much patients can participate in decisions about their own treatment; 2. It prioritizes the avoidance of suffering and death above all other values; and 3. It is fetishistic about technology. An *ad hoc* apologetic exchange between a Christian and a non-Christian, then, might take these common concerns as a point of departure, with the Christian taking this as an opportunity to show how, for the Christian tradition, suffering and death are not the final word and, thus, need not be a governing motive in medical treatment. In this way, a Christian can use a shared experience with common concerns to point a person of another tradition to one of the most salient aspects of Christian belief, namely the hope of resurrection. These sorts of opportunities present themselves in numerous contexts—workplace ethics, approaches to education, community concerns, politics, and so on. In each of these spheres of discussion, Christians have opportunities to find points of agreement with those of different backgrounds and to use these commonalities as impetus for sharing theological insights unique to the Christian tradition that may prove helpful to those of another tradition.

Another example of an interpersonal approach to interreligious dialogue can be found in the works of Randall M. Falk and Walter J. Harrelson, authors of *Jews and Christians: A Troubled Family* and *Jews and Christians in Pursuit of Social Justice*. These books emerged from a series of seminars that Falk and Harrelson taught jointly at the Vanderbilt University Divinity school with the intention of emphasizing the shared concerns of Jews and Christians over issues of social justice. This is a core theme of our shared scriptures, where the Hebrew prophets repeatedly admonish us to "seek justice, rescue the oppressed, defend the orphan,

---

2. See Werpehowski, "Ad Hoc Apologetics," and Placher, *Unapologetic Theology*.

3. Placher, *Unapologetic Theology*, 167.

plead for the widow" (Isa 1:17), and call for "justice to roll down like waters, and righteousness like an ever-flowing stream" (Amos 5:24).

In *Jews and Christians in Pursuit of Social Justice*, for example, Falk and Harrelson devote each chapter to a specific social issue, providing first a Jewish, then a Christian perspective on each. The chapters canvas issues of marriage and family values, including issues of single parenting, mixed marriages, and homosexuality; as well as issues of religious liberty, racial tension, and civil rights; war and peace; and relationships among Jews, Christians, and Muslims. They also address economic justice and ecology, focusing on our responsibility for the care of the earth and the ways that Jews and Christians have been active in movements concerning issues such as the National Energy Strategy.

In identifying points of commonality and difference among Jews and Christians on these shared areas of concern, Falk and Harrelson provide an invaluable model for the interpersonal approach to interreligious dialogue. Enough cannot be said for their contribution, as it is imperative that we continue to seek common ground and ways to work together toward a common future. The more that people of various traditions can find points of commonality for the purpose of collaboration, the better. We live in an increasingly pluralistic world where people of differing backgrounds must learn to live together peaceably or else run the risk of allowing our differences to tear us apart in ways that will continue to have negative implications for our local communities and our international relations. This seems especially true for the Abrahamic faiths, given our shared histories and our shared understanding of God's vision for the world, which entails, as Falk and Harrelson state, "working together for the establishment of God's kingdom of justice and peace on earth."[4]

While interreligious dialogue will always incorporate an element of the *ad hoc*, interpersonal approach, ultimately it falls short of providing a more comprehensive analysis of traditions *in toto*. The position of deep pluralism that I am proposing recognizes that all beliefs, personal or otherwise, are dependent on the rational resources of larger traditions. In pursuing broader questions of truth from a philosophical perspective, then, it is not enough to engage at the individual level alone. What is required is an approach that allows us to evaluate the rational resources of the larger traditions, themselves. Only then can we assess the extent to which each tradition provides resources that are adequate for its

---

4. Falk and Harrelson, *Jews and Christians in Pursuit of Social Justice*, 124.

participants and, potentially, for the adherents of other traditions, the goal being to find ways in which the various traditions can help each other toward fuller and clearer descriptions of reality.

Mutual Constructive Engagement

Mutual constructive engagement differs from the interpersonal approach in that it seeks a more systematic approach to interreligious dialogue than impromptu, one-on-one discussions. One of the problems with the foregoing approach is that progress is necessarily incremental, having to show "bit by bit that this construal of the world fits better than others."[5] Mutual constructive engagement, however, seeks to find a way of bringing entire traditions into conversation in a way that is holistic, taking into consideration each traditions' views of cosmology, science, ethics, theology, and so on. Because this approach is much broader in scope, it is also something that can hardly be done by one or two individuals. It requires entire communities of faith entering into dialogue in a way that allows for a comprehensive analysis of each tradition. Thus, this form of dialogue will require the participation of historians, theologians, philosophers, scientists, clergy, as well as lay participants, all of whom are committed to humble and empathetic engagement with those of another tradition.

The goal of mutual engagement: truth

The goal of mutual constructive engagement, as I am presenting it, is to aid one another across religious traditions to move toward a clearer understanding of the truth of the way things are. This is not unlike the debates among scientists of competing scientific theories. In our everyday, ordinary understanding of science there is generally a presumption that the world is intelligible and that it can be explained rationally, despite heated debate over varying theories (see, for example, debates on quantum physics). Nevertheless, those debates presume the possibility of consensus, otherwise, we would refrain from debate altogether. Something similar seems possible for interreligious dialogue. We have varying experiences and descriptions of the divine, but is it possible to help each other toward some kind of consensus, at least on particular issues and concerns?

5. Murphy, *Reasoning and Rhetoric in Religion*, 260.

Ironically, as I mentioned in the previous chapter, the starting point for consensus and for humility is the denial of relativism. If it is the case that every tradition is equally true in its description of reality, then there is little need for dialogue, at least not the sort of dialogue that fulfills anything more than general curiosity about other cultures and traditions. If our various descriptions of God and the world are the same, then we have little reason to learn from each other in a way that challenges us to grow past our own beliefs and practices. As Veli-Matti Kärkkäinen cleverly states: "just consider how useless and uninteresting a task it would be to compare two items that are alike!"[6] There is a certain arrogance in relativism that presupposes everyone to be right and above error or correction. However, if individuals and communities can admit that it is possible to be wrong, then it is possible to remain open to learning from others.

The question arises as to how anyone can know that they are wrong or, conversely, how anyone can know that they are right. The problem is that we can never step outside our own tradition and evaluate it from the outside, from a God's eye perspective, so to speak. So how do we know if our rational resources are true (or at least adequate) or not? In the previous chapter, I introduced the notion of epistemological crises, occasions where our rational resources no longer seem to navigate us adequately. I compared traditions to submarines that rely on sonar as an indirect means of navigating the ocean depths. We cannot step outside the "submarine" to test our theories about God and the world directly; but if our theories continue to navigate us well, then, at the very least, we have reason to trust them, to view them as reliable. This is especially true if those resources can navigate a tradition through unexpected crises that pose a threat to its fundamental beliefs and practices. If the rational resources of a tradition can adequately circumnavigate unexpected difficulties and challenges, then we have reason to believe that our "sonar" is giving us a truthful report of the world around us. It is only when a tradition encounters a problem that its resources are not able to resolve that the participants of that tradition will have cause to question their beliefs and practices and, thus, the reliability of their own rational resources.

Successfully resolving an epistemological crisis provides a tradition with a unique vantage point. To continue the analogy of the submarine, to have come through a naval minefield is to know the state of things, even (and especially) if you have hit some mines along the way. This

---

6. Kärkkäinen, *Trinity and Revelation*, 364.

provides a certain perspective that one's tradition did not have prior to the crisis, and a vantage point that other traditions may not have acquired yet. We know we are approaching the goal of truth when we can explain the limitations of our own perspective and that of others; that is, when we can look back and see why certain rational moves did not work and why they will likely not work for others, we can trust that our rational resources are accurately describing the way things are. Thus, a tradition's description of reality following the successful resolution of a crisis can be relied upon as true, at least as it pertains to the particular set of issues under consideration, since the tradition will be in a better place to judge what works and what doesn't concerning that issue.

Alasdair MacIntyre calls this the *correspondence theory of falsity*.[7] We cannot always anticipate in advance which of our beliefs are true; the most we can typically claim is that they are reliable (or justified). However, we can look back on our former beliefs and judge them clearly as *false*. As they say, hindsight is 20/20. However, 20/20 hindsight helps improve foresight, for when we learn from our mistakes, this helps us sharpen our beliefs in a way where we are able to avoid this sort of mistake in the future.

In order to reach the point where a tradition can resolve an epistemological crisis successfully and move forward with confidence in the truth of its own claims, the participants of that tradition must be able to create what MacIntyre calls a *dramatic narrative*, an account of "history understood in a particular way."[8] Only this kind of narrative can help the adherents of a tradition to understand (1) how they could have intelligibly held their former beliefs, (2) how they could have been so drastically misled by them, and (3) how they can avoid this sort of crisis going forward.[9] A dramatic narrative, then, must be able to explain three salient features of a tradition's crisis and its resolution.[10] First, it must be able to explain how their rational resources failed in the first place. This requires a good measure of humility and self-awareness on the part of the participants of the tradition to be able to assess honestly how well their own resources have or have not been working in response to certain points of conflict and tension.

---

7. MacIntyre, *Whose Justice? Which Rationality?* 356.
8. MacIntyre, "Epistemological Crises," 56.
9. MacIntyre, "Epistemological Crises," 56.
10. MacIntyre, *Whose Justice? Which Rationality?* 362.

Second, this narrative must be able to provide a new solution, one that not only resolves the crisis but ensures that it will be avoided in the future. This is crucial. If a tradition cannot offer an adequate explanation for how its former beliefs failed them *and* how their new beliefs will remedy the problem, then the tradition has not clearly assessed its own crisis and, in effect, cannot have learned from its own mistakes. Only a solution that can confidently avoid this same problem in the future will demonstrate that the tradition has adequately assessed and resolved its crisis and can continue making progress. Finally, this narrative will need to show how its revised description of the world remains consistent with the overall beliefs and practices of the tradition to this point. This third criterion is particularly important when borrowing from another tradition, otherwise, what is the difference between having solved the problem and having ceded that the other tradition is right?

If a tradition can meet these three criteria, then it can have some confidence that it has adjusted its "sonar" to be more reliable. More importantly, since the adherents of that tradition will have fixed the sonar in such a way that they are now confident it will not make this mistake again, they can also be confident that the input they are receiving from it going forward, at least on this particular issue, is truthful. So, to repeat: only when we look back on our previous beliefs and are able to explain how they misled us and how our new beliefs will help us avoid the same problem in the future can we judge the former beliefs as false and the new beliefs as true.

When solving a crisis, a tradition has two options, both of which require humility. One route is to scour the existing resources of one's own tradition to find existing resources in the tradition that might resolve the problem. However, since it is the primary resources of the tradition that have failed in the first place, this process will likely require listening and learning from dissenting voices within the tradition—marginalized voices that have been largely ignored or unconsidered to this point. Examples of this in the Christian tradition include feminist and womanist theologians, liberation theologians, black theologians, all of whom have helped identify shortcomings in Euro-centric ways of doing theology. This, of course, requires those in the majority to humble themselves enough to listen to these neglected voices in the first place.

The other option, however, is to listen to the resources of another tradition, for it is at this point that the adherents of two or more traditions may find themselves in a vulnerable enough position to be willing to learn from each other in a way that is not merely theoretical, but mutually constructive. This sort of dialogue will be far more communal and comprehensive than the *ad hoc*, interpersonal approach. It requires communities within each tradition taking stock of their own rational resources and evaluating how well they have served the tradition to this point. They will then need to construct narrative accounts for each tradition with detailed histories of the previous advances and defeats that each tradition has faced regarding their respective crises. Juxtaposing these narrative histories may then reveal points of *asymmetry*, whereby one tradition was able to resolve certain problems and incoherencies that the other could not.

Again, this requires a careful balance of empathy and dialogue. When constructing these narratives, the goal is to understand the opposite tradition on its own terms. We cannot evaluate another tradition based on our own standards of rationality. Either their rational resources are working on their own merit or they are not. Only members of a given tradition can evaluate this accurately. Thus, it is imperative for the members of a given tradition to construct their own narrative of progress as honestly as possible, so that they can have a reliable inventory of assets and liabilities. The responsibility of those of a foreign tradition is to understand the other tradition as empathetically as possible, to understand its rational resources on their own terms. As I will discuss in detail below, this requires something like dual citizenship, where we understand the other tradition so intimately that when we identify a potential problem for its members, it is not from the outside looking in, but rather as an insider, one who is familiar enough with the other tradition's standards of rationality to be able to anticipate potential pitfalls that they would identify for themselves. If the adherents of a tradition can honestly admit their own failings and shortcomings, they may find themselves in a position to learn something from those of another tradition that might help them avoid potential crises down the road.

This sort of mutual constructive engagement admits of at least two possibilities. The first entails a tradition-in-crisis searching out resources from another thriving tradition in order to resolve its own crisis; the second entails a thriving tradition proactively seeking to assist the adherents of another tradition, either by helping them anticipate a potential crisis or by providing resources for resolving an existing one. I will consider both possibilities in turn.

A tradition-in-crisis seeking assistance

In terms of the first, if a community is not able to find adequate resources in its own tradition to resolve an impending crisis, they always have the option of looking to another thriving tradition to find conceptual resources to aid them. This very thing happened in the thirteenth century when St. Thomas Aquinas drew on the work of a number of Muslim (and Jewish) philosophers to assist him in integrating Aristotelian philosophy into the Augustinian Christian tradition. At the end of the Roman empire, most of the ancient works of Greek philosophy were lost, many burned by Christians who were threatened by "heathen" texts; others were smuggled into Syria and Persia, where they were translated into Syriac and Farsi. When the works of Aristotle were rediscovered in the Christian West during the medieval period there was naturally a desire to integrate them into Christian thought. However, Aristotelian philosophy was utterly incompatible with Augustinian theology, which dominated Christian thought in the West at the time.

The core issue had to do with the nature of reason. Augustine believed that our ability to reason is corrupted by sin until it is illuminated by God's saving grace. Aristotle, however, held no such notion and maintained full confidence in the ability of human reason without divine assistance. However, the very fact that Aristotle's system was so successful challenged the central tenet of the Augustinian tradition that knowledge cannot occur independent of faith. As Nancey Murphy puts it: "if the Aristotelian system is (even largely) true, its very existence falsifies the Augustinian. If the Augustinian system is true, then it predicts that the Aristotelian system *must* be false."[11] This constituted an epistemological crisis for the Christian tradition.

It so happens, however, that the Islamic tradition had encountered a similar crisis nearly four hundred years earlier. As I will discuss in more detail in chapter 6, the works of Aristotle first made their way from ancient Greece and Rome through Syria and Persia into the Islamic tradition around 800 CE. This initiated a three-hundred-year Golden Age of Islamic philosophy and science, where Islamic scholars such as al-Kindī, al-Fārābī, Ibn Sīnā (Avicenna), and al-Ghazālī wrestled with a similar problem, namely how and to what extent to integrate the works of Aristotle, much of which was incompatible with the Qur'ān and Islamic belief. Averroës was technically born a quarter of a century after the Islamic

11. Murphy, *A Philosophy of the Christian Religion*, 31. Her emphasis.

Golden Age, but his writings on Aristotle became so well known in the West, that he came to be known as "*the* Commentator." His commentaries often accompanied most Latin translations of Aristotle in the West, and provided an invaluable resource for medieval scholastics seeking to integrate Aristotle into the Augustinian tradition.

Here we have a prime example of a tradition-in-crisis deliberately seeking the aid of a thriving tradition in order to resolve its crisis. In fact, one wonders if Aquinas did not go far enough. Medieval scholastics were influenced more heavily by Averroës than by Avicenna or al-Ghazālī, both of whom were considered more influential in Islamic thought than the former.[12] Furthermore, it was a significantly Latinized Averroës that became influential in the West, resembling the actual Averroës but little. One wonders what difference it would have made if Aquinas had had good translations of Avicenna and al-Ghazālī. Would it have better enabled mutual constructive engagement between these two traditions?

A thriving tradition proactively assisting another

The second possibility for mutual constructive engagement suggests that the adherents of a thriving tradition may proactively seek to assist those of another tradition, either by helping the members of that tradition anticipate a potential crisis or by assisting them in a current one. The reasons for cooperative interaction along these lines are as numerous as the reasons for interreligious dialogue in the first place. There may be a desire for a truthful account of reality and a recognition that cooperative dialogue can aid in that pursuit. There may also be interest in addressing common problems, such as growing concern over global environmental ethics or humanitarian rights, as reflected in the work of Falk and Harrelson. There is also the simple desire to live peaceably with those of other faith traditions. Regardless of the motivation, any attempt to assist another tradition proactively should be accompanied by humility and empathy. The days of volleying cannon balls over the bows of each other's ships is behind us. If we are going to be of any assistance to those of other traditions, it requires not only coming alongside those of another tradition, but also adopting their tradition in such a way that it becomes second only to our own.

---

12. Nasr, *Science and Civilization in Islam*, 54.

Here, again, the example of Aquinas is instructive. In addition to the help he received from the Islamic tradition, Aquinas also had an intimate familiarity with the Aristotelian tradition that other scholastics of his time did not. He was in a unique position, largely due to his philosophical training under Albertus Magnus, who had studied both the Augustinian and Aristotelian traditions closely, to understand both traditions from the inside out, so to speak, as though each were his own. His unique situation gave him a "rare gift of empathy," which allowed him to see points of conflict and convergence that others could not.[13] He had become so familiar with the language and background of the Aristotelian tradition, that it was as if he had "become a child all over again" and learned "this language—and the corresponding parts of the culture—as a second first language."[14] Adopting a foreign culture and language as one's own, gives one an insider's perspective, an ability to see strengths and weaknesses of the tradition as a native member of that tradition would see it.

Only when we understand another tradition empathetically, from the inside out, can we truly hope to provide anything of value. Otherwise, it is merely an attempt to convince those of another tradition to see things our way, on our terms. If, however, we can understand a tradition on its own terms, we may be in a better position to help its adherents anticipate certain epistemological crises that might pose problems for them in the future.

Islamic philosopher Seyyed Hossein Nasr is another good example of this kind of approach. Nasr was born in Tehran, but has spent much of his adult life and academic career in the United States. He studied physics and philosophy of science at M.I.T. and Harvard and is currently Professor Emeritus of Islamic Studies at George Washington University. He is a product of two cultures—Iran and America, the Middle East and the West, Islam and Christianity. Several of Nasr's writings focus on the inability of Western science to address ecological concerns adequately. He argues that the current ecological crisis in the modern West arises from a loss of a sense of the sacred in nature, a conception that he maintains the Islamic tradition has preserved.[15] According to Nasr, the only way for the Western scientific tradition to resolve its current crisis is to adopt a similar notion of the sacred found in the Islamic tradition. His

13. MacIntyre, *Whose Justice? Which Rationality?* 167.

14. MacIntyre, *Whose Justice? Which Rationality?* 374.

15. See Nasr, *The Need for a Sacred Science* and Nasr, *Religion and the Order of Nature*.

tradition-dependent response to a problem inherent in another tradition is a prime example of the sort of cooperative engagement I am proposing. Nasr has identified a conceptual category that is present in his tradition, but missing in ours and that might benefit us if we were willing to engage in mutual constructive dialogue. I will return to a fuller of discussion of Nasr in chapter 6.

Practical Hospitality

The second and third parts of this book will attempt to model the kind of mutual constructive engagement that I have outlined above. There I will consider an epistemological crisis that each of the major world religious traditions have encountered and the ways that each has stood to learn from the other. At this point, however, I want to consider some practical suggestions for how local communities might begin to engage in this sort of dialogue. It should be noted that offering practical suggestions for mutual constructive engagement as I have outlined it is difficult since it is designed to be more communal and comprehensive. As I noted above, it requires the contribution of experts in various fields from each tradition working collaboratively to create comprehensive narratives for each tradition to reveal points where one tradition has demonstrated strengths that another has not. This is not the sort of enterprise that the average lay community is prepared to do. Nevertheless, I think there are some steps that faith communities (churches, mosques, synagogues) can begin incorporating that may move us in this direction.

First, since mutual constructive engagement is designed to be communal, it is imperative that different religious communities begin engaging one another. We must be deliberate about this. We must invite members of other religious communities to our places of worship for meals and discussions. We must make these gatherings as inviting and non-threatening as possible. We must learn to be sensitive to the observances and dietary restrictions of those we are inviting and try to accommodate their needs. We should strive to be as hospitable as possible and make them feel like honored guests in our own home. In our discussions, we must seek points of commonality. We should not be afraid to discuss differences, but we must be careful to remain respectful and hospitable. Also, we must remember that we probably share more in common with each other than we think. It is easy to focus on the fact that we are from different religious backgrounds with different cultural and religious practices. But we must remember that these are members of our community who participate in many of the same communal activities that we do. Their children likely attend the same school systems, the same community sports leagues; their families likely frequent the same restaurants and markets. So look for basic human commonalities and build relationships from there.

Johns Creek United Methodist Church has engaged in this sort of interfaith discussion on a few occasions. We began by hosting a five-week series during the summer of 2017, where we invited representatives of different faith communities to come each week and share their faith tradition with us so that we could begin to get to know them better. Out of this series, we developed a particularly close relationship with a local Muslim community, whom we invited back to have a more intimate luncheon and discussion. They, in turn, invited us to an Iftar meal at their Mosque. These were occasions for mutual edification. At each event, we allowed time for both formal and informal discussion. During the meals, members of both communities had informal opportunities to eat and talk to each other, after which, we set aside a time for formal discussion, where the leaders of the communities would facilitate a seminar-style discussion, asking each other questions and taking questions from those gathered. This allowed us to begin crossing cultural and religious boundaries in order to build relationships of trust and mutual concern. It also allowed a space where members of both communities could respectfully ask questions about the other as a means of finding clarity and understanding.

Second, we must begin adopting another tradition's language as a "second first language." I mean this in two senses. First, in a literal sense, we need to begin learning the language of other traditions. Begin by learning individual terms; focus on the ones that the members of the other community deem important to understanding who they are as a tradition. This will go a long way in building understanding, providing insight into how those of another tradition understand God and the world. Second, in a more figurative sense, we need to begin learning another tradition's ways of understanding the world. What do they see as important and why? How do they understand the divine? How do they understand the world and our place in it? How do these beliefs shape their understanding of how we should live in the world? What are similarities and differences that we share? These sorts of questions, asked sympathetically, can lead to mutual understanding.

Third, we should consider adopting some of the practices and customs of another tradition. Corrie ten Boom offers this kind of example in *The Hiding Place*. When the ten Boom family housed Jewish families in their home during the Nazi occupation of Holland, they not only provided them with food and shelter, they offered them dignity by beginning to honor some of their practices and observances—reading from the shared Hebrew and Old Testament scriptures, learning to read Hebrew, and even celebrating Hanukkah in addition to Christmas.[16] Adam Hamilton offers another good example. In a talk that he gave at First Honolulu United Methodist Church, he noted that in preparing his book *Christianity and the World Religions*,[17] he deliberately chose one practice from each tradition that he would be willing to adopt into his spiritual practices.[18] From the Islamic tradition, he decided to incorporate the five daily prayers (*selah*). I have adopted a similar practice. While I do not pray five times a day, I do pause at least two or three times each day to pray and meditate, and when I do, I prostrate myself in a way not unlike Muslims. As I do, I often think about my Muslim brothers and sisters and our mutual spiritual connection.

Finally, above all, we should strive for friendship. We should deliberately seek out those who are different from us and build relationships. It is easy to make friends with those who are like us, who share our cultural background and our interests. It is another thing, altogether, to "love your neighbor as yourself" (Luke 10:28), especially when your neighbor is not like you. Yet this is one of the central aspects of the Christian message. "If," as Jesus says in the Sermon on the Mount, "you love those who love you, what reward do you have? . . . And if you greet only your brothers and sisters, what more are you doing than others? . . . Be perfect, therefore, as your heavenly Father is perfect" (Matt 5:46–48). If we consider ourselves Christians, we must reach out beyond our parochial communities and seek those who are different from us. If we don't, we fall short of what it means to be Christian in the first place.

---

16. Ten Boom, *The Hiding Place*, 117, 123, 134.
17. Hamilton, *Christianity and World Religions*.
18. Hamilton, "The Britt Lecture."

Conclusion

In this chapter, I have argued for two approaches to interreligious dialogue—the *ad hoc*, interpersonal approach and what I have termed mutual constructive engagement. Both approaches are indispensable to interreligious dialogue. The first looks for interpersonal opportunities to build toward points of agreement and consensus. The second entails a more comprehensive analysis of religious traditions, whereby scholars, religious leaders, and lay communities engage each other across religious lines to help each other anticipate and avoid potential crises and, in doing so, aid one another toward a more accurate description of God and the world. This requires humility to admit where we may be wrong in our descriptions of the world, and empathy to understand those of another tradition on their own terms. Relativism, the belief that every position is equally true, presupposes that we cannot be wrong. But experience does not bear this out. We are all capable of error—as individuals and as communities. Being humble enough to admit this is the starting point for authentic interfaith dialogue.

Finally, I offered some practical suggestions for interreligious engagement. These suggestions may be more in keeping with the interpersonal approach, but they are a first step in the process of building relationships that aid in interreligious dialogue. As I noted above, the second and third parts of the book will attempt to model mutual constructive engagement, bringing Christianity into conversation with each of the major world religions and looking for places that might allow for mutual edification between the traditions. In the next chapter, however, I will consider what role missions continues to play in light of the approach to interfaith dialogue outlined thus far.

Chapter 4

Humility, Hospitality, and Missions

"Untold millions are still untold, until we tell them."[1]
—JOHN WESLEY

Introduction

THE PREVIOUS TWO CHAPTERS have focused on the need for humility in dialogue, but have also attempted to preserve an aspect of interreligious dialogue that is often overlooked, especially in pluralistic approaches to interfaith discussions, namely the notion of *truth*. One of the main tasks of this book has been to find a middle way between two extremes—acknowledging authentic religious experiences, on the one hand, as a basis of genuine dialogue, but also recognizing the limits of human descriptions of God and the world, on the other. Another way of asking the question is this: How do we honor the authentic spiritual experiences of people in other religious traditions while, at the same time, recognizing that not every description of God and the world is equally true? The distinction is a tricky one, but important, philosophically speaking. It is a distinction that we are often more comfortable making in the natural sciences than in matters of religious belief, but the motivation is not

1. Wesley, attributed.

entirely different—an earnest desire to describe the world as accurately and truthfully as possible.

In the last two chapters, I have tried to make a case for how to walk this line, first by arguing in chapter 2 that our focus should remain at the level of descriptive language rather than that of the experiences themselves, recognizing that experiences may be authentic while descriptions can change over time. I also argued that it is the possibility of error in our descriptions that allows for more authentic dialogue, for only when we are willing to admit that we may be wrong are we then also willing to learn from others. Then, in chapter 3, I outlined my proposal for mutual constructive engagement that would allow participants of two or more traditions to enter into honest discussion of how accurately each tradition is describing the nature of God and the world. Taken together with the argument I made in chapter 1 that interreligious dialogue is not principally about conversion, the preceding chapters may raise the question for some readers as to the role of missions in the Christian tradition. Do we still need Christian mission and outreach if the authentic religious experience of others is taken as a given and if the goal of conversion is either precluded or, at least, minimized?

I contend that there is still a place for Christian mission, but that, again, the focus should shift primarily to the level of descriptive language rather than that of personal religious experience. That is, the function of missions is not necessarily to introduce religious experiences where once there were none; rather the role of missions is to provide better descriptive language for the authentic religious experiences that indigenous peoples have already had. This presupposes a theological belief that God is already present in these contexts prior to the arrival of the missionary, and that indigenous peoples have already experienced God's presence and activity, though they may lack the epistemic language to describe it and to live into it fully. This is the precedent set by the apostle Paul who, while attending a Greek worship at the Areopagus, acknowledges the authentic devotion of the people gathered there, but also recognizes the need to name the "unknown God" that they worship (Acts 17:16-34). It was not their lack of religious piety that concerned Paul; rather it was the fact that they lacked the descriptive, epistemic language to describe the religious experience they were already having. As Paul states: "What therefore you worship as unknown, this I proclaim to you" (17:23b).

Missionary outreach has not always been good on this point. Regrettably, missions has garnered the reputation—not without merit—of cultural imperialism, concerned with spreading Western supremacy, rather than the gospel itself. However, missions has come a long way in the recent past, especially in the United Methodist Church, largely in an attempt to correct the sins of the past. There is a growing awareness that God is already active in mission contexts long before missionaries arrive, and that the role of the missionary is not to impose spirituality onto others, but rather to help them describe their own spiritual experiences with the language of the Christian tradition. The World Council of Churches, for example, maintains that the work of the Holy Spirit is already present in the lives of non-Christians, working to prepare people for the gospel of Jesus Christ.[2] John Wesley called this prevenient grace, God's presence in the lives of all people irrespective of their religious standing.

In this chapter, I want to consider the role of missions in light of the approach that I have been presenting throughout this book, that of mutual constructive engagement. Considering missions in this way will help highlight several aspects of the discussion. First, it will underscore ways in which we can continue to honor the authenticity of the religious experience of other traditions. This is imperative in interreligious dialogue. The moment that we discount the authenticity of the religious experiences that others have had in their religious traditions, we relinquish any humility or empathy, and fall back into proselytization, antipathy, or worse. Second, this chapter should highlight the ongoing need for missions in the Christian tradition. Honoring the religious experience of others does not discount the missionary need. As Christians we are called to carry the message of Christ to the ends of the world. My argument, however, is that the missionary call should focus on augmenting what God is already doing in other places by giving others the epistemic language that is missing in their tradition.

I begin by looking at the biblical account of Peter and Cornelius in the book of Acts. It is one of the earliest conversion accounts in the early church and sets a similar precedent to the one noted above with the apostle Paul, namely honoring the authenticity of another's religious experience and providing the epistemic language to describe it better. I then argue that Christian mission should be based on our biblical understanding of the incarnation, the fact that Christ, in all respects, was one of us, adopting our forms of life, our language, our cultural identity, all so that we could know God. Christ's example provides us with a paradigm for

---

2. World Council of Churches, "Mission and Evangelism in Unity Today," 11–13, sec. 4, pts. 59–62.

what many have called incarnational missions, an approach that respects the distinctiveness of indigenous cultures and their religious experience, while at the same time bringing a clearer description of God into those contexts.

God's Prevenient Grace: Acts 10:1–48

The biblical account of Peter's encounter with Cornelius in the book of Acts provides a good example for how we, as Christians, should approach people of other faith traditions without discounting the authenticity of their religious experiences, on the one hand, or disregarding the real, descriptive differences, on the other.[3] In this account, Peter is forced to overcome his own biases against those outside his own religious tradition in order to recognize the saving presence of God in their lives. In this text, God does not call Peter to bring the message of salvation to Cornelius and his family, but to offer a better description of the experience that they have already had.

The story begins with Cornelius, a high-ranking centurion in the Roman regiment. The fact that he is a gentile is critical to the story. By definition, gentiles were non-Jewish (literally, "the nations") and, thus, fell outside the salvation history of the Jewish people. Historically, only Jews or converts to Judaism could participate in the covenant relationship with YHWH. Despite this, Cornelius, along with the rest of his family, is described as "devout and God-fearing" (Acts 10:2 NIV).[4] "God-fearing," in this context, carries the technical meaning of a "non-Jewish seeker who is simply interested in the beliefs and practices of Judaism."[5] It is often contrasted with the term proselyte, referring to one who has completed the necessary rites of initiation and is considered a full convert to Judaism. Thus, Corneilus would have been familiar with Jewish belief and practice, but would not have been a full convert. Moreover, Luke's emphasis in this passage is on Cornelius' moral character and religious devotion, rather than on his religious or political status. It is his *piety* that is "the causal relationship between his character and conversion,"[6] his

---

3. This section is adapted from my article, "Rationality and Religious Traditions," 273–293.
4. I will be using the New International Version (NIV) in discussing Acts 10.
5. Wall, "The Acts of the Apostles," 162.
6. Wall, "The Acts of the Apostles," 164.

regular prayer and almsgiving that are received as a "memorial offering before God" (10:4b).

All of this points to the authentic spiritual experience of Cornelius and his family. God clearly honors the faithfulness of this non-Jewish, non-Christian believer. The fact that he is neither a Jew nor a Christian is important, here. One of the central tensions of the early church is the extent to which it would welcome those outside of the Jewish nation. In many ways, this is a continuation of the ongoing debate that Jews had from the beginning—the extent to which God's covenant extends to those of other nations. Cornelius is a double-outsider. He is not a Jew and thus (in the understanding of the early believers) is also precluded from becoming a Christ-follower. Yet God's recognition of Cornelius' piety and devotion, in this passage, is a reminder that God—since the time of the covenant, itself—has honored those such as Rahab, Ruth, Melchizedek, the entire city of Nineveh, who were faithful to God despite not being a part of the chosen people. Indeed, when Peter tells Cornelius later in the passage that Cornelius' prayers and alms have been "remembered before God," the use of the term "remember" is covenant language, whereby God recalls the promise that the gentiles would participate in Israel's blessings (Gen 12:1-3; 17:1ff). Thus, even though Cornelius and his family are not part of the Jewish tradition, they are still able to have a genuine, transformative experience of God, one that is recognized by God as "devout and God-fearing."

However, God is not content to leave it at this, and instructs Cornelius to send for Peter, with the intent, as becomes clear later in the passage, of having Peter explain the content of his religious experience. That is, while Cornelius has had an authentic experience of God based on sincere religious practices and at least partial knowledge of the God of Israel, he still lacks the language to describe this experience accurately and to identify that it is the God revealed in Jesus Christ who he has been serving and worshiping with his piety.

Peter, for his part, must overcome certain prejudices against those outside his own faith tradition in order to help Cornelius account for the revelation he has received from God. The preparation for this encounter with Cornelius comes in the form of a vision where three times God sends a blanket of unclean food and instructs Peter to "Get up . . . and eat" (9:13). Each time Peter refuses, declaring that he will not eat anything that is impure or unclean. According to Jewish law concerning ritual purity, anything "unclean" is considered profane, and thus unacceptable to

God. However, when Peter refuses the third time, God declares, "Do not call anything impure that God has made clean" (10:15). The full meaning of this pronouncement remains obscure until Peter meets Cornelius and acknowledges that it concerns people too (10:28b). On the surface, the tension here is cultic not cultural. That is, Peter's concern is over ritual purity, not religious or ethnic identity. However, Peter's admission later is telling, when he declares to Cornelius: "I now realize how true it is that God does not show favoritism but *accepts from every nation the one who fears him and does what is right*" (10:34–35). For Peter, the tension is more than ritual purity. His concern is with Cornelius' ethnic identity as a gentile.

The vision that Peter receives, however, makes it clear that one's spiritual status does not depend on one's ritual purity, much less one's ethnicity or religious affiliation, but rather on God's determination. God alone decides who has been faithful to the revelation one has received. Cornelius and his family were faithful to their limited understanding of God, and God honored that faithfulness. Equally clear, however, is that our descriptions about our religious experiences are also important. While Cornelius had an authentic spiritual experience, he lacked the epistemological language and categories to describe that experience. It is for this reason that God instructs Cornelius to send for Peter. Although Cornelius' pious devotion was accepted by God, it was insufficient for fuller knowledge of who God is as revealed in Jesus Christ, and for fuller knowledge of who Cornelius is called to be in light of that revelation. Without the epistemic tools to describe his experience, Cornelius would be hindered in his ongoing faithfulness, for he would not be able to identify the one whom he serves and why. The role of Peter in this story, then, is not to introduce Cornelius to a saving religious experience of God or even to convert him to Judaism. Instead, his role is to provide the descriptive language necessary to account for Cornelius' religious experience and to allow Cornelius to continue more fully in that experience.

The fact that Cornelius' conversion culminates in baptism for him and his family serves as their inclusion into the Christ community and is the obvious next step. This is in keeping with the argument of this book. As discussed in earlier chapters, to accept another community's epistemic explanation of reality is to accept the basic rightness of that community and, in essence, to become part of it. It is interesting to note, for example, that Alasdair MacIntyre has become a Roman Catholic not on the basis of a spiritual conversion, *per se*, at least not in the colloquial sense of that term, but rather on the basis of his acceptance of the intellectual correctness of the Thomistic-Aristotelian tradition with its particular understanding of virtue and epistemology.[7] The same is true for Cornelius. Having already accepted the praxis of the Christ community, once he was introduced to its *doxa* and accepted it, there was nothing left but to join that very same community.

Thus, there is still a need for missionary outreach. However, I am arguing that missionary outreach might benefit from shifting its focus from conversion alone to helping others better describe their own religious experiences by providing the language and epistemological categories of the Christian tradition. I do not mean to suggest that discussions of conversion and salvation should be eliminated altogether. The World Council of Churches (WCC), for example, acknowledges that "there is place both for the proclamation of the good news of Jesus Christ and for dialogue with people of other faiths," and that whichever end of this spectrum is accentuated depends on "the situation and the charisms of Christians in that situation."[8] I mean only to suggest that missionary outreach, in general, might be better served by striving for the same balance that I am arguing for in this book—the balance that acknowledges the authenticity of the spiritual experience of religious others, on the one hand, and the need for Christian descriptive language and epistemological categories to shape and guide those experiences, on the other. This is particularly important for Wesleyans, who believe in God's prevenient grace. Wesley preached that God's presence as an initial form of grace comes to each of us before we are aware of it, and that it does not depend on our knowledge or understanding of it. We are responsible to respond in faith (to the best of our understanding) to the grace that has been received.

This is the experience of countless missionaries in the United Methodist Church, who recognize the experience of God's presence in mission contexts prior to their arrival. This is also the testimony of the WCC, which acknowledges that missionaries tend to "discover 'glimpses' of God's presence and activity among people of other religious traditions."[9]

---

7 MacIntyre, *Whose Justice? Which Rationality?* 393–95; see also Cornwell, "MacIntyre on Money," online. In this interview, MacIntyre explains his conversion to Catholicism as a "result of being convinced of Thomism while attempting to disabuse his students of its authenticity."

8. World Council of Churches, "Mission and Evangelism in Unity Today," 12, sec. 4, pt. 61.

9. World Council of Churches, "Mission and Evangelism in Unity Today," 12, sec. 4, pt. 59.

An approach to mission evangelism that is humble and hospitable, then, is one that remains open to God's prevenient presence in all places and seeks to engage with the mission of God (*missio dei*) as it already exists there. This approach to missions is not imperialistic, but rather open to the cultural and religious idiosyncrasies of particular mission contexts. As the WCC states, this approach to missions presupposes

> our *presence* with them, *sensitivity* to their deepest faith commitments and experiences, *willingness* to be their servants for Christ's sake, *affirmation* of what God has done and is doing among them, and *love* for them.... We are called to be witnesses to others, not judges of them.[10]

In the remainder of this chapter, I will explore some of the current trends in missionary outreach and how missionaries are already seeking to incorporate this approach.

Incarnational Approaches to Missions

Recent attempts in the field of missions to strike this balance between respecting the authenticity of religious others, on the one hand, while still providing Christian language and categories, on the other, is most clearly reflected in the model of incarnational mission. According to Alan Neely, the term "incarnational mission" was first used by Frederick D. Maurice in 1838 to describe "those who in Christ's name bury themselves in the lives and struggles of another people, missionaries who serve the people, learn to speak their language, develop the capacity to feel their hurt and hunger, and 'who learn to love them personally and individually.'"[11] This approach to missions marks a sharp departure from older, imperialistic approaches.

Indeed, our understanding of missions has changed dramatically in the last hundred years.[12] In 1910, for example, the Edinburgh Missionary Conference was held with 1,200 representatives of Protestant missionaries. For those gathered, the understanding of a missionary was a "paid professional, either male or female, who needed advanced

---

10. Davies and Conway, eds. "Witness among the People of Other Living Faiths," 274. Originally: Wilson, *The San Antonio Report*. His emphasis.

11. Neely, "Incarnational Mission," 475.

12. The remainder of this chapter is adapted from the Rev. Dr. Judy Y. Chung's dissertation, "Leading a Bible Study on Incarnational Mission."

graduate training in theological disciplines, or in medical and educational administration."[13] Missionaries were mainly evangelistic Westerners who advanced colonial-era structures such as mission stations, medical and educational institutions, and the emerging nation-state. The purpose of missions was "both to make converts and to establish Christian churches and civilizations."[14] The prevailing biblical understanding of mission was to export Christian teachings and lifestyle to non-Christian nations, often ignoring or devaluing the indigenous culture and traditions.

This understanding of mission was at times motivated by factors and influences that have led to negative stereotypes and pernicious expectations among the missionaries, the receiving communities, and the sending agencies. Johannes Verkuyl, in *Contemporary Missiology: An Introduction*, describes these motivations as "impure," rooted more in self-serving interests—imperialism, commercialism, and cultural and ecclesiastical colonialism—than in a genuine desire to fulfill the scriptural mandate to spread the gospel. In seeking to impart their knowledge and predominantly anglicized understandings of faith, missionaries have often confused their cultural particularities with the gospel message itself, thus squelching the indigenous expressions of faith and denying the preservation of the cultural identity of other people. Verkuyl notes that even as imperialism came to an end, missionaries continued to "impose the model of the mother church on the native churches among whom they [were] working rather than give the people the freedom to shape their own churches in response to the gospel."[15]

This approach to missions has been challenged, not merely on grounds of imperialism or cultural insensitivity, but on biblical grounds. Many argue that the incarnation of Christ itself provides grounds for an incarnational approach to missions, one that seeks to model itself on the indwelling presence of God among us *as one of us*. In the incarnation, Christ divested himself of his divinity to become human and to meet humanity on its own terms. Philippians 2:6–8 states that Christ,

> Who, though he was in the form of God, did not regard equality with God as something to be exploited, but emptied himself, taking the form of a slave, being born in human likeness. And

---

13. Roberts, "Rethinking Missionaries," 1.
14. Roberts, "Rethinking Missionaries," 1.
15. Verkuyl, *Contemporary Missiology*, 173.

being found in human form, he humbled himself and became obedient to the point of death—even death on a cross. (NRSV)

The incarnational mission that Jesus models for us, then, is this: he is Emmanuel, God *with us*. Before he preached his first sermon, before he performed his first miracle, before he proclaimed the kingdom of God, Jesus learned to walk, talk, eat, and live as a Palestinian Jew. He was born as an infant in a particular time and place to a particular family within a particular cultural and religious context. He observed and absorbed the culture around him before doing any teaching or evangelizing. In doing so, he has shown us that mission is not about unilaterally imparting our knowledge or imposing our culture and expressions of faith on another culture and people. Rather, mission is about coming alongside others, living with them, learning from them, and sharing ourselves with them. Indeed, as Michael Pocock, Gailyn Van Rheenen, and Douglas McConnell contend, "just as Jesus Christ was incarnated as a person, so missionaries, it can be said, need to incarnate themselves into a new context. They cannot enter as newborns, but they can learn the language and the culture of their new context in such a way that they behave like those who were born in the culture."[16]

The incarnation, then, is the example *par excellence* of missionary outreach. In his willingness to transcend his own divinity and to become fully human, Christ demonstrated what it means to offer a ministry of presence that is motivated by love and lived out in humility.[17] Darrell Guder contends that incarnational mission is "the understanding and practice of Christian witness that is rooted in and shaped by the life,

---

16. Pocock, Rheenen, and McConnell, *The Changing Face of World Missions*, 15.

17. While I acknowledge God's involvement in other traditions, I refrain from discussing the degree to which God is involved. I argue for missions precisely because I believe in the fundamental truth of the Christian tradition, that God has been working uniquely in the history of the Jewish tradition, preparing the way for the full revelation of God in Jesus Christ. My entire claim is that other traditions may have had experiences of God, but that those experiences may also be limited or incomplete because they lack the specific revelation of God in Jesus Christ. Thus, there is still the need of missionary outreach. Incarnational mission assumes this—that God has been revealed fully in the incarnation of Jesus Christ and that we are to bring this fuller revelation to other people who may have received some partial revelation, however full or incomplete. One very real problem at the heart of this book, however, is that *every* tradition feels that it has *the unique* revelation. So how do we demonstrate which one really does?

ministry, suffering, death, and resurrection of Jesus."[18] In this understanding of mission, there is no room for any ulterior motives of political domination, economic profit, or cultural superiority. Jesus showed us that the only true motive for mission is to love the world in obedience to God's will. He showed us that mission is about incarnational living that begins with the willingness to cross boundaries and is accomplished through living with and among the people—sharing bread and wine at the common table, listening to their stories and questions, embracing those who were marginalized, and teaching in ways that are relevant to the culture and context to which we are called.

In his *Philosophical Fragments*, Søren Kierkegaard provides equally good reason for incarnational missions. He argues that God's love for humanity can neither be expressed by elevating humans to an equal status with God, nor by revealing Godself to humanity in all God's glory and majesty. The first option would only make humans feel disingenuous because they would always know that they were not truly equal with God, like a peasant woman who found herself suddenly married to a king. The second option would compel humans to love God, not out of genuine devotion for who God is, but rather for God's splendor and majesty. Neither option produces a true relationship of mutual love and devotion. Kierkegaard concludes that the only option available is for God to become equal with us, to become truly human, like a king who relinquishes his crown and his kingdom to live among a poor peasant village just so that he may earn the love and trust of a single peasant maiden. Therefore, God must

> appear in the form of a *servant*. But this servant-form is no mere outer garment, like the king's beggar-cloak, which therefore flutters loosely about him and betrays the king; it is not like the filmy summer-cloak of Socrates, which though woven of nothing yet both conceals and reveals. It is his true form and figure.[19]

Only then will the servant accept the king as he is without feeling either disingenuous or unworthy. Only then will there be a true reciprocal relationship between the king and the maiden. The same is true for God and us. Only by coming as a true servant could God hope to have a genuine relationship with us. Christ's example, then, should be our model for missions. Only when we, like Christ, come as servants, can we

---

18. Guder, *The Incarnation and the Churches Witness*, xii.
19. Kierkegaard, *Philosophical Fragments*, 29. His emphasis.

hope to have a genuine love relationship with those we are ministering to, one that will result in true mission evangelism. It is this sort of humility, the humility that respects the distinctiveness of the other, that must characterize mission outreach.

In addition to the incarnational approach to missions, it should be noted that there has also been a shift based on trinitarian theology. I noted in the introduction to this book that the World Council of Churches (WCC) has come to recognize the presence of God in other religions through the doctrinal commitment to the Trinity, the belief that God is manifested not only in Christ, but also in the Holy Spirit. This opens the possibility for recognizing that God's presence may be available in various communities and cultures by means of the Holy Spirit, even when they have never heard the specific name of Jesus Christ. The scholarship on this is vast, and I will not attempt to trace it here. Suffice it to say, this is in keeping with what was said earlier regarding John Wesley's notion of prevenient grace, which, in many ways anticipates the recent trinitarian approach, that God's presence is available to all people before we are aware of it.

Recent Changes in Missions

In this section, I want to explore several specific ways in which missions is seeking to incorporate incarnational approaches, by recognizing God's presence in other communities through the Holy Spirit and by modeling Christ-like humility in its interactions with people of other cultural and religious backgrounds. Specifically, I will look at two ways in which contemporary Christian mission reflects this new approach: (1) the fact that Christian mission has become multi-directional and (2) the empowering of indigenous and diaspora leaders to minister in their own contexts.

Multi-directional missions

First, contemporary Christian mission has become multi-directional in the sense that it is no longer dominated by the global North with the United States taking the lead in sending missionaries. Countries such as South Korea and Brazil have become leaders in mission outreach, with South Korea now the second largest missionary-sending nation and Brazil right behind them. The stereotype of Christianity as the religion of the "West" or the global North no longer reflects reality. According to Philip Jenkins, "the center of gravity in the Christian world has shifted inexorably southward, to Africa, Asia, and Latin America."[20] His research shows that this trend will continue in years to come as "many of the fastest-growing countries in the world are either predominantly Christian or else have very sizable Christian minorities."[21] Moreover, the declining and stagnant population in historically Christian countries has resulted in the decline of Western mainline Protestantism. Jenkins asserts that "the era of Western Christianity has passed . . . and the day of Southern Christianity is dawning."[22]

Indeed, of more than 320 missionaries of the General Board of Global Ministries (GBGM) of the United Methodist Church, almost 50 percent are from a country other than United States. Many of these countries are now sending missionaries to the global North, ministering to the indigenous population and to the *diaspora*, those from one's native country living abroad. Missions today is no longer unilateral; rather as stated in the "Guiding Principles of Missionary Service" for GBGM, missionaries today are *from everywhere to everywhere*, willing to transcend multiple cultures to engage in God's mission in a spirit of humility and mutuality to build appropriate, active, transforming relationships that lead both to personal salvation and social and cosmic transformation.[23]

Examples of this multilateral approach to Christian mission abound. For example, GBGM has sent a second-generation Korean American couple to serve in Kazakhstan, ministering to indigenous clergy and lay leaders, assisting the United Methodist Church to grow and expand in Eurasia. One of the significant people-groups that they are ministering to are third- and fourth-generation Koreans who have migrated from Korea to Kazakhstan, via Russia. Thus, missions in this context is not unilateral, with predominantly Caucasian Westerners ministering to the indigenous population of some foreign country; rather missionaries from Korea are ministering to ethnic Koreans in Kazakhstan who are culturally Kazakhstani in terms of their language and customs.

Likewise, in Cambodia there are seven United Methodist missionaries of four different ethnicities serving alongside one another. Among

20. Jenkins, *The Next Christendom*, 2.
21. Jenkins, *Next Christendom*, 2.
22. Jenkins, *Next Christendom*, 3.
23. General Board of Global Ministries. "Guiding Principles for Missionary Service."

them is a woman from Bangladesh working with impoverished children; a Cambodian-American couple who came to the United States as refugees and have now returned to their mother country to plant churches; a Kenyan woman coordinating volunteers in mission; a Filipina woman serving as a treasurer and a Filipino-American pastor providing leadership as the Country Director. These missionaries have traveled from three different continents to serve in the same location for the common purpose of God's mission, demonstrating that today's missions truly are from everywhere to everywhere.

This multi-directional dimension of missions reflects the incarnational model because it signals a drastic move away from imperialistic approaches to missions. The focus is no longer on exporting Western culture and customs to "inferior" or "uncivilized" peoples. Rather, the focus is on creating a "global network of persons called to witness to the 'Christ event' across multiple frontiers or boundaries."[24] There is no longer an air of superiority, where white Westerners condescend to those in developing nations. Rather, it is an interconnected web of mission outreach where people from diverse cultural backgrounds travel to any mission location to spread the gospel. This sometimes includes missionaries *from* developing nations being sent *to* places in the West.

Missions of indigenous and diaspora leaders

Second, one of the critical issues that many new and young churches are identifying is the need for trained and educated indigenous leaders who can continue to carry out the mission work initiated by foreign missionaries. This reality indicates that there are limitations to the work that a foreign missionary can do. It takes a long time for a foreigner to build trust and to establish roots in a community. Not only are there limitations of culture and language that are challenging, but there is only so much that one missionary or a small group of missionaries can do. However, these limitations are significantly reduced or even eliminated when local people are equipped and empowered to be in mission in their own context. When local people are engaged in mission, they are able to reach more people in more places, significantly increasing the impact in that context.

---

24. Orchard, *Missions in a Time of Testing*, 164.

This need grows out of the recognition of cultural imperialism in the history of missions and the need to cultivate mutual partnership through community-building rather than imposing our solutions on others. Miriam Adeney shares a story that best depicts the receiving community's perspective of mission. On one occasion, a Christian from Africa asked his Western friend if he would like to know what it is like to do missions with Americans. The Westerner was interested, so the African told him this story:

> Elephant and Mouse were best friends. One day Elephant said, "Mouse, let's have a party!" Mouse agreed, and they invited all their friends. Animals gathered from far and near.
> They ate. They drank. They sang. And, they danced. And nobody, but nobody, celebrated more and danced harder than Elephant.
> After the party was over, Elephant exclaimed to his best friend, "Mouse, did you ever go to a better party? What a blast!"
> Mouse didn't answer.
> "Mouse, where are you?" Elephant called. He looked around for his friend, and then shrank back in horror.
> There at Elephant's feet lay Mouse. His little body was ground into the dirt. He had been smashed by the big feet of his exuberant friend, Elephant.

The African concluded, "Sometimes, that is what it is like to do missions with you Americans. It is like dancing with an elephant."[25] Christian mission can have a damaging if not detrimental impact on the community that we are seeking to help. Sometimes the best form of hospitality is respectful distance. It is sometimes better, then, to train indigenous people to carry the gospel to their own people than to send foreign missionaries.

The story of the Samaritan woman at the well in the Gospel of John is a good example of this. After her encounter with Jesus, she returns to her hometown to invite others to "come and see" (John 4:29). She becomes the first missionary recorded in the Gospels, and her primary mission field is her own home context. Indeed, the passage makes it clear that, while the harvest was plentiful in the Samaritan village (4:35), the disciples were unable to see it, much less reap it. Only the Samaritan woman could be a missionary to her own people. As a result of her witness to the good news of Jesus and her invitation to the people of the town, many came and believed. Similarly, a local person can have a far

---

25. Adeney, "When the Elephant Dances."

greater missional impact than a foreign missionary in many parts of the world. Thus, it is important for missions to empower indigenous leaders to engage in mission in their own home context.

Often, well-meaning Christians engage in mission out of a desire to help others. However, these Christians tend to identify the needs of a community based on their own criteria and standards, which are influenced by their own culture and context. When indigenous people are trained to minister in their own context, they can do so without imposing cultural expectations that are alien to the home community. Training indigenous missionaries, however, requires mutuality—an initial willingness on the part of the foreign missionary and the local recipient to work together toward a shared understanding of the kingdom. This concept of mutuality in mission is best described by the Greek word *koinonia*, or "fellowship." Glory and Jacob Dharmaraj discuss *koinonia* and the role of mutuality in missions in their book, *A Theology of Mutuality*. They state:

> In his letter to the church in Philippi, Paul introduces a few key mission concepts such as fellowship, partnership, relationship, and mutuality.... The words *partnership* and *partakers* come from the Greek word, *koinonia*, "fellowship," which Paul mentions in Philippians 2:1; 3:10; 4:3, 14, and 15 as well. Paul uses the word *fellowship* not as an exclusive one but in a larger context...."[26]

Glory and Jacob Dharmaraj further assert that "mutuality should not rob the recipient of dignity nor serve as a platform for the donor or representative to act as an emancipator. Mutuality is built on trust, respect, openness, readiness, and a commitment to change as everyone involved is willing to listen and acts as one entity, which has no room for monopoly."[27]

Mission that is mutual is about cultivating equal partnership that values what each partner brings to the relationship. It is about building communities that are not *co*dependent, but *inter*dependent, honoring one another for the gifts each other brings. This does not mean that missionaries do not have an evangelical role; they do. As I argued above in connection with the story of Peter and Cornelius, that role is primarily to provide epistemic language to help religious others better understand and better live into the religious experiences that they have already had.

---

26. Dharmaraj and Dharmaraj, *A Theology of Mutuality*, 81.

27. Dharmaraj and Dharmaraj, *A Theology of Mutuality*, 82.

However, mutual, incarnational mission seeks, above all, to listen to the needs of the receiving community in sensitivity to them and to the leading of the Holy Spirit in that context. Mutual missions starts with God and with the people that we are being sent to serve.

Conclusion

In this chapter, I have argued that missions still has a place in the approach to interreligious dialogue outlined in this book. However, I have argued that the focus of mission, as with interreligious dialogue, should shift from one of conversion, only, to providing religious others with better descriptive language for understanding the religious experiences they have already had and living into them more fully. I have tried to show that Christian missions, especially in the United Methodist Church, but among the World Council of Churches more broadly, have sought to do this by adopting the biblical model of the incarnation, where missionaries seek to adopt the cultures, languages, and customs of their mission fields, becoming the embodiment of Christ to them, in the same way that Christ was embodied for us. I then showed that this shift in approach has been characterized by a move away from Western imperialism toward multi-directional missions and by a spirit of mutuality, where indigenous people are encouraged to minister to their own communities and cultures without the imposition of foreign cultural customs.

In the second part of this book, I will return to the primary topic under consideration, that of interreligious dialogue. I will take each of the three Abrahamic religions in turn and attempt to apply the process of mutual constructive engagement that I have outlined in the preceding chapters. Taking deep pluralism as a given, I will attempt to show that traditions in constructive mutual engagement have something to learn, in humility, from each other and that in doing so, we can aid one another, across religious lines, toward a fuller understanding of the way things are.

Part II

Abrahamic Faiths in Mutual Constructive Engagement

Overview of Part II:
Abrahamic Faiths in Mutual Constructive Engagement

IN PART I, I outlined my proposal for mutual constructive engagement. In this second part, I will attempt to apply this approach in a practical way, by bringing the three Abrahamic traditions—Judaism, Christianity, and Islam—into conversation with each other. Recall that this approach to interreligious dialogue is intended to be more comprehensive than the interpersonal approach. The goal is not to offer techniques for how individuals can have one-on-one dialogue or even small-group discussions with members of other faith traditions. Rather, the goal is to evaluate the rational resources of each tradition in a comprehensive way, looking for places where each tradition can benefit from the others. As I noted in chapter 3, this requires constructing narrative histories of each tradition, setting them side-by-side, and looking for points of *asymmetry*, points at which one tradition may have exhibited greater success in anticipating and resolving an epistemological crisis than the others. Again, this requires deliberately looking for epistemological crises, those places where the rational resources of a tradition have failed to guide its members adequately or that demonstrate some potential for failing to do so in the future.

In this part of the book, then, I will consider an epistemological crisis that each of the Abrahamic traditions has faced and then examine the ways in which each has stood to learn from the others as a result of these vulnerabilities. The issue that I will be considering is that of providence—how we explain God's particular action in the world given modern scientific understandings of the universe. Since each of the three Abrahamic traditions has a vested interest both in God's particular action in the world and in modern scientific accounts of the world, each shares a similar vulnerability to the challenges raised by the latter for the former. However, the problem is more than a mere conflict between science and religion. The epistemological crisis is this: if modern science rules out the possibility of God's special providence, then, by extension, it also calls into question the possibility of revelation and, with it, any theological knowledge derived from revelation. That is, if special providence is precluded, then so too is the reliability of any particular knowledge about God, and the lack of reliable knowledge is, by definition, an epistemological crisis.

While the Jewish and Islamic traditions have not faced this crisis in the modern period in the same way that the Christian tradition has, all three traditions have encountered a similar crisis during the medieval period with the adoption of Greek philosophical and scientific conceptions of the world that constrained notions of God's action in the world, resulting in a similar crisis to that of the modern period. Moreover, during the medieval period all three traditions exhibited a form of mutual constructive engagement that allowed each to benefit the others in such a way that helped them to resolve their shared crisis. In the following chapters, then, I hope to show how these three traditions have aided one another in overcoming a shared epistemological crisis in the past and how they stand to benefit from each other today in resolving the current crisis.

Here, I want to make two caveats. First, in talking about *the* Christian, Islamic, or Jewish traditions, I do not mean to suggest that each is a strict monolith. This is certainly not the case. Each tradition has its own unique sub-traditions that deserve careful attention. Unfortunately, the scope of this book does not allow for that sort of detail. Instead, I will be looking at the some of the dominant strands of thought from each tradition (*Protestant* Christianity, *Sunni* Islam, and *Reform* Judaism) within particular historical contexts, principally the medieval (700–1200 CE) and modern (1650–1900s CE) periods.

Second, I will do my best to consider this issue from the perspective of each tradition, endeavoring to identify the crisis in such a way that the participants of each tradition would recognize it for themselves. Recall, that MacIntyre encourages us to develop empathy to the point that the language of the other tradition becomes a second first language. The goal is not to point fingers, to identify discrepancies that *we* see in another tradition. The goal is to help the participants of another tradition identify and articulate the crisis as they would recognize it *themselves*, and then to enter into dialogue in such a fashion that the participants of each tradition can stand to benefit from one another's insights as a means of resolving the crisis moving forward. The overriding goal is mutual constructive engagement, how we can learn from each other's crises in such a way as to help each other toward a clearer understanding of God and the world.

Chapter 5

Christianity and Providence

There is scarce any doctrine in the whole compass of revelation, which is of deeper importance than this [providence]. And, at the same time, there is scarce any that is so little regarded, and perhaps so little understood. Let us endeavor then, with the assistance of God, to examine it to the bottom; to see upon what foundation it stands, and what it properly implies.[1]

—JOHN WESLEY

Introduction

THE CONCEPT OF PROVIDENCE has been a part of the Christian tradition from at least the time of St. Augustine (354–430 CE). It is the belief that God is governing the world in all its aspects, working in both general and particular ways to bring about God's purposes for the world and for human history. The doctrine of providence, however, raises two seemingly conflicting positions about divine and human causation. On the one hand, it holds that God is all-powerful, sovereign over all creation, so that nothing happens without God's involvement, while, on the other hand, it holds that the created order—humans in particular—are endowed with autonomous causal powers, capable of acting independently of God's

---

1. Wesley, "Sermon 67," 315, par. 7.

providence. Reconciling these two positions has always been a matter of balance. If, at any point, more weight is given to one side than the other, an epistemological crisis is bound to ensue.

If, for example, the former is granted more weight, and God is understood to be the only true agent, then the result is *occasionalism*—the belief that all events in the world are mere occasions for God's action. Such a position exacerbates, among other things, the problem of evil, making God solely responsible for everything in the world, including all suffering. If, by contrast, the latter position is granted full weight—that the world possesses its own independent, causal agency, and God has little or no involvement—then the result is *deism*, the belief that God created the natural world, but has no ongoing involvement in it.[2]

The rise of Western science during the modern period (ca. fifteenth to mid-seventeenth centuries) tipped the scale toward deism. Over time, more and more causal power was attributed to the created order, leaving less and less room for God's involvement. This has posed one of the greatest challenges to Christian theology, undermining classical language about God's action in the world, particularly as it pertains to miracles, given scientific accounts of the world that seem to preclude such language in the first place. Moreover, this issue poses an epistemological crisis because it threatens the very reliability of the tradition's truth claims about God. Particular, theological knowledge of God is predicated on divine revelation, which, in turn, is dependent on God's ability to act in the world in particular ways. If divine action of this sort is precluded, then so too is any special revelation and, along with it, any justification for Christian belief (theology) and practice.[3]

---

2. It is interesting to note that while most of the founders of America are typically regarded as "Christian," they were, in fact, deists, believing that God created the natural world and then left it to run its own course. Thomas Jefferson, by way of example, notoriously edited his own version of the Bible that discarded the entirety of the Old Testament and much of the New Testament, especially anything related to miracles, whittling it down to the teachings of Jesus and the apostles. See Jefferson, *The Jefferson Bible*.

3. This is one of the reasons for the movement in liberal theology toward demythologizing Christian belief. If we cannot say unequivocally that God acts in the world the same way that scripture recounts, then how do we justify religious belief and practice? We "demythologize" it, meaning that we remove the literal sense of the phrase, "God acts," and shift the grounds for theological belief and practice from divine action to something like ethics or morality. But how far can we go in this direction without substantially gutting the tradition? See, for example, Bultmann, "Jesus and the Word." See also, Gilkey, "Cosmology, Ontology, and the Travail of Biblical Language."

In this chapter, then, I will discuss how the issue of providence became an epistemological crisis for the Christian tradition during the modern period. I will begin by discussing, in more detail, the historical understanding of providence and its importance in the Christian tradition. I will then provide an overview of the rise of modern science and how it came to pose a problem for Christian notions of providence. Finally, I will conclude by looking at the tradition's most promising attempt to resolve the crisis.

Creation and Providence

Historically, the Christian tradition has understood God's action in the world in terms of two distinct, though related, doctrines: creation and providence. The first is the belief that God is the ultimate source of all that is, that in an act of sovereign will and love, God called the entire created order into existence from nothing (*creatio ex nihilo*). The doctrine of creation also tends to entail the belief in *creatio continua*, the affirmation that creation continues to be dependent on God for its existence as well as for its ongoing novelty. *Creatio continua* maintains that creation does not stop at the moment of the world's inception, but rather is an ongoing process, worked out through the unfolding of divine action and natural processes. In this way, *creatio continua* acknowledges the divine right to bring about new realities, both natural (e.g., evolution) and spiritual (e.g., Christ's resurrection). Finally, in addition to *creatio ex nihilo* and *creatio continua*, the doctrine of creation also implies, at a basic level, that the world is the primary arena of God's action as creator. It is the locus of God's immanent action, the context in which God brings about the divine purposes—God's providence.[4]

The doctrines of creation and providence, then, are closely related to each other, specifically in regard to divine intent. The doctrine of creation holds not merely that the world was created by God, but that it was created by God *for a purpose*. Movement toward this divine end is accomplished only by means of God's ongoing acts of providence, whereby God acts in general and specific ways to guide creation toward its fulfillment. For this reason, classical theology of the Middle Ages maintained that the doctrine of providence entails three dimensions: preservation,

---

4. Russell, *Cosmology: From Alpha to Omega*, 112–13.

concurrence, and governance.⁵ Preservation is closely related to the doctrine of *creatio continua*, God's ongoing sustaining activity in the world. It is through preservation that God keeps the world in existence. Indeed, classical theology maintained that if God were to withdraw divine support, the world would cease to exist altogether. This dimension of providence, then, is requisite for all others; without God's preservation there would be no context in which God's purposes could be realized.

Concurrence is the commitment to God's self-limiting restraint in overriding created causality. It is the belief that God cooperates with the secondary powers of creation, "allowing them to act as they do within certain set spheres of activity."⁶ Concurrence is the fulcrum of the balance, noted above, between occasionalism and deism, the fundamental belief that God's power, though absolute, does not override the causal powers of the created order. It complements preservation in that, as Veli-Matti Kärkkäinen states, it suggests that the latter "does not mean frustrating the relative independence of creatures."⁷ Although there have been sharp disputes over the extent to which God's will complements or overrides created volition—as in those defining debates between Calvinists and Arminians, the former placing more causal consequence on God's providence than the latter—the Christian tradition has historically affirmed the belief that God has deliberately created free choice, a world in which creatures are capable of diverging from God's will.

Governance, or "providence proper," refers to the overarching rule of God—God's loving guidance of the world toward its divine *telos*.⁸ It is the root of the Christian hope that the world has meaning, that it has been created for a purpose and is being divinely directed toward that end. It is also the locus of the Christian hope concerning questions of theodicy, that evil—moral evil, in particular—will be put right through the unfolding of the kingdom of God and the final consummation of the kingdom at the end of time. Indeed, it is this belief in God's ultimate governance that supports the central claim of the Christian tradition, that God, in loving devotion to creation, has sought to redeem it from the ravages of sin and evil through the life, death, and resurrection of the incarnate Son.

5. Grenz, *Theology for the Community of God*, 116.
6. Grenz, *Theology for the Community of God*, 116.
7. Kärkkäinen, *Creation and Humanity*, 167.
8. Grenz, *Theology for the Community of God*, 116.

Finally, the working out of God's providence, in all its dimensions, has traditionally admitted of two broad possibilities: general and special divine action. God's general providence is closely associated with preservation and *creatio continua*. It is God's uniform, undifferentiated, and ubiquitous presence to creation as a whole, sustaining it and guiding it. There is no aspect of creation, for example, that receives more or less divine preservation than another. It is spread evenly like a coat of paint on the wall. The whole is necessarily sustained uniformly by God's general divine action. Likewise, God's general governance can be understood in terms of an overarching lure or divine persuasion,[9] whereby God directs creation in its entirety toward God's desired end. Such an understanding does not require God to act in particular events with regard to particular people or communities. In fact, as will be examined more closely below, during the modern period general divine action came to be associated with *immanentism*, the belief that God works in and through the natural processes of creation in such a way that it is nearly indistinguishable from those processes. General providence, however, is not enough to provide particular theological knowledge. It may be enough to secure general beliefs such as the existence of God or even the goodness of God, but it is not enough to provide particular beliefs such as the divinity of Christ, the triune nature of God, the resurrection, the kingdom of God, and so on.

Special providence, by contrast, refers to God's particular acts in creation—distinct acts that directly effect the events of nature and history by employing specific events or people at particular times and places to bring about some specific divine end. Unlike general divine action, special providence is not ubiquitous or undifferentiated. It betides particular people or communities in the form of localized revelations such as the call of Abraham, the word of the Lord to the prophets, the annunciation of Mary, and so on. These acts of providence have traditionally been understood to be both *objective*, capable of being discerned and agreed on by all who observe or experience them, and *effectual*, altering the course of events from what they would have been had God not acted in this way, at this time. As a distinct subset, special providence also entails that class of divine acts identified as "miracles" or the "mighty acts of God." These are the *extraordinary* acts that disrupt the ordinary course of things in order to bring about something truly novel or exceptional, such as the parting of the Sea of Reeds or the resurrection. In *The Concept of Miracle*,

---

9. Cobb, *God and the World*, 90.

Richard Swinburne offers both a broad and narrow definition of the term. Broadly construed, a miracle is "an event of an extraordinary kind, brought about by a god, and of religious significance."[10] More narrowly it has been understood, throughout the modern period, in particular, as "*a violation of a law of nature by a god.*"

For the most part, the doctrines of creation and providence remained relatively unproblematic from the time of their formulation in the Middle Ages until the early to mid-1700s and the advent of the modern scientific worldview. In later chapters, I will argue that this was not entirely the case, that certain conceptions of Neoplatonic metaphysics presented challenges for divine action even for medievals. However, the shift to the mechanistic philosophy of nature in the modern period presented its own unique challenges. God's causal agency became more difficult to explain. As the picture of a causally-closed universe, functioning deterministically from the lowest constituent parts of reality to the highest, came to dominate the modern scientific (and metaphysical) imagination, it became increasingly more difficult to account for God's ongoing action in the world, especially in regard to special providence, miracles in particular. As Brian Hebblethwaite states:

> It is the doctrine of providence rather than the doctrine of creation that is most problematic here. . . . Nor is a doctrine of general providence too difficult to reconcile with contemporary scientific, sociological, and historical conceptions of reality. It is possible to hold that God has built into the nature of things a certain grain of tendency, a latent teleology, that is bound to realise God's purposes, one way or another, in the course of time. Such theological interpretations of the data of experience do not necessarily conflict with purely naturalistic descriptions. It is the notion of *special providence*—of particular divine acts within the created world—that raise the difficulties. . . . Can we continue to believe that things have happened in the world that would not have happened had not God himself taken action (over and above his basic creative action) . . . ?[11]

Yet belief in God's mighty acts is so central not only to the Christian tradition, but to all the Abrahamic faiths—from the Jewish confession that God led the Israelites out of Egypt by parting the Sea of Reeds, to the Islamic claim that Muḥammad received direct revelations from the

10. Swinburne, *The Concept of Miracle*, 1.
11. Hebblethwaite, "Introduction," 2.

angel Gabriel while praying and meditating in the caves of the mountains near Mecca, to one of the strongest claims of the Christian tradition that Jesus of Nazareth was raised from the dead on the third day after his crucifixion. Indeed, the picture that emerges from these various scriptural accounts is one of God's total sovereignty over all of history, not only in its general course, but in its particulars. All of nature and history are utterly dependent on God not only for their ongoing existence, but for their moment-to-moment operations. They are interdependent on God's activity, such that historical processes and God's actions constitute an interwoven tapestry. Moreover, the very possibility of theological knowledge depends on the possibility of special divine action and special revelation. Without special revelation there can be little in the way of theological knowledge about God, which would constitute an epistemological crisis of the first order for the Christian tradition.

The Rise of Early Modern Science

So what happened after the 1800s that made talk of God's action in the world so problematic? Is it simply the case, as the standard account goes, that modernity superseded archaic thinking—that the "light of reason" dispelled the "darkness" of myth and ignorance? Yet, Aristotle was no mythologizer. His cosmological model was a sophisticated scientific account of nature and the operations of the heavens, one that continued to be influential, not only through the Middle Ages, but right up to the dawn of the modern period, where it was initially rejected, as we shall see below, not on grounds of mathematical simplicity, alone, but on the grounds that there was an alternative to Aristotle's *metaphysical* backing, specifically that of Neoplatonic Pythagoreanism. Copernicus' belief—and that of Kepler and Galileo after him—that the universe is fundamentally mathematical was arrived at not empirically, but because of a shift in metaphysics.

It is well-attested that the scientific revolution came about as the result of the careful mathematical work of Copernicus, Kepler, Galileo, and Newton. What is not often acknowledged are the underlying *metaphysical* assumptions governing their work. E. A. Burtt argues that Copernicus, in particular, was led to his hypothesis about the heliocentric universe, not strictly by his mathematical calculations, but by broader assumptions of his time. One of these assumptions was that astronomy was considered to be a subset of geometry; therefore, anything that was geometrically true, had to be true of astronomy, as well. This meant that if a simpler geometrical model could be devised to represent the motions of the planets, as Copernicus' model did, then it must accurately reflect astronomy. This was reinforced by a second assumption—the rediscovery of Pythagoreanism (via Plato's *Timaeus*), which provided an alternative metaphysic to the prevailing Aristotelianism. Based on this Platonic-Pythagorean influence, which viewed numbers as metaphysical entities existing eternally in their own right, Copernicus became "convinced that the whole universe was made of numbers, and that whatever was mathematically true was really or astronomically true."[12]

Notice, however, that neither of these assumptions are strictly mathematical *per se*. Rather, they are *metaphysical*, implying a new picture of the world. If geometry is not merely mathematical, but ontologically representative of cosmology, then the world is essentially mathematical, and that which is "real" must be so in terms of its mathematical quantifiability. It is this metaphysical commitment that allowed Copernicus and his successors, particularly Kepler, to see the power in using geometry in the analysis of natural phenomena. Kepler, for example, argued that the real world is comprised only of quantifiable objects—qualities such as number, magnitude, position, and motion, which are governed by mathematical rules. These he called *primary* qualities; the rest *secondary*. Again, what is important to note is that the primary justification for this mathematico-conception of reality and its primary-secondary distinction is the *a priori* adoption of Neoplatonism as a metaphysic, and the belief that it could be applied rigorously to the natural world.

Kepler's primary-secondary distinction is perpetuated and enlarged by the adoption of the atomic theory of matter. The revival of atomism in early modern science, however, was also an *a priori* choice on the part of philosophers such as Pierre Gassendi (1592–1655) and René Descartes (1596–1650), who were attracted to the ancient Greek atomism of Leucippus, Democritus, and Epicurus. By assuming that all matter is reducible to infinitely small and indivisible atoms, these early modern natural philosophers began to view atoms as the primary stuff of reality. That is, since everything else in the world was taken to be a mere aggregate of these smaller atoms, the atoms themselves seemed to take ontological priority over everything else. The only way to understand any physical

12. Burtt, *The Metaphysical Foundations of Science*, 55.

object, then, is to reduce it to its constituent parts (atoms) and explain it in terms of those parts.

This metaphysical commitment to atomism was compounded by at least two further metaphysical assumptions—*causal reductionism* and *determinism*. Causal reductionism is the belief that atoms, in addition to being the only real things, are also the sole source of all motion and change. Thus, all causation in the universe is *bottom-up*, beginning with the smallest constituents of reality effecting the whole. Composite bodies—persons, animals, complex machines—are not causal agents in their own rights, only the atoms. Furthermore, it was believed that these atoms behaved deterministically, having no choice in how they behave. This too was another carry-over from Democritean atomism. Together, then, atomism, reductionism, and determinism implied a causally-closed cosmological system, where all the component parts determine the whole, not unlike a clock functioning vis-à-vis its own internal mechanisms.

Think of a billiard ball table. Early moderns assumed that if you could know the precise initial conditions of the game—the placement of the balls, the angle of the cue stick, the force and velocity of the first strike—*and* if you knew that all the variables would behave deterministically, then, in theory, you could predict the trajectory of every ball and, thus, the entire outcome of the game. This same thinking came to predominate modern conceptions of the universe. Thus, I am not sitting here in front of my computer writing this fascinating chapter on philosophy because I have studied philosophy most of my adult life and am enthralled by the subject. Rather, *my atoms*, which were set in motion at the very beginning of time, have been moving and vibrating in deterministic ways over the millennia, eventually forming my particular body and resulting in this particular moment, where I am sitting in front of this computer writing this chapter.

It is this metaphysical picture of the world as law-governed, mechanistic, and deterministic that came to preclude God's special divine action. If all events in the world are determined bottom-up by the smallest constituents of matter, and if the behavior of these atoms is determined by the initial conditions of the universe, then what room is there for God to act? During the modern period, then, there were only two viable options for God's providence in the world—*interventionism* and *immanentism*. Conservative theologians tended toward the former, maintaining that, in addition to ordaining the laws of nature, God also reserves the right to suspend or break those laws in order to bring about miracles.

Although conservative theologians did not deny that God works through the natural processes, they held that God was not *bound by those laws*, and that the laws, themselves, though regulative, were not immutable. Immanentism, by contrast, is the belief that God works strictly through the natural processes of nature, honoring the laws of physics that were divinely ordained in the first place. Liberal theologians thought it inconsistent and self-contradictory of God to create laws of nature only to break them whenever God saw fit. Why would God create such an orderly world only to violate that order on a regular or semi-regular basis?

Neither of these two options proved satisfactory. The main problem with interventionism has already been noted, but the problem with immanentism may be more damning. Without a thoroughgoing account of God's special providence, much of scripture and its understanding of God becomes unintelligible. Doctrines that have been central to orthodox Christianity have either been mythologized or altogether rejected by liberal theology. More importantly, without an account of special revelation, we can have no particular knowledge of God. If we can have no reliable knowledge of God, then all Christian theology and practice is utterly called into question, constituting an epistemological crisis.

The irony is that the law-governed, mechanical picture of the world that developed during the modern period was thought to be more conducive to the biblical conception of God as creator. The natural theologies of early physico-theologians such as Robert Boyle, Nicolas Malebranche, and even George Berkley sought to *de*-deify nature and to establish natural science on biblical grounds. By these lights, nature is not a "separate agent," as the ancients presumed, with its own organismic agency, but rather "a system of rules."[13] As Hooykaas explains:

> A world organism has been generated; a world mechanism has been *fabricated*. That is why the latter fits in more suitably with a biblical view of the world. So seventeenth-century mechanical philosophy was not a new compromise of Christianity, . . . but rather a step towards the Christianization and the emancipation of natural science.[14]

Robert Boyle, in particular, sought a radical distinction between Creator and creation and wanted to secure "a twin emphasis upon divine

---

13. Hooykaas, *Religion and the Rise of Modern Science*, 17.
14. Hooykaas, *Religion and the Rise of Modern Science*, 15.

transcendence and the radical contingency of creation."[15] Because of Boyle's voluntarist theology, which allowed creation to be distinct from, but also dependent on the Creator, he was able to secure an ontological picture of the world that allowed for systematic empirical investigation, which entailed waiting on "concrete processes" and attending to "particular phenomena." Most importantly, it entailed a search for "positive laws . . . based on the presupposition that God's will was published in creation as a lawful order."[16] Unfortunately, over time the view of natural law would lose its metaphysical foundation in Christian belief, and become associated with independent laws of nature—yet another metaphysical assumption of the modern period—once more swinging the pendulum toward the total autonomy of creation and resulting in the current epistemological crisis.

Attempts to Resolve the Crisis

So far I have been arguing that an epistemological crisis concerning the issue of providence was bound to occur for the Christian tradition insofar as the balance between divine and created causality was lost, and that this is precisely what happened during the modern period due to the development of the legal-mechanical worldview that shifted the balance toward created autonomy. More importantly, I have argued that without special providence, there can be no reliable theological knowledge, constituting an epistemological crisis. The question that concerns us now, then, is whether or not the Christian tradition has the rational resources to resolve this problem. Recall that for a tradition to resolve an epistemological crisis, it must be able to create a narrative that explains three things: (1) how the rational resources of the tradition led to this crisis, in the first place; (2) how the new solution will not only resolve the crisis, but also ensure that this problem will not recur in the future; and (3) how the new solution remains consistent with the overall beliefs and practices of the tradition. The first part of this chapter has been devoted to addressing number 1 above. In this section and the next, I will address 2 and 3.

There is a long history of attempts to provide a resolution to this crisis. A full account of all the options would exceed the scope of this short chapter. Instead, I will focus on what I believe to be the most promising

---

15. Klaaren, *Religious Origins of Modern Science*, 149.
16. Klaaren, *Religious Origins of Modern Science*, 123.

proposal that has been offered in the recent past. Over the course of about two decades (1991–2008), there was a consortium of scientists, philosophers, and theologians, who met over six times, resulting in six publications that focused specifically on questions of providence and the natural order.[17] The goal of this consortium was to find an account of providence that is in keeping with our best current theological and scientific understandings of the world. Robert J. Russell, one of the principal organizers of the conference, outlined a set of criteria that he maintains would resolve the problem for the Christian tradition if they were adequately met. He calls his proposal Non-Interventionist, Objective Divine Action (NIODA), and outlines the following criteria for a successful theory:

> For non-interventionist objective divine action to be intelligible in light of science, the events that result from God's action must occur within a domain of nature in which the appropriate scientific theory can be interpreted philosophically in terms of *ontological indeterminism*. The events must be considered as *direct*, *mediated*, and *objective acts of God*.[18]

This is a highly technical definition and requires some explanation. I will consider the above italicized terms in backwards order.

First, in order for an event to be considered an *objective* act of God it must meet at least two criteria—(1) it must be an event where God acted differently than God would have otherwise, and (2) it must be an event that would not have occurred had God not acted in this particular way. Both criteria are counterfactual in nature. That is, God must be said to have acted uniquely and deliberately to have brought about a different set of circumstances than otherwise would have occurred.

Second, the term *mediated* suggests that God is able to act in and through created causes in order to bring about particular divine ends. This is an attempt to avoid both interventionism and strict immanentism. If God can bring about special providential acts in conjunction with the created order, then God does not have to "break into" the natural order, as assumed by interventionism, nor is God "restricted" by the natural order, as assumed by immanentism. Rather God can be said to work in conjunction with the created order to bring about God's particular ends.

---

17. See Russell, Murphy, and Stoeger, *Scientific Perspectives on Divine Action*.

18. Russell, Murphy, and Stoeger, *Scientific Perspectives on Divine Action*, 125. His emphasis.

Finally, the fact that God's actions can be mediated through nature, implies that there is some point in the natural order where God can act *directly*. That is, there must be some openness in nature itself that allows for God's action in the world. It cannot be the closed, mechanical model of Newtonian physics, otherwise, we would be left with the dual options of interventionism and immanentism. For this reason, much of the work of this consortium focused on developments in scientific research that indicate a shift in the Newtonian worldview. Russell argues that by 1930, an account of God's objective, non-interventionist special divine action was conceivable in light of three specific scientific advances—special relativity (1905), general relativity (1915), and quantum mechanics (1900–1930), all three of which radically challenged the prevailing mechanistic and deterministic metaphysic of Newtonian science. These advances simply went unnoticed by most of the theological community until the relatively recent past.

Perhaps the most promising area of scientific research for the question of divine action is that of quantum physics. George Ellis, Nancey Murphy, and Thomas Tracy have all argued that the erratic nature of particles at the quantum level has led to the possibility of openness in the natural order that was not presumed to be there in Newtonian physics. As scientists have studied atoms, electrons in particular, they have found that these elementary particles do not behave at all like tiny billiard balls. Instead, they behave quite bizarrely. To note a few examples: electrons can jump energy levels without moving across space, simply disappearing from one level and reappearing instantaneously at another. Electrons can act as both waves and particles; that is, when a scientist shoots a single electron (a particle) at a screen, what appears on the screen is not a single dot, but a distribution pattern (a wave). Electrons can exhibit quantum entanglement across vast distances, so that what you do to one electron will affect another entangled electron, even if that second electron is on the other side of the world.

All of this is strange stuff, even for advanced physicists. However, perhaps the most baffling aspect of quantum physics, and the most interesting for this discussion, is the indeterminate nature of electrons. Every electron exists in what is called a state of *superposition*, meaning that every electron exists at multiple places at once, inhabiting all probabilistic states simultaneously, and there is no way to determine where a given electron will be in advance. There are multiple explanations for this phenomenon and little agreement. However, one of the most widely accepted accounts is the Copenhagen interpretation, first proposed by Niels Bohr in 1920. This interpretation suggests that electrons remain in their state of superposition *until they are observed*. That is, our observation of an electron determines where it will be at any given moment, and we cannot know in advance of observing it where an electron will be. All we have are probabilistic calculations (the *wave function*) to help us identify the probabilities of where it might be. This is known as the Heisenberg uncertainty principle.

If the Copenhagen and Heisenberg principles are true, then there are two important implications. First, atoms do not operate the way that modern natural philosophers thought they did. They do not obey the same basic laws of physics that we assumed applied to all other physical objects. Second, the behavior of these atoms is *not* deterministic. Rather, their behavior is open and unpredictable. Contrary to what modern philosophers assumed, you cannot calculate the position of all the atoms from the initial conditions of the universe, like billiard balls following the trajectory of their initial strike. Rather, electrons remain in a state of suspended superposition where their future state is undeterminable until they are actually observed.

The theological proposal in broad outline, then, is this: God, as the omniscient observer, "acts in quantum events to bring about, or actualize, one of several potential outcomes."[19] Quantum events then become the result of both divine and natural causality. Nancey Murphy, who has provided perhaps the clearest and most compelling theological argument for the application of this theory to divine action, argues that God is the "hidden variable," the one who "induces [electrons] to take one course of action rather than the other . . . ."[20] God's action at higher levels of order, then, such as natural phenomena and human consciousness, is primarily through bottom-up causal processes. God acts at the quantum level, thus, initiating an otherwise ordinary chain of causation that, then, results in higher-order processes such as cognition, memory, human interactions, natural events, and so on. The indeterminacy of the quantum level, however, avoids the problem of making God a competing cause with other natural processes. Since electrons require an observer to determine their course of action, they are insufficient on their own. They require

---

19. See: Russell, Clayton, McNelly, and Polkinghorne, *Quantum Mechanics*, 187.
20. Murphy, "Divine Action in the Natural Order," 341–42.

participation on the part of some observer, of which God could constitute the most important one.

To say that God works in all quantum events, however, is not to say that God is solely and directly responsible for them. This would be a version of occasionalism. Instead, Murphy insists that to have created some-*thing* is, by definition, to have endowed it with "some measure of independence and a nature of its own, including inherent powers to do some things rather than others."[21] This applies even to the smallest constituents of reality. God's action, then, is *non-coercive*, cooperating with every created entity, no matter how simple or complex, by respecting their natural rights. This means, however, that God's action becomes more constrained the farther up the scale of complexity. God can lure an electron more easily than a human, because a human has more complexity and, thus, greater degrees of freedom—freedom to say no to God, for example, or to ignore God altogether. However, it also suggests that creatures at higher levels of complexity have a greater capacity for reciprocity and cooperation, making them more capable of responding positively to God's action.

The Adequacy of the Proposal

I contend that the foregoing account of divine action at the quantum level not only meets the criteria for a successful theory of NIODA, but that it also effectively resolves the current crisis of divine action for the Christian tradition. In terms of the former, insofar as quantum physics is open and indeterminate, God's action can truly be said to be direct, mediated, and objective. It is *direct* in the sense that God does not have to initiate a causal series in order to effect a quantum event; rather, since quantum processes are necessary but insufficient causes in their own right, they require something else's (e.g., God's) direct participation to be fully actualized.

Similarly, God's action is *mediated* in the sense that God's action at the quantum level will have causal consequences at higher levels of complexity. Thus, insofar as God acts in all quantum-level events, it goes without saying that God must necessarily be a participant in every resultant macro-level event. Here, Murphy also contends that there is a

---

21. Murphy, "Divine Action in the Natural Order," 341.

subsidiary role for chaos theory.[22] Since chaotic systems are sensitive to initial conditions, including those at the quantum level, and since they are statistically unpredictable they provide room for God to work "undercover," so to speak. While chaotic systems are not indeterminate in the same way as quantum events and thus do not provide the same sort of opening for God's action in the world, they can work in tandem with quantum events to provide a veil for God's providence at higher levels of complexity. This is one of the reasons why God's work in our lives is always open to interpretation.

Finally, God's action is *objective* precisely in the sense outlined above, whereby God does, indeed, act in such a way that (1) is different from God's normal, sustaining action, by responding uniquely to particular sub-atomic events; and (2) produces a genuinely counterfactual set of circumstances that, otherwise, would not have occurred had God not acted. When God deliberately interacts at the quantum level to bring about a particular quantum event, God has done more than general preservation; God has acted to bring about something that would not otherwise have occurred. The collapse of the wave function is complete and irreversible—all other potentialities are abandoned. Thus, all subsequent series of events will necessarily be different than they would have been had God not acted to elicit this particular event. Added to what has already been said about direct and mediated action, events at the quantum level will, subsequently, have counterfactual consequences for higher levels of complexity.

This account of direct, mediated, objective divine action, however, does more than meet the criteria of NIODA; it resolves the present crisis concerning the issue of divine action. Insofar as God is able to work within the causal structures of the world at the lowest level of complexity in order to bring about changes at higher levels, then any degree of change that comports with nature, however grand or trivial, is conceivable. The extraordinary acts of God, then, can be understood as ways in which God's action at the quantum level is mediated and amplified through the causal structures either to augment something already latent in creation or to create something entirely new. By way of example, Russell argues that the resurrection can be viewed—both scientifically and

---

22. Murphy, "Divine Action in the Natural Order," 348.

theologically—as a "new creation," an event in nature that displays both continuity and discontinuity with the created order.[23]

Notice that this position also avoids the traps of both interventionism and immanentism. God does not have to "break into" the created order to bring about counterfactual changes, nor is God's action simply subsumed in the natural order. God and nature are distinct and autonomous. However, because there is genuine openness at the level of quantum physics, there is the real possibility of collaboration between God and the world. Also, insofar as this account allows for God's ongoing, particular action in the world, we have also resolved the major epistemological crisis concerning the issue of providence, for if God can act in particular events, then special revelation is also possible and so is particular knowledge of God. Thus, our confidence in our epistemological resources as a tradition is retained.

Conclusion

Having established the epistemological crisis concerning the issue of providence for the Christian tradition in the modern period and some of the tools that the tradition has for resolving it, I will spend the remainder of Part II looking at how this issue has presented itself in the other two Abrahamic traditions. While neither Islam nor Judaism has had to deal directly with this crisis in the modern period, both are, nonetheless, susceptible to it. Furthermore, all three of the Abrahamic traditions dealt with a similar crisis in the medieval period, where all three stood to benefit from each other. Thus, in the subsequent chapters, I will consider the ways in which all three traditions have benefited from each other in the past, during the medieval period, and how they stand to benefit from each other today.

---

23. Russell, *Cosmology: From Alpha to Omega*, 312.

Chapter 6

Islam and Providence

> ... we here speak of that superintending providence which regards the children of men.... The outermost circle includes the whole race of mankind, all the descendants of Adam, all the human creatures that are dispersed over the face of the earth. This comprises, not only the Christian world, those that name the name of Christ, but the Mohametans also, who considerably out-number even the nominal Christians.[1]
>
> —JOHN WESLEY

Introduction

I NOTED IN THE previous chapter that when it comes to the issue of divine providence, there are two theological commitments that need to be kept in balance—God's total sovereignty, on the one hand, and creaturely autonomy, on the other, particularly human free will. Whenever this balance is lost, theology winds up tipping toward one extreme or the other, either *occasionalism*, the belief that all events are occasions for God's action, or *deism*, the belief that God created the world, but has no further involvement in it. Historically, the Islamic tradition has tended to emphasize God's sovereignty and, thus, has leaned heavily toward occasionalism. At

---

1. Wesley, "Sermon 67," 318–19, par. 16.

stake for Muslims is the central theological belief in *tawḥīd*, commonly stated as the affirmation: "there is no god but Allah." *Tawḥīd*, however, is a much stronger claim than this. Seyyed Hossein Nasr contends that in its strongest sense, this affirmation states that "there is no reality outside of the Absolute Reality, thereby negating all that is other than Allah."[2] The implication is that God is the primary and, in some sense, the *only* true reality and, thus, has total control over all things. However, like Christianity, the Islamic tradition also believes that humans are responsible for their individual choices, particularly when it comes to sin. Thus, even for the Islamic tradition there is some measure of balance that must be preserved between God's agency and human agency. The same challenge that modern science posed for Christian theology, then, is also a real possibility for the Islamic tradition as it seeks to integrate Western science.

The Islamic tradition was once the leader in scientific and philosophical thought. For a period of about three hundred years, from about 800 CE to 1100 CE, Islam experienced a Golden Age of science and philosophy, while the Christian West was still in the throes of the so-called "Dark Ages."[3] However, its contributions in these areas declined late in the medieval period, and it has only been in the relatively recent past that the Islamic tradition has regained interest in modern science. Consequently, it has not yet had to deal with the crisis concerning the issue of divine action in the same way that the Christian tradition did during the modern period. Nevertheless, the Islamic tradition did encounter a similar crisis during the medieval period, one that also involved the adoption of a foreign metaphysic that wound up constraining notions of God's general and special providence. Again, the epistemological crisis for the Islamic tradition was not unlike the one for the Christian tradition in the modern period—if God's special providence is precluded, then so too is any divinely revealed theological knowledge.

Equally important for our purposes is the fact that the Jewish and Christian traditions also encountered this same crisis during the medieval period, and, in order to resolve their respective crises, both relied heavily on the resolution that the Islamic tradition reached. Thus, it is an example, *par excellence*, of the sort of mutual constructive engagement I

2. Nasr, *An Introduction to Islamic Cosmological Doctrines*, 5.

3. Something of a pejorative misnomer, as they were not as "dark" as the name suggests. Many of the chapters in this book take seriously the intellectual contributions of the Middle Ages—from the Muslim, Jewish, and Christian traditions.

am considering. In this chapter, then, I will consider the crisis concerning the issue of divine action as it developed for the Islamic tradition in the medieval period. I will begin by looking at the development of Islamic notions of providence, how those notions were then called into question with the integration of Greek philosophy, and the resolution that was offered by the tradition's preeminent medieval scholar, al-Ghazālī. I will conclude by considering some ways that the Christian and Islamic traditions have stood to benefit from each other both in the medieval and the modern periods.

Islam and Providence in the Medieval Period

For Muslims, Jews, and Christians, alike, medieval science and philosophy has its beginnings with the rediscovery of ancient Greek texts that had been lost after the fall of Rome. In the seventh century, as the early Islamic tradition expanded its territorial presence into areas such as Persia and Syria, it encountered texts of Aristotle and Plotinus that had been smuggled there at the end of the Byzantine empire. The texts had been translated from Greek into Syriac and Farsi and were then translated from all three sources, though mainly from Syriac, into Arabic. Unfortunately, in the process of so many translations, many of the texts became muddled, resulting in translations that sometimes bore little resemblance to the originals. For example, Aristotle's *Metaphysics*, an already difficult text in its original Greek, became "gibberish" in the process of so many translations.[4] More troublesome, however, was the fact that Plotinus' *Enneads* was translated under the title of "Aristotle's Theology,"[5] confusing two very different cosmological systems into a hybrid Neoplatonic-Aristotelianism. Consequently, it was this confused hybrid that became widely influential among Muslims, Jews, and eventually Christians.

The principal metaphysic of this Neoplatonic-Aristotelian system was the doctrine of *emanation*, the belief that reality is a series of cascading spheres that emanate from one "primordial unity," which Plotinus called "the One."[6] The adoption of this metaphysic presented a problem for traditional Islamic belief in God's action in two ways. First, since the doctrine of emanation held that every sphere in the chain is a necessary

---

4. Matson, *A New History of Philosophy*, 266.
5. Pessin, "The Influence of Islamic Thought."
6. Black, "Al-Fārābī," 188.

outflow of the preceding one, it suggested that God's creation of the world was *necessary* and not an act of divine choice, as Muslims believed. Second, the doctrine of emanation also implied that each sphere in the chain could only influence the next sphere immediately following it, implying that God's action would be limited only to one sphere, the next one directly in succession. This would rule out any direct involvement in the world of human affairs, including special divine action and miracles. This constituted the very sort of epistemological crisis we have been considering, for again, if God's particular providence is precluded, then so too is any revelatory knowledge of God.[7]

In this section, then, I will begin by looking at the development of Islamic thought on providence itself. I will then consider in more detail how the doctrine of emanation posed a problem for Islamic notions of providence. I will conclude by looking at the preeminent medieval Islamic philosophical-theologian, al-Ghazālī, who is typically credited with resolving the crisis.

Development of Islamic thought on providence

For the Islamic tradition, questions about divine and human causation first developed during the early Umayyad period (661–750 CE) amidst concerns over what constitutes inclusion in the community, that is, who is considered to be a "true believer" and to what extent sin precludes one from being considered so. The earliest and most stringent sect to address this issue was the Khārijites, who argued that "the decision is God's alone," implying that all who had committed a grave sin were destined for hell and belonged to the people of hell.[8]

One of the primary issues in these debates over inclusion in the community, however, pertained to the question of *qudra*, or power: how

---

7. It should be noted that Eric Perl argues that it is a common misunderstanding of Neoplatonism to see God at the top of the chain of being. Instead, Perl argues that for Plotinus, all levels of being participate directly in the One, though to varying degrees. If this is true, then Plotinus's position presents no substantial problem for theories of divine action, since, theoretically, God is present to all things and all things participate in the divine being. Nevertheless, since Plotinus' position was mischaracterized throughout the Middle Ages, my current argument still stands. Insofar as Muslims, Christians, and Jews of the Middle Ages understood God as the top of the chain of being, however mistakenly, it presented certain challenges for conceiving God's action in the world. See Perl, *Thinking Being*.

8. Watt, *Islamic Philosophy and Theology*, 12.

much power does God possess and how much do humans? On this point, the Qur'ān affirms two seemingly contradictory positions—(1) that God, alone, is omnipotent, responsible for all human action, even their choices to believe or disbelieve (Q 2:7), and (2) that humans are, nevertheless, responsible for their actions, receiving God's judgment in the afterlife for sinfulness and reward for faithfulness. Some argued that since God determines everything, humans cannot help but sin, resulting in an attitude of moral complacency. This elicited reactions not only from the Khārijites, but from other more moderate sects as well, who argued that humans do, in fact, have free will (*istiṭāʿa*), the choice to sin or not. Two groups, in particular—the Muʿtazilites and the Ashʿarites—tried in different ways to preserve the balance between God's power and human responsibility.

The Muʿtazilites argued that ascribing all human action—good or bad—to God not only fosters moral complacency, it negates the justice of God. That is, it would be unjust for God to determine all human actions and still hold them morally responsible. Consequently, the Muʿtazila not only defended human free will, they argued that God is subject to the same moral laws as humans, that "that which is just or unjust for us . . . is the same for God."[9] This conclusion contained two additional commitments: First, because they claimed that humans have control over their own voluntary actions, the Muʿtazila denied predestination.[10] There can be no predetermined fate for humans if their future choices are yet undetermined. Second, since God is bound by the same moral law as humans, God must necessarily "reward those who have merited His reward and punish those who have merited His punishment."[11] God is not free to reward and punish as God sees fit; rather the "principle of divine justice (*ʿadl*) imposes on God the moral imperative of doing what is already known by reason to be just and good."[12]

At the beginning of the tenth century, a dissenting Muʿtazilite, Abu'l-Ḥasan al-Ashʿarī (d. 935/36 CE) argued, conversely, that it would be *unjust* for God *not* to determine the choices of human actions. Al-Ashʿarī argued that, given Muʿtazila reasoning, God would be as liable for the sinner who is permitted to persist in sin despite the fate of eternal damnation as God would be for the infant who dies before she can merit

---

9. Gimaret, "Muʿtazila," 789.
10. Gimaret, "Muʿtazila," 790.
11. Gimaret, "Muʿtazila," 790.
12. el Omari, "Muʿtazilah."

reward in the afterlife.[13] To make his point, al-Ash'arī tells the story of three brothers: one good, one wicked, and one who dies in childhood. When each receives his eternal judgment, the third, who is in limbo, complains that he had no opportunity to merit paradise. The response is given that God caused him to die early in order to prevent the life of wickedness he otherwise would have led. Upon hearing this, the second brother, who is in hell, asks why he was not also permitted to die young before his life of sin. To this there is no response.[14] The parable's underlying concern is one of divine negligence. If God knows the eternal fate of the righteous and the unrighteous and neglects to alter the course of their actions, then God is, by implication, culpable. Al-Ash'arī and his followers sought to preserve God's justice by ascribing all power exclusively to God.

Al-Ash'arī also argued, in opposition to the Mu'tazila, that God's action is constrained by nothing outside of Godself. It is God who determines whether something is right or wrong, not reason (*'adl*). Subsequently, God is not obligated to punish the wicked and reward the virtuous; these judgments are left to God's discretion, based solely on God's determination.[15] For al-Ash'arī and his followers, the only motive for God's actions is "what He wills . . . because He wills."[16] Osman Bakar argues that the uniqueness of Ash'arite theology stems from the fact that, out of so many divine attributes, "it chose to concentrate on just one of them for the purpose of constructing a worldview," namely the limitless omnipotence of God.[17]

The problem for al-Ash'arī, however, is in how to preserve human culpability in the face of God's total sovereignty. Richard M. Frank argues that for al-Ash'arī the question of *qudra* is not one of individual free will, *per se*, but one of the metaphysical structure of efficient causality, in general, and that the key to understanding al-Ash'arī's metaphysic is his conception of atoms and accidents.[18] Ash'arite atomism is a modified understanding of Mu'tazilite metaphysics. The Mu'tazila were one of the earliest *mutakallimūn*, those who engaged in speculative theology (*kalām*), to adopt and apply Greek philosophical concepts. They were

---

13. Griffel, *Al-Ghazālī's Philosophical Theology*, 125.
14. Watt, *Islamic Philosophy and Theology*, 68.
15. Watt, *Islamic Philosophy and Theology*, 68.
16. Bakar, *The History and Philosophy of Islamic Science*, 84.
17. Bakar, *The History and Philosophy of Islamic Science*, 84.
18. See Frank, *Beings and Their Attributes*.

"particularly rich in attempts to explain physical processes" and, as a result, they developed both an atomism of physical matter and an atomism of time.[19]

In terms of the former, the Muʿtazila had developed something very similar to Hellenic atomism whereby all physical objects are composed of smaller constituent parts, the smallest of these, the atom, being indivisible (*lā yatajazzaʾu*). According to the Muʿtazila, atoms have no attributes in isolation, only when assembled into larger bodies. They argued that atoms, by themselves, are "completely powerless and have no predetermined way of reacting to other atoms or to accidents" (Griffel, 125). Some Muʿtazilites speculated that the movements of physical processes are not continuous, but rather "consist of smaller leaps (sing. *ṭafra*) that our senses cannot detect and whose sum we perceive as continuously flowing movement" (Griffel, 126). It was this latter theory, in particular, that led to the development of an atomistic theory of time among some of the Muʿtazila, some arguing that time itself is not continuous, but rather a "fast procession of 'moments' (sing. *waqt*), which again is concealed from our senses" (Griffel, 126). The Muʿtazila already maintained that accidents cannot subsist from one moment to the next and must be created anew by God in each new instance. By extension, since bodies cannot exist without accidents, these too must be recreated, anew, in every moment. As Griffel states: "In order for an atom to exist from one moment to another, God has to create the accident of 'subsistence' (*baqā*) every moment He wants the atom to persist" (Griffel, 126). For al-Ashʿarī, then, atoms (physical and temporal) are *occasions* for God's action in the world; thus, the term *occasionalism*.

It is this basic understanding of atoms and accidents that underlies al-Ashʿarī's conception of *qudra*. For al-Ashʿarī, *qudra* does not refer to the intrinsic power or potentiality of a created being to change, in the way that the Greek term *dynamis* (power) implies.[20] Instead, it is understood to be an "accident" (*ʿaraḍ*), an attribute that is created anew in the agent for each event "so that one speaks in terms of the single act of *qudra*."[21] Every moment is a new act of creation. In this sense, God is the cause of our generated causality, which accounts for God's ultimate sovereignty;

---

19. Griffel, *Al-Ghazālī's Philosophical Theology*, 125. Going forward, I will refer to Griffel parenthetically.

20. Frank, "The Structure of Created Causality According to al-Ashʿarī," 18.

21. Frank, "The Structure of Created Causality According to al-Ashʿarī," 27.

all power to act ultimately derives from God and the divine creation of *qudra* in each moment.

As for human culpability, however, al-Ash'arī and the rest of the Mu'tazila diverged significantly. The Mu'tazila argued that *qudra* provides the direct power to act or not to act in a given instance. Thus, while the *power* to execute a given event comes from God, the *choice* of so acting is determined by an act of the will on the part of the agent. For al-Ash'arī, this was far more constricted. *Qudra* is the accident that determines specifically which of the two poles (to act or not to act) will be actualized. Nevertheless, al-Ash'arī argues that while God is, in the strictest sense, the cause of our generated causality, and thus the creator of every event, God is *not* the cause of our efficient causality. Rather, since the created accident belongs to the human agent and since it is from this created causality that the event takes place, it is still the human agent who is responsible for its efficient causation.

In this sense, al-Ash'arī's position is not strict occasionalism; that is, it does not deny secondary causality or the reality of human agency, at least not in any simplistic sense. Actions belong entirely to the human agent since it is the agent who performs them; however, they are "really initiated originally by God, who allows us to participate in those actions."[22] Nor does Ash'arī deny the reality of natural causes or secondary causation other than human; "rather, since such causality does not fall within the range of the problem of *qudra* as it was universally understood, he simply does not discuss it."[23]

Epistemological crisis posed by ancient Greek philosophy

It was this Ash'arite understanding of *qudra* that came to predominate in the Islamic tradition, preserving, as it did, the belief in God's total sovereignty and human culpability. Since God provides *qudra* to each person at every moment, God has total sovereignty, yet individuals are still responsible for their choices based on the *qudra* that is given at that moment. More importantly, it was this notion of *qudra* that was called into question with the adoption of Neoplatonic emanationism (see Fig. 1). For some Islamic scholars, such as Al-Fārābī and Ibn Sīnā (Avicenna), the doctrine of emanation seemed to preserve Islamic notions

---

22. Leaman, "Ash'arī," 221.
23. Frank, "The Structure of Created Causality according to al-Ash'arī," 25.

of sovereignty and *tawḥīd*, God's ultimacy and oneness. Al-Fārābī, for example, argued that the doctrine of emanation made up for what was lacking in Aristotle's metaphysics. He argued that Aristotle's account of physics focused on the principle of change (*kinesis*), viewing God as the first cause of motion in the universe, but not with the principle of existence (*wujūd*).[24] For al-Fārābī, the doctrine of emanation resolved this by focusing on "divine beings and their causal links to the sublunar world."[25] However, emanation also allowed al-Fārābī to preserve the doctrine of *tawḥīd*, maintaining that from the one divine, unchanging source, only one other sphere can emanate, "thus protecting divine simplicity and unity."[26] As a consequence, the multiplicity in the world is only apparent, not real—"all existence is unified in God, the source of all."[27]

The central problem in al-Fārābī's adoption of emanation is the conclusion that the world is eternal, having no definitive beginning, thus, calling into question Qur'ānic belief in creation by divine decree. Here, al-Fārābī is influenced by Aristotelian notions of causation, which maintain that "every effect is necessary in relation to its efficient cause," meaning that if a cause is sufficient, needing nothing else, its effect must issue *eo ipso*, necessarily and instantaneously. As Griffel puts it: "If all conditions are fulfilled for a certain cause to have its effect, the connection between the cause and effect must occur and cannot be suspended" (Griffel, 139). It is this line of reasoning that leads to the conclusion that the world must be coeternal with God. If God is the only sufficient cause, then there can be no delay between God's existence and the effect, creation. The world "must have existed for as long as God has existed. God and the world exist . . . from eternity" (Griffel, 135). This, however, undermines the Ash'arite commitment to God's total sovereignty by removing the divine choice of creation.

Thus, the doctrine of emanation restricted God's action in several important ways. First, it made the creation of the world the necessary result of God's existence, a necessary byproduct. This form of *necessarianism* also severely limited God's actions and knowledge—God's action, because God cannot choose to act one way rather another, particularly when it comes to the creation of the world (general providence); God's

24. Druart, "Al-Fārābī and Emanationism," 28–29.
25. Black, "Al-Fārābī," 188.
26. Sonn, "Tawḥīd," 334.
27. Sonn, "Tawḥīd," 332.

knowledge, because if the world cannot be any different than the way it is, then God's knowledge of the world cannot be any different either. God can only know the world as it was *necessitated* to be, not as God would *will* it to be.

Second, the doctrine of emanation restricted God's action to only one sphere of influence. In the Neoplatonic model, the chain of causation is only between connecting spheres. Each sphere can only influence the one right below it (see Fig. 1). God, as the first cause, acts directly on only one other being—the first intellect (mind or *nous*). This first intellect, in turn, causes the emanation of a third sphere directly below it and acts solely on that sphere. This process is continued with each succeeding sphere, constituting the chain of causation through which God's creative activity is mediated. So according to this understanding of emanation, God does not act directly in the physical world or in the lives of humans (special providence); rather God acts only *indirectly* through a chain of spheres, each of which emanates from the other.

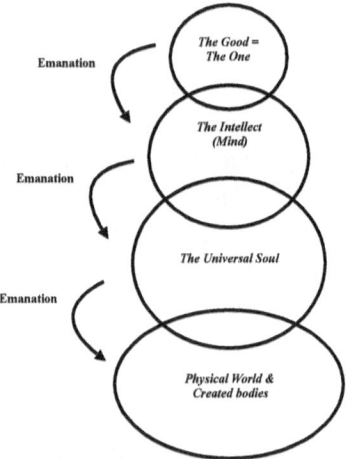

Figure 1 Neoplatonic Emanation

The epistemological crisis for the Islamic tradition in the medieval period, then, is not radically different from that of the modern period. The doctrine of emanation limited God's general providence and altogether precluded God's special providence, thus calling into question the kinds of claims the Islamic tradition could reasonably make about God. It was the prominent Persian philosopher, al-Ghazālī, a life-long adherent of the Ash'arite tradition, who perceived this crisis the clearest and who, ultimately, provided a definitive resolution to it.

Al-Ghazālī's resolution to the crisis

It is interesting to note that al-Ghazālī possessed that rare gift of empathy discussed above (chapter 3) in relation to Thomas Aquinas. Al-Ghazālī was in a unique position to understand both the Ash'arite and the Greek traditions intimately. Born in Ṭus, Iran (1058 CE), al-Ghazālī received his initial education under the al-Ḥarāmayn Abu'l-Maʿālī al-Juwaynī, the most distinguished Muslim scholar of his time. In his education, al-Ghazālī was exposed both to *kalām*, to which he would remain faithful all his life,[28] and Greek philosophy (Griffel, 30). In fact, al-Ghazālī's greatest contribution was not that he refuted Greek philosophy altogether, but rather that he was able to integrate Aristotelianism into Ash'arite *kalām* to make a suitable synthesis.

It is primarily the doctrine of emanation and its accompanying tenet of *necessarianism*, the necessary connection between causes and their effects, that al-Ghazālī attacks, arguing that the *falāsifah*—philosophers such as al-Fārābī and Avicenna—had stripped God of both will and knowledge. His most influential work, *The Incoherence of the Philosophers*, draws on Ash'arite belief to argue that it is God who creates the causal connection between things and, indeed, God can create one without the other—satisfaction without eating, burning without fire, light without sun, and so on. Al-Ghazālī's goal, of course, is to preserve the Islamic (Ash'arite) commitment to God's total sovereignty, expressed in the doctrine of *tawḥīd*. If al-Ghazālī can show that there is no necessary connection between causes and their effects, then he can show (1) that God is not constrained in God's actions or knowledge when it comes to the creation of the world, and (2) that God can act directly in the world to bring about miracles, thus preserving both general and special providence.

The *Incoherence* is divided into twenty discussions, each one dealing with a Greek metaphysical proposition that al-Ghazālī refutes. Of these twenty philosophical propositions, seventeen he condemns as heretical innovations and three he claims fail to agree with Islam in any respect.[29]

28. Campanini, "Al-Ghazālī," 259.
29. Al-Ghazālī, *The Incoherence of the Philosophers*, 10–11.

It is the seventeenth discussion where al-Ghazālī focuses on the *falāsifah's* commitment to *necessariansim*. In the introduction to the seventeenth discussion, al-Ghazālī states that insofar as one subscribes to the necessary connection between cause and effect one renders miracles impossible (Griffel, 163). More than this, al-Ghazālī views the issue of causality as "a problem of Qur'ān interpretation" (Griffel, 148). That is, if al-Ghazālī can show that there is no necessary connection between causes and their effects, he can secure not only the possibility of miracles, but also the truth of God's revelation in the Qur'ān. Notice, then, that al-Ghazālī, at some level, recognizes this as an epistemological crisis. The denial of special revelation calls into question the reliability of the Qur'ān, and thus any other knowledge about God.

Throughout the seventeenth discussion, al-Ghazālī offers several arguments against *necessarianism*. I will focus on three. First, al-Ghazālī argues that cause and effect are not givens; rather they are created by God. To illustrate his point, he uses an example of fire burning cotton. Al-Ghazālī argues that "[something's] existence *with* a thing does not prove that it exists *by* [that thing]."[30] When we observe cotton burning on contact with fire, for example, this observation does not prove either that there is any causal connection between these two events or that fire is the *only* cause. For al-Ghazālī, if it can be shown that what we observe as regular causal connections are not necessary in themselves, then we can attribute some, if not all, of those connections to God. Second, al-Ghazālī argues that the consistency that we observe in these causal relationships is not the result of independent causal forces, but due to God's reliable *habit*. God chooses to maintain causal regularity or suspend it as God sees fit. When God chooses to enact a miracle, God is not constrained by outside causal forces, but only by God's own habitual action in the world.

It is interesting to note that there is strong resemblance between al-Ghazālī's argument and David Hume's later argument against induction. There is even some indication that Hume might have been familiar with at least some of al-Ghazālī's arguments through the Latin translation of Averroës' *Incoherence of the Incoherence*, a refutation of al-Ghazālī's *Incoherence*, as well as Maimonides' *The Guide for the Perplexed*, which likewise provides a thoroughgoing account of Ash'arite *kalām*.[31] Notice, however, that al-Ghazālī employs his argument against the empirical

---

30. Al-Ghazālī, *The Incoherence of the Philosophers*, 167.
31. Bakar, *The History and Philosophy of Islamic Science*, 100–101.

reliability of causality as a means of preserving God's absolute power, whereas Hume does quite the opposite. While Hume agrees that there is no necessary connection between causes and their effects, he attributes the link to *our* habit; al-Ghazālī attributes it entirely to God's.

The third argument against *necessarianism* to consider presently is directed at Avicenna and his adoption of Aristotelian notions of what is possible and what is not. Griffel contends that modern understanding admits of three logical possibilities: (1) that which is logically *necessary* and obtains in all alternative states of affairs, (2) that which is *possible* and obtains in some alternative states, and (3) that which is *impossible* and does not obtain in any state of affairs. For Aristotle, however, the options were much more constricted. Notions of possibility were connected principally to "temporal indefinite sentences" (Griffel, 167). As Griffel states:

> To explain a temporally unqualified sentence of the form "S is P" contains an implicit or explicit reference to the time of utterance as part of its meaning. If this sentence is true whenever uttered, it is necessarily true. If its truth-value can change in the course of time, it is possible. If such a sentence is false whenever uttered, it is impossible. (Griffel, 167)

It is this form of modality that leads Aristotle to speculate over the truth-value of such sentences as: There will be a sea battle tomorrow.[32] In Aristotle's understanding, this sort of statement can only be either true or false on the occasion that it is uttered; it cannot be *possible*, in our modern sense.

Avicenna held a model very similar to Aristotle's, adding one important change. For Avicenna, the possible—that which neither holds always nor holds never—pertains both to things in the world *and* to things in the mind. Consequently, *existence in the mind* is one of two legitimate forms of existence for Avicenna. Furthermore, Avicenna maintained that anything that exists (in the mind or in the world), exists *necessarily*. In this way, Avicenna argues that, while everything is possible in itself, everything is ultimately *necessitated* by something else, namely God. As Griffel states:

> God's creative activity . . . makes the existence of these beings necessary. Once a thing that is only possible by virtue of itself comes into being, it is necessary by virtue of something else (*wājib al-wujud di-ghayathi*). It is, first of all, the necessary effect

---

32. Aristotle, "De Interpretatione," 30.

of its proximate efficient cause. That cause, however, is itself the necessary effect of other efficient causes, which proceed in a chain of secondary efficient causes from God. Everything that we witness in creation is possible by virtue of itself and necessary by virtue of something else, ultimately necessitated by God. (Griffel, 169)

Al-Ghazālī, however, argues that in eliminating the distinction between existence in the mind and existence in the world, Avicenna eliminates another important distinction, namely "whether possibility and necessity exist in things outside of our mind, or whether they are simply predicates of our judgment" (Griffel, 171). For al-Ghazālī, it is the predicates of our judgments that allow us to conclude that something is possible or impossible. The same is true regarding our judgments concerning God's action. The fact that we can conceive of God having acted differently or having created an alternative state of affairs leads us to conclude that causal connections are *not* necessary. They are contingent, whether God ever chose to act differently or not. In this way, al-Ghazālī is able to preserve Ash'arite conceptions of God's absolute will and knowledge without rejecting secondary causation, only the necessary connection of those secondary causes.

It is this in this way that al-Ghazālī is able to resolve the epistemological crisis, denying the necessary connection between causes and effects and, thus, preserving Ash'arite notions of God's absolute power (*tawḥīd*). Moreover, he was able to do so in a way that did not entirely jettison Aristotelian philosophy. Indeed, while many have concluded that al-Ghazālī's attack on philosophy in the *Incoherence* ended the peripatetic tradition in Islam, a closer reading indicates something similar to a Thomistic synthesis. F. E. Peters argues that while it is true that philosophy (*falsafa*) as an academic discipline wanes after al-Ghazālī's treatment of it in the *Incoherence*, the philosophical bent in Islam is not altogether lost, but rather is transmuted and assimilated into the *kalām* tradition. As I noted at the outset of this section, one of al-Ghazālī's greatest contributions was in showing that most of the philosophical commitments of ancient Greek philosophy were, in fact, neutral to Islamic belief. In so doing, he made it possible for "the more rationally-minded theologians" to accept much of Aristotle's work, including his logic and some of his metaphysics.[33]

---

33. Watt, *Islamic Philosophy and Theology*, 90.

Islam and Christianity in Mutual Constructive Engagement

So far, I have argued that the Islamic tradition encountered a similar epistemological crisis in the medieval period that the Christian tradition faced in the modern, one where the adoption of an alien, Greek metaphysic restricted theological notions of God's general and special divine action. The comparison, however, is not simply between the Islamic medieval period and the Christian modern period. The Christian tradition also faced this same crisis in the medieval period and the Islamic tradition, with its more recent adoption of Western science, stands to face the one posed by the modern period. Thus, in this section, I want to highlight some of the ways that the Islamic and Christian traditions have stood to benefit from each other in both periods.

Engagement in the medieval period

When it comes to the question of science, religion, and providence during the medieval period, the Christian tradition is indebted to Islam in several significant ways. First, it was largely through the Islamic tradition that the Christian West re-encountered many of the lost works of Greek philosophy in the first place, particularly those of Aristotle, leading to a renewed interest in ancient philosophy in the West. Much of ancient Greek philosophy, Aristotle in particular, came into the Christian tradition through Islamic scholarship. Second, and more importantly, the Christian tradition was significantly aided by the Islamic tradition in its interpretation and integration of these sources. As I noted in chapter 3, Christian scholastics relied heavily on Averroës' extensive commentaries on Aristotle as they sought to integrate his philosophy.

Perhaps one of the clearest places where Aquinas responds to the position of *necessarianism*—that it is impossible for God to precede the world in time, thus, the world must be coeternal with God—is in "On the Eternity of the World."[34] There, Aquinas argues that the eternity of the world and its dependence on God are not mutually exclusive. That is, "there is no contradiction in principle between the world's being created and its being eternal."[35] As Aquinas states:

---

34. Aquinas, "On the Eternity of the World." My Emphasis.
35. Schindler, *The Catholicity of Reason*, 156.

> We thus ought to determine whether there is any contradiction between these two ideas, namely, to be made by God and to have always existed. And, whatever may be the truth of this matter, *it will not be heretical to say that God can make something created by him to have always existed.* . . . However, if there is no contradiction involved, then it is neither false nor impossible that God could have made something that has always existed, and it will be an error to say otherwise.[36] (Aquinas, "On the Eternity.")

Aquinas' reasoning is that a cause (God) does not have to precede its effect (creation) *in time*. Rather, the important distinction is one of a metaphysical prioritization, not a temporal one. There does not have to be a "before" and "after" in a temporal sense for the effect to be metaphysically dependent on its cause.[37] As Aquinas states:

> we should show that it is not necessary that an agent cause, in this case God, precede in time that which he causes, if he should so will. This can be shown in several ways. First, no cause instantaneously producing its effect necessarily precedes the effect in time. God, however, is a cause that produces effects not through motion but instantaneously. Therefore, it is not necessary that he precede his effects in time.[38]

In this way, Aquinas is able to preserve notions of creation *ex nihilo* without insisting that it be *de novo*, that is with a particular starting point. This is a distinction that eluded Avicenna, al-Ghazālī, and Averroës, but one that Aquinas could only reach by remaining in dialogue with their contributions.

In the next chapter, I will show how Aquinas relied on Avicenna and Moses Maimonides, the prominent Jewish medieval philosopher, to resolve the remaining problem of divine action in the medieval period, namely, God can work directly in the created order itself. For the present, it is enough to note that in addressing both aspects of this crisis, Aquinas treats Islamic (and Jewish) medieval scholars as interlocutors, conversation partners that allow him to wrestle with this crisis in such a way as to reach a satisfactory conclusion. Regrettably, however, Aquinas may not have gone far enough in this respect. While Aquinas was heavily influenced by Avicenna and, to a lesser extent, Averroës, it was al-Ghazālī

---

36. Aquinas, "On the Eternity of the World." My Emphasis.

37. See Schindler, *The Catholicity of Reason*, 156 and Burrell, "Aquinas and Islamic and Jewish thinkers," 73.

38. Aquinas, "On the Eternity of the World."

who is considered the more influential in Islamic thought.[39] One wonders, then, what significance it would have made had Aquinas and the other scholastics of the late Middle Ages had access to good translations of al-Ghazālī as well as Avicenna and Averroës.

It should also be noted that the Christian tradition may have also benefited from Islam in the very *process*, itself, of adopting and translating Greek philosophical texts. In the Islamic tradition, this process is sometimes referred to as the Islamization of science, meaning that the language and conceptual categories of the Greek tradition could not be adopted into the Islamic tradition uncritically. To have done so would have constituted its own form of epistemological crisis, one quite distinct from the issue of providence. The problem for the translators was more than linguistic; it was epistemological. In wrestling with matters of translation, the Islamic tradition was seeking to guard against adopting concepts so foreign to its language and tradition that an entirely *new* language had to be constructed. Think of the vast difference between the Arabic term *qudra* and the Greek term *dynamis*. Each of these terms carries entirely different metaphysical meanings with vastly different implications for theology and philosophy. To substitute one for the other would potentially undermine Islamic conceptions of reality. In a MacIntyrean sense, to have done so would have signaled a failure on the part of the Islamic tradition's own rational resources, namely its inability to identify in its own language with its own conceptual resources the truths expressed in another, alien tradition.

The same challenge presented itself to the Christian tradition. I noted in chapter 3 that Aquinas encountered a similar problem in synthesizing the Augustinian and Aristotelian traditions. The language and conceptual categories of the two traditions were not only different but, in many ways, diametrically opposed, such that the adoption of one meant the negation of the other, and vice versa. By virtue of familiarizing himself with the points of conflict and possibility between the Islamic and Aristotelian traditions through the writings of Avicenna and Averroës, Aquinas would have been aware of these dangers and may have benefited from some of the same philosophical moves that they used to avoid them.

---

39. Nasr, *Science and Civilization in Islam*, 54.

Engagement in the modern period

In the centuries following the writings of al-Ghazālī, the Islamic scientific tradition waned for reasons that are still widely disputed. In some ways, al-Ghazālī brought a finality to the conversation about how to integrate Greek philosophy into Islamic thought. It was truly a resolution to the vexing epistemological problem that had plagued the tradition for three hundred years. After al-Ghazālī, Islamic scholarship became a synthesized blend of both Greek philosophy and Islamic theology, "faithful in principle to the revelation of the Qur'ān, but unmistakably the product, in shape and procedure of the Hellenic tradition in philosophy, orthodox and at the same time Aristotelian."[40] However, as modern science was on the rise in the West, Muslim nations began to experience what Muzaffar Iqbal calls a "catching up syndrome," where Muslims sought to match the progress of Western science and technology.[41] This has led to a new set of tensions, this time between Islamic belief and modern Newtonian physics.

Perhaps no one has articulated the tensions between Islam and Western science better than Seyyed Hossein Nasr, professor of Islamic studies at George Washington University. Born in Tehran (1933) and raised in the United States from the age of thirteen, Nasr possesses an intimate knowledge of both traditions. According to Nasr, the central problem for the Christian tradition in the modern period is the loss of the *sacred* in modern Western science's view of the world. Nasr argues that sciences of other cultures seek to explain the physical nature of the world, yet still retain a sense of the sacred, what he calls *scientia sacra*, or sacred science.[42] Modern Western science is unique in its rejection of this sacred component.

According to Nasr, *scientia sacra* involves the "illumination of the heart and the mind" leading to wisdom (sapience), rather than mere knowledge (science).[43] Traditional cultures, in Nasr's view, understand knowledge of the natural world and knowledge of God to be interconnected.[44] That is, when a traditional culture strives to understand nature, it is also striving to understand God, and *vice versa*. This is due in large

---

40. Peters, *Aristotle and the Arabs*, 187. His emphasis.
41. Iqbal, *Islam and Science*, 203.
42. Nasr, *Knowledge and the Sacred*, 190.
43. Nasr, *Knowledge and the Sacred*, 190.
44. Nasr, *An Introduction to Islamic Cosmological Doctrines*, 2.

measure to the fact that God is understood to be connected to all things. It is at this point that Western science radically differs from the sciences of other traditional cultures, according to Nasr. There is no sense of God's presence in anything, and nothing needs to be understood in its interrelationship with the divine. In fact, it is only through isolating and reducing phenomena to quantifiable data in compartmentalized disciplines that Western science proceeds.

For Nasr, solving this problem requires adopting something like the Neoplatonic hierarchy of emanation, discussed above, consisting of: (1) Creator, (2) Intellect, (3) Universal Soul, (4) matter, (5) nature, (6) body, (7) the spheres, (8) the elements, and (9) beings of this world.[45] The loss of this sort of hierarchy, according to Nasr, has had two significant consequences. First, it has led to the "confusion between *vertical* and *horizontal causes*."[46] Here Nasr is criticizing the treatment of the physical world as though it were detached from God. This emphasis on the distinction between vertical and horizontal causality, however, indicates the real underlying concern for Nasr, which is one of providence. Nasr maintains that any scientific understanding of the universe that does not take God's vertical causality (providence) into consideration is not complete. This is a question of divine action—how and to what extent can God act in the physical world.

The rejection of this sort of hierarchy, according to Nasr, has also resulted in the "denial of life as an animating principle or energy which has penetrated into the physical realm."[47] Again, this is also related to the question of providence. First, according to Nasr, the loss of the World Soul as the animating principle of the world has resulted in a shift from notions of God directing the course of human events to notions of the movement of history as something independent of God's involvement. Second, the loss of the animating principle, according to Nasr, has made it difficult to resolve questions related to the origin and meaning of life. In this respect, Nasr is particularly critical of evolutionary explanations of human origins, arguing that "many nineteenth-century thinkers felt that they had to choose between either the creationist view or the Darwinian theory of evolution and naturally chose the latter as appearing more

---

45. Nasr, *An Introduction to Islamic Cosmological Doctrines*, 1–2.
46. Nasr, *An Introduction to Islamic Cosmological Doctrines*, 207. My emphasis.
47. Nasr, *An Introduction to Islamic Cosmological Doctrines*, 207.

'plausible' in a world which had forfeited the view of permanence and immutability to that of constant change, process."[48]

Finally, Nasr is also critical of Western science's commitment to both the uniformity of the laws of nature (uniformitarianism) and reductionism. According to Nasr, reductionism is an "inversion" of the traditional view of nature.[49] Whereas the traditional view of the cosmos understands God working top-down in the world, the modern Western cosmology reverses this order, making the primary causation bottom-up, so that the smallest constituents of reality control the higher-order reality. This is also closely related to the uniformity of the laws of nature. Since the smallest particles of reality control everything bottom-up, the regularities of nature are determined by these smallest bits of matter, *not* by the larger "cosmic cycles" that God directs and regulates.

Overall, I am in general agreement with Nasr's critique of modern Western science, and find it to be in keeping with similar criticisms raised by the Christian tradition (see chap. 5). As such, these criticisms serve as a source of agreement between the Christian and Islamic traditions, points at which we can engage in mutual constructive dialogue, rather than disagreement or debate.

Where I challenge Nasr is on his insistence that we need to adopt the Neoplatonic hierarchy to resolve the problems beset by modern science. This model does not seem congruent with either Islamic or Christian thought. In both the Qur'ān and the Christian scriptures, there are only two arenas of interaction—God and the world. Neither the Qur'ān nor the Bible require mediating spheres for God to interact with the rest of creation. Moreover, as discussed above, al-Ghazālī rightly argued that this kind of model restricts God's ability to work directly in the world and, thus, rules out the possibility of God's special providence. The doctrine of emanation implies that God can only work indirectly in the world, mediated through the chain of emanating spheres. This seems diametrically opposed to Islamic and Christian views of the God-world relationship.

I contend that a better way forward is to challenge the law-like, reductionistic, and deterministic understanding of the world that developed in the modern period, which is the root of the common concern for both traditions. To be clear, this is not to reject modern science altogether, but rather to reject some of the underlying *metaphysics*. Part of

---

48. Nasr, *An Introduction to Islamic Cosmological Doctrines*, 169.
49. Nasr, *An Introduction to Islamic Cosmological Doctrines*, 211.

doing so will require drawing on more recent discoveries in science, as discussed in the previous chapter, which indicate intrinsic openness in the world, making discussion of God's direct action more plausible.

Conclusion

In the last two chapters, I hope to have shown that the Islamic and Christian traditions are not as far apart on questions of providence as we may assume. This is no small feat, given the fact that God's action in the world is a central theological commitment. Demonstrating points of commonality go a long way toward confirming our respective views of reality. In particular, I argued that the Islamic tradition encountered a similar crisis concerning the issue of divine action in the medieval period that the Christian tradition encountered in the modern. In both instances, the respective traditions adopted metaphysical conceptions of the world from ancient Greek philosophy that placed significant restrictions on notions of God's general and special providence. The epistemological crisis for both traditions lies in the fact that without special divine action, there can be no special knowledge of God, thus calling into question the fundamental beliefs and practices of both traditions.

I also argued that both traditions have stood to benefit from each other, both in the medieval and modern periods in regard to this crisis. In this chapter, I have tried to show how the crisis developed for the Islamic tradition during the medieval period, in the first place, and the resources it used for resolving it. I then considered some of the ways the Christian tradition benefited from the Islamic tradition in the medieval period, and points of mutual constructive engagement for both traditions in the modern. In the next chapter, I will examine this same epistemological crisis and the possibilities for mutual constructive engagement between the Jewish, Islamic, and Christian traditions.

Chapter 7

Judaism and Providence

Nothing is so small or insignificant in the sight of men as not to be an object of the care and providence of God, before whom nothing is small that concerns the happiness of any of his creatures.[1]

—JOHN WESLEY

Introduction

THE JEWISH TRADITION HOLDS an important place alongside the Islamic and Christian traditions during the medieval period amid discussions of emanation and divine providence. Since Jews at this time were dispersed throughout both the Islamic and Christian worlds, they found themselves at the center of intellectual life in both contexts, first in major Islamic centers such as Baghdad, Cairo, and Córdoba, and later in Christian territories such as Spain, Sicily, Italy, and Provence.[2] In the Arabic-speaking world, Jews were fully immersed, adopting Arabic as their primary language and engaging in the broader culture. As this coincided with the Islamic Golden Age of science, Jews living in these areas were equally engaged in discussions of science and philosophy.[3] Consequently, two of

---

1. Wesley, "Sermon 67," 314–15, par. 6.
2. Rudderman, *Jewish Thought and Scientific Discovery*, 17.
3. Freudenthal, "Assimilation of Greco-Arabic Learning," 14.

the central, overriding concerns that confronted medieval Jewish scholars, such as Ibn Gabirol and Moses Maimonides, were the very questions that confronted Islamic thinkers of this period, that of the eternity of the world and God's providence in it. Jewish scholars were recipients of the same philosophical tradition as their Muslim neighbors with its emanationist view of the cosmos, which held that the entire universe issued instantaneously from God by necessity. This was just as problematic for the Jewish tradition as it was for the Islamic.

Jews, like their Muslim and Christian counterparts, tend to espouse the doctrine of *creatio ex nihilo*, the belief that the universe was created from nothing as an act of divine fiat, a deliberate and conscious choice of God's will, not an incidental by-product of God's existence; and that God is free to act in creation as the domain of God's providence. However, as discussed in the previous chapter, emanationist philosophy constrains both options, removing both the possibility of divine choice in creating the world and that of God acting directly in the particulars of creation. Emanationist philosophy, then, challenges general and special divine action, such that God cannot act in history or the lives of individuals, as the Torah, the Qur'ān, and the Christian scriptures all profess. While, for medieval thinkers the inherent problem with emanation had to do with the restrictions placed on God—God's knowledge, power, will, even God's oneness; from our vantage point, it is easy to see that this also constituted an epistemological crisis. If God cannot act directly in the world, then there can be no special revelation, and without revelation, there can be no direct theological knowledge of God. By definition, the lack of reliable knowledge constitutes an epistemological crisis.

In this chapter, then, I will examine how the Jewish tradition addressed the problem of emanation during the medieval period, looking at the resources it both gleaned from and proffered to its religious neighbors. I will begin by considering the responses to this issue by two prominent Jewish medieval philosophical-theologians—Ibn Gabirol and Moses Maimonides and their influence on the Latin West, particularly on that Thomas Aquinas. Finally, I will look briefly at how the Jewish tradition has dealt with the issue of special divine providence in light of modern science.

Medieval Judaism and Science

The beginning of Jewish philosophy in the medieval period began with the assimilation of the Arabic language as their vernacular. The adoption of literary Arabic, or Judeo-Arabic, began with translations of the Hebrew Bible, culminating in the commentaries (*tafsir*) of Sa'adiah ben Yosef Gaon (or Saadia Gaon), a tenth-century rabbi and philosopher.[4] Known as the founder of Judeo-Arabic literature, Saadia Gaon increased the literary knowledge of Arabic among Jews and the fluency among Jewish thinkers with the Arabic-translated philosophical texts. In so doing, he introduced to Jewish scholars the prevailing concerns of science, philosophy, and Muslim theology. As a result, Jewish scholars in Islamic areas of influence had access "to the entire corpus of Greco-Arabic learning," such as it was at the time, and began to weigh in on the prevailing tensions between medieval Aristotelianism and biblical faith, resulting in distinctly Jewish works that sought to balance the two. Again, one of the central issues along this line was the tension between emanation and *creatio ex nihilo*. Presently, then, I will consider two of the most prominent medieval Jewish thinkers who sought to resolve this tension in their own ways—Ibn Gabirol and Moses Maimonides.

Solomon Ibn Gabirol (Avicebron)

Solomon Ibn Gabirol, known to medieval philosophers in the West as Avicebron, was an eleventh-century poet and Jewish Platonic philosopher who was born in Málaga, Spain during the Córdoba Caliphate. He wrote in Arabic and was influenced particularly by Arabic translations of Plato. His most important philosophical work, *Fons Vitae*, was largely influential in the Latin West, rather than among his Jewish contemporaries. It was originally written in Arabic as *Yanbu' al-Hayat* in the form of a Platonic dialogue between a teacher and his disciple. What is most interesting for our purposes is the fact that Ibn Gabirol accepts both creation (*creatio ex nihilo*) *and* emanation, viewing them both as a means of God's divine will (*Irāda*).

While Ibn Gabirol accepted the basic Neoplatonic scheme of emanation, he, like so many medieval thinkers, was uncomfortable with the

---

4. Freudenthal, "Assimilation of Greco-Arabic Learning," 13.

implications of this model for Jewish biblical understandings of God.[5] Ibn Gabirol sets out to provide a systematic response to this problem. His response is comprehensive and seeks to hold several strands together. First, Gabirol is principally interested in the nature and purpose of being human, that is, he argues that we must first understand what we are (our nature) in order to understand how to live and act (our purpose).[6] For Ibn Gabirol this is as much a theological question as it is a philosophical one. He is chiefly interested in how devout Jews are to live their lives in obedience to God in light of Torah and their best philosophical reasoning. It is with these concerns in mind that Ibn Gabirol considers larger metaphysical questions about the nature of reality and metaphysics. Thus, the broader backdrop for Ibn Gabirol's discussion of human purpose is the doctrine of emanation, not only of the world emanating from God, but also the doctrine of Neoplatonic Return, whereby the created intellects, humans in particular, are motivated by a desire to return to the ultimate source and to live in accordance with the nature of that source (see Fig. 2 below).

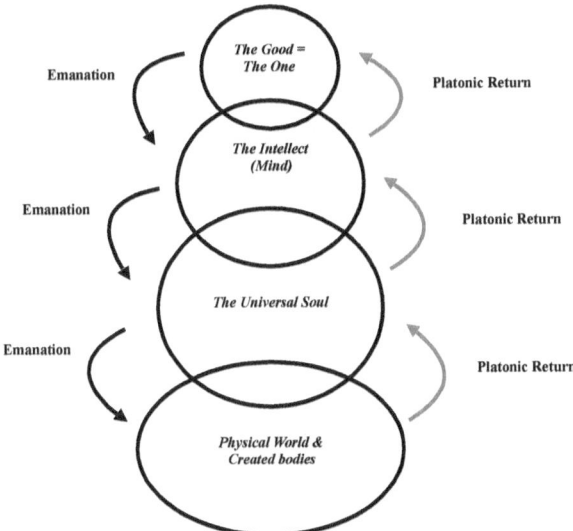

Figure 2 Neoplatonic Emanation and Platonic Return

5. Klausner, "The Philosophy of *Fons Vitae*," v.
6. Pessin, "Solomon Ibn Gabirol [Avicebron]."

For Ibn Gabirol, it is God's will (*Irāda*) that is responsible both for the creation of all things and for their restoration with God.[7] Thus, in Ibn Gabirol's system, there are three aspects that must be held together—(1) God (Prime Being), (2) the will (*Irāda*), and (3) matter and form. God, of course, is the source of all things, and all things, for Ibn Gabirol, are made of matter and form. Indeed, Ibn Gabirol is uniquely known for arguing that *all things*, not just physical things, but soul and intellect, too, are comprised of matter and form. What connects God and the rest of the world (1 and 3 above) is God's will (*Irāda*). Will is the mediating principle between God and everything else. Here we come to Ibn Gabirol's understanding of divine action and his attempt at resolving the crisis posed by emanation. For Ibn Gabirol, the will (*Irāda*) is diffused throughout the world in the same way that the soul is diffused throughout the body, and its function is similar. As Ibn Gabirol states:

> Matter and form may be likened to body, the atmosphere and the soul; and Will that binds them and is diffused through them is like the soul in body, luminosity in the atmosphere, and reason in the soul, for when Will permeates the whole matter of reason, that matter becomes knowing and encompasses the form of all things; and when it is diffused throughout the whole matter of the soul, this becomes a living matter, mobile and cognizant of forms in the measure of its potency and its relative placement away from the source of truth and form; and when it permeates the matter of nature and of body it endows this with motion, shape and form. (*FL* 5.38, 292)

Of course, the question arises as to *how* God's will (*Irāda*) is able to interact in the material world. This is part and parcel of the problem of emanation. If God, as the source, is one and is spirit, having no physicality and no separable attributes, then how can God act in any other sphere of existence comprised of matter and multiplicity? Here Ibn Gabirol is responding to the Greek assumption, adopted by Muslim philosophers such as Avicenna, that since God is pure being, God must be one and unchanging. Consequently, God, by nature, cannot have multiple attributes or interact directly with complex processes, otherwise this would introduce multiplicity into the divine being, making God less than simple, less than complete.[8]

---

7. Ibn Gabirol, *Fountain of Life*, 1.2, 4–5. Going forward, references to *Fountain of Life* (*FL*) will be noted parenthetically.

8. Avicenna, "Metaphysics," 214. See 2.5 "On the Simplicity of the Necessary."

This is where Ibn Gabirol's unique position that all created things are comprised of matter and form is so important. By identifying matter and form in all things—physical and non-physical (spiritual)—he can identify at least some spiritual in all physical things and at least some physical in all spiritual things. In this way, he can explain the interdependency between spiritual and physical, between God and the world. As historian, Joseph Klausner, states: "Gabirol *must* think thus; for if not, how is the gradation from highest spirit to lowest matter possible?"[9] For Ibn Gabirol, then, there is no inherent contradiction between creation and emanation. The notions of creation, emanation, and *Irāda* go "hand in hand in hand."[10] As Ibn Gabirol himself states:

> The whole of philosophy is divided into three parts . . . the science of matter and form, the science of will and the science of the primary Existent. . . . [A]nything created requires a cause and some intermediary between. Now the cause is the primary Existent; what has been created is matter and form; and the intermediary is will." (*FL* 1.7, 11)

And:

> "Therefore will (*Irāda*) must occupy an intermediate position between the supreme Existent and the form that has sprung from will." (*FL* 4.19, 227)

For Ibn Gabirol, then, God is the first essence as described in the emanationist scheme, with the world of matter and form issuing from God's nature. However, God's will (*Irāda*) serves as the mediating element between God and the world, both causing (or creating) its emanation and allowing for God's purposes (or providence) to manifest in it.[11]

In this way, Ibn Gabirol views himself as not only resolving the tension of how God works in the created world in an emanationist metaphysic, but also bringing together his two major foci—God's will in the world and our nature and purpose as humans. The goal of all things is to return to the source, the one, and join in its likeness. This is achieved principally through the will (*Irāda*). It is *Irāda* that gives motion to all things, and the motion of all things is that of desire and love, the desire to move closer to God in order to unite with the one, the source of all things.

9. Klausner, "The Philosophy of *Fons Vitae*," xiii.

10. Pessin, *Ibn Gabirol's Theology of Desire*, 60.

11. Pessin, *Ibn Gabirol's Theology of Desire*, 62. See also: Klausner, "The Philosophy of the Fons Vitae," vi–vii.

Ibn Gabirol's entire system then, can be summarized as a desire "*to unite with the Godhead via the will.*"[12] As Ibn Gabirol states: "The motion of everything, therefore, is for the sake of Goodness, which is the one [God]. Now the proof of this is that no existent longs to be multiple; rather, all yearn to be one. All, therefore, desire unity" (*FL* 5.32, 284).

Moses ben Maimon (Maimonides)

Moses ben Maimon, or Maimonides, was born in Córdoba, Spain, during the Almoravid rule of the Iberian peninsula. At the time, Córdoba was considered one of the great intellectual centers of the world. From an early age, Maimonides studied the Torah and Talmud, under the tutelage of his father. He also developed a strong interest in philosophy and science, reading the Greek philosophers available in their Arabic translations. At the age of thirteen, he and his family were forced to flee Spain due to the rise of the Almohad dynasty. They settled in Cairo, Egypt where he and his brother, David, became jewel merchants until his brother's death in a shipwreck in the Indian Ocean. After this, Maimonides gave up the merchant business and turned to medicine, eventually becoming the appointed court physician for the ruler Saladin—"the same Saladin who defeated Richard the Lionhearted in the Third Crusade."[13]

Maimonides wrote several works of great import. It was his commentary on Jewish law, the *Mishneh Torah* (literally, second Torah) that established Maimonides' importance within the Jewish community, constituting a complete systemization of the Oral Law.[14] However, his most important treatise for philosophical purposes is *The Guide for the Perplexed*, which was addressed, quite literally, to those who were perplexed as to how to harmonize both Jewish Law and Greek philosophy. *The Guide* was controversial from the start because it seemed to give too much credence to the philosophers (Aristotle and Al-Fārābī, in particular) than to Torah and biblical prophecy.[15] Nevertheless, in *The Guide*, Maimonides sets out to do precisely what al-Ghazālī did before him and what Thomas Aquinas did after him—to bridge theological and

---

12. Klausner, "The Philosophy of *Fons Vitae*," x.
13. Baird and Kaufmann, "Moses Maimonides," 261.
14. Leaman, *Moses Maimonides*, 6.
15. Seeskin, "Maimonides."

philosophical descriptions of the world, specifically in reference to its creation and God's ongoing role in it.

I will begin by looking at Maimonides' response to the challenge of emanation, followed by his response to questions of providence. In terms of emanation, Maimonides sets out to show that *creatio ex nihilo* is plausible by demonstrating that the philosopher's arguments for the world's eternity do not amount to proofs. Part of his reasoning is that neither *creatio ex nihilo* nor emanation can be demonstrated conclusively. In fact, he maintains that Aristotle recognized this too, and, thus, never intended to prove emanation in the first place.[16] However, Maimonides reasons that if he can show that the arguments for the eternity of the world have substantial flaws, then he will have gone a long way toward showing the plausibility of the doctrine of creation.

According to Maimonides, there are eight arguments made by philosophers for the eternity of the world (*GP*, 2.14, 174–76). However, there are three that he identifies as being primary, and a fourth that he gives considerable attention to. I list all four together: (1) that there can be no "transition from potentiality to actuality" in God's nature, (2) that God cannot change God's will; (3) that whatever God creates is necessarily created *eo ipso* (instantaneously) (*GP* 2.18, 181–83); and (4) Aristotle's assumption that (a) anything indestructible must be eternal and, by extension, anything eternal must be indestructible, and (b) anything destructible must *not be* eternal, thus anything *not* eternal must be destructible (*GP*, 2.14, 174). Arguments 1 and 2 derive from ancient and medieval assumptions about multiplicity and simplicity. That is, if God is one—simple and unchanging—then how can God bring about the complexity of the created world? To do so would suggest either a change in God's nature (God's oneness) or that God was not one and unchanging in the first place. Here Maimonides is particularly influenced by Islamic Neoplatonic philosophers, such as al-Fārābī and Avicenna as well as Almohad and Muʿtazilite theology, all of which held God to be "a kind of pure being so utterly unified that it transcends any internal divisions."[17]

Arguments 3 and 4 assume the cosmological argument—the belief that nothing comes from nothing, but that the causal series of events cannot go on *ad infinitum*. Consequently, there must be some prime mover, an eternal, unchanging source that is, nonetheless, the cause of all other

16. Maimonides, *Guide for the Perplexed*, 2.15, 176–77. Going forward, references to *Guide for the Perplexed* (*GP*) will be noted parenthetically.

17. Pessin, "The Influence of Islamic Thought on Maimonides."

motion in the universe. Emanationist philosophers used this reasoning to argue that if nothing comes from nothing, and if everything that exists is the immediate effect of its sufficient cause, then everything that exists must issue *eo ipso* from its sufficient cause. Furthermore, if this reasoning applies to all things, then it must also apply to creation, itself. That is, the universe is no exception. It must be the immediate effect of its sufficient cause, i.e., God.

Kenneth Seeskin summarizes the above arguments this way: arguments for the eternity of the world assume that there is either something in God's nature (arguments 1 and 2) or in the nature of the world (3 and 4) that makes creation *ex nihilo* impossible.[18] In response to the first line of argument—that creation would constitute a change in God's nature—Maimonides argues that this does not have to be the case if creation were always a part of God's original intent. Only if a change were necessitated by something outside of God would this constitute a fundamental change in God's nature. However, if God had always intended a thing, then bringing it about, even if at a different time, implies no such change (*GP*, 2.18, 182–83). Furthermore, Maimonides argues that the doctrine of emanation is not a very adequate solution to the problem of multiplicity. If God is one and simple, then anything that arises from God must also be one and simple. So even the second sphere could not have multiplicity, nor any succeeding sphere after it. Such complexity cannot come about as a necessary by-product of God's existence. Rather, it must have been *created* to be this way (*GP*, 2.22, 192–93).

In terms of the cosmological argument (arguments 3 and 4 above), Maimonides contends that the assumption that nothing comes from nothing breaks down when we consider the creation of something truly novel. He argues that since creation is by definition something new, it need not follow the same pattern of change that we see in the rest of the natural world. As Maimonides states: "[the world's] genesis is not like that of the things produced from it, nor its destruction like theirs; for it has been created from nothing, and if it should please the Creator, he might reduce it to absolutely nothing" (*GP*, 2.17, 180). In this way, Maimonides secures at least the possibility that God freely created the world, raising substantial doubts about emanationist arguments for the necessity and eternity of the universe.

---

18. Seeskin, "Maimonides."

In terms of the constrictions that the doctrine of emanation places on notions of providence, God's ability to act directly in the world of human affairs, Maimonides responds to a line of reasoning that originated with Avicenna. Avicenna argued that since God is one and unchanging, God can only know the universals of creation, not the particulars. Again, this stems from theological and philosophical assumptions about God's oneness. If God is utterly simple, then God cannot have multiple ways of knowing, for this would be "just as faulty as the assertion that [God] has multiple acts."[19] God's knowledge is one. It is unchanging and atemporal, and it cannot "consist of individual cognitions (*'ulūm*) that refer to multiple objects."[20] Furthermore, since God can only know the universals of creation, not the particulars, God cannot *act* on the particulars, either, thus, eliminating the possibility of special divine action. As Maimonides puts it, the philosophers declare that

> it is impossible that God should have a knowledge of earthly things, for the individual members of a species can only be perceived by the senses, . . . but God does not perceive by means of any of the senses. . . . [F]urthermore, knowledge of individual beings, that are subject to change, necessitates some change in him who possesses it, because this knowledge itself changes constantly. (*GP*, 3.16, 281)

Maimonides attempts to resolve this in at least two ways. First, he is emphatic that descriptions of God's actions are *homonymous*. That is, we cannot assume that when we use the word "act" in reference to God's action and creaturely action that we are using it in the same way. The two uses bear at most a family resemblance.[21] God's ways are beyond our comprehension. Indeed, Maimonides takes an apophatic position regarding theological language altogether. That is, we can only arrive at knowledge about God by acknowledging what God is *not*, because we can never definitively state what God *is*. Thus, we cannot speak unequivocally of God's action in the world. For Maimonides, this frees Torah-believers

19. Avicenna, "Metaphysics," 2.18, 216.

20. Griffel, *Al-Ghazālī's Philosophical Theology*, 136.

21. Aquinas makes a similar argument in both *The Principles of Nature* (6:37, 419) and *Summa Theologica* (1.13.5, 354–55). There he argues that language about God must be considered analogical, rather than univocal or equivocal. Thus, when we speak of God's action in the world, it is an analog to our own action, recognizing that we cannot fully comprehend God's mode of acting since it is so radically different from our own.

to continue using biblical and theological language about God's action, recognizing that it implies no contradiction since we cannot fully understand God's mode of acting in the first place.

Second, Maimonides argues that in the lower spheres (the sublunar world), God's action extends only to humans, principally through the intellect, and not to "other living beings" (*GP*, 3.17, 286). He reasons that divine providence is essentially "Divine intellectual influence," and thus only extends to other rational beings capable of using the intellect. God's action, then, is primarily along moral lines, interacting only with those who have the capacity to make moral choices meriting "reward or punishment" (*GP*, 3.17, 287). Maimonides states that on this position he is in agreement with Aristotle, but that he is drawing explicitly on his own faith tradition—the Torah and the Prophets, not "on demonstrative proof" (*GP*, 3.17, 286). However, by deferring to his own fideistic commitments, Maimonides fails to show *how* his account is possible from a philosophical or scientific perspective. Furthermore, by limiting God's action only to humans, Maimonides restricts God's action in the world in a way that neither the Jewish, Christian, nor Muslim scriptures do, all three of which acknowledge God's providential action in all created things, not just humans. As we will see below, it is Thomas Aquinas who sharpens Maimonides' response, not by contradicting it, but by adding to it.

Influence of Ibn Gabirol and Maimonides on Aquinas

Regrettably, the experience of Jews in the Latinized West was markedly different from their relationship to the Muslim world. As already noted, Jews lived amicably with Muslims throughout much of the Golden Age of Islamic science and philosophy. However, in 1121 CE when the Almohad dynasty came to power in Iberia, the attitude toward non-Muslims changed drastically. The Almohads rejected the Islamic doctrine of legal protection for non-Muslims (*dhimmī*), and many Jews were forced either to convert or leave. As a result, many Jews migrated to other areas of Europe, such as northern Spain, France, Italy, and even the Orient.[22] This resulted in a transition from Arabic as the dominant language to Hebrew and, eventually to Latin and other languages of Christianized West.

---

22. Sela, *Abraham Ibn Ezra*, 6.

Judeo-Arabic philosophy and science was first introduced into the Hebrew-speaking and reading communities in the West through the works of Abraham Bar Hiyya and Abraham Ibn Ezra. The diaspora of Jews during the Almohad period, however, resulted in a second wave of Judeo-Arabic works, making their way into southern France (the Midi), where many Jews found refuge in Provence. This process lasted more than two centuries and included both translations of Jewish religious philosophy, such as Saadia Gaon's *Beliefs and Opinions* and Maimonides' *Guide for the Perplexed*, as well as works of science and philosophy by Greek and Muslim writers. As a result, "displaced Jewish intellectuals found themselves in the advantageous position as translators and cultural intermediaries between Muslims and Christians," stimulating interest in philosophy and science among Jews already living in Europe.[23] Furthermore, it was largely through these Jewish scholars that Aristotle was reintroduced to medieval scholastics in Western Europe. Nowhere is this influence more prominent than in the writings of Thomas Aquinas.

Aquinas, then, is as concerned with questions of emanation and divine providence as his religious counterparts, particularly with the question of how God can act directly in the world and in the lives of individuals. In addressing these concerns, Aquinas remains in constant dialogue with Maimonides, Avicenna (the Commentator), and Aristotle (the Philosopher) throughout the *Summa Theological* and other writings. He engages Ibn Gabirol briefly, but substantively, in "On Being and Essence," one of Aristotle's earliest writings on metaphysics. There he dismisses Gabirol's argument that all things are made of matter and form, maintaining, that intellectual substances such as intelligences (incorporeal beings) and souls must be entirely free of matter. He argues this for two reasons. First, Ibn Gabirol's position does not comport with the teachings of the philosophers. Second, it defies the very need for the categorical distinction between matter and form in the first place. We only make this distinction because we consider form to be something other than matter and its material conditions.[24] As Aquinas states: "*corporeal form*, like other forms, is only intelligible *because it can be abstracted from matter.*"[25]

---

23. Rudderman, *Jewish Thought and Scientific Discovery*, 18.
24. See Kerr, "Aquinas: Metaphysics."
25. Aquinas, *On Being and Essence*, 52; chapter 4. My emphasis.

It is Aquinas' engagement with Ibn Gabirol in this chapter of "On Being and Essence," however, that leads him ultimately to borrow a distinction made by Aristotle and adopted by Avicenna between existence (*esse*) and essence, a distinction that will also allow him to respond to the shortcomings in Maimonides' position. Recall that Maimonides' explanation of God's providence is limited both by his inability to provide a philosophical (metaphysical) account for it, in the first place, and by his insistence that God's action applies only at the level of human intelligence. In both respects, Aquinas sharpens Maimonides' contribution. By distinguishing between existence (*esse*) and essence, Aquinas argues that God is not simply the only pure being (*esse*), but also the *source* of all being (*esse*). As the source, God participates directly in the existence (*esse*) of *all things*, not just humans. As David Burrell states:

> since "*esse* itself is the most common effect [of God], first and more intimate [to each thing] than all other effects, it belongs to God alone according to its peculiar power." . . . So in giving each individual thing its existence, God may be said to be intimately present to each. From there it is a short step to maintain that "everything falls under divine providence, not merely in its universality but in its particularity."[26]

In so doing, Aquinas is able to address both shortcomings in Maimonides' argument. First, in his distinction between *esse* and essence, Aquinas provides a rich metaphysical account for how God's providence can extend to all things, since there is a necessary link between God's own *esse* and that of all other created things. Second, this same metaphysic allows Aquinas to preserve God's providence in *all* created things, not merely humans.

In this way, Aquinas resolves, at least for the Christian tradition, the crisis posed by emanation for divine providence, but in doing so, benefits directly from the contributions of his co-religionists Avicenna, Ibn Gabirol, and Maimonides, and indirectly from a host of others, not least of which al-Fārābī and al-Ghazālī. Indeed, while in one sense Aquinas stands as the culmination of these efforts, he does so only as a result of these efforts. It was only through the protracted dialogue between Muslims, Jews, and Christians of the medieval period, that these three traditions were able to reach such a formidable conclusion. Aquinas could

---

26. Burrell, *Knowing the Unknowable God*, 94. Burrell is quoting Aquinas' *Summa Theologica*, 1.22.2.

only arrive at a philosophical account of God's providential presence in a Neoplatonic framework by building on the prior contributions of those from other religious traditions, bound in a common effort to resolve a shared problem. It is this sort of mutual constructive engagement that I have been proposing throughout this book, encouraging members of multiple traditions to work together on common problems in pursuit of joint solutions that bring us closer to a shared account of the truth. What would it look like if we deliberately entered into this sort of engagement today?

Judaism and Modern Science

Tracing the history of Judaism and science during the modern period, specifically as it pertains to the question of divine action, proves to be more complicated than doing so for the medieval period. First, while Jews remain actively involved in science, technology, and medicine throughout the modern and contemporary periods, making significant contributions to scientific enquiry and technological development, their specific concern for the question of divine action dwindles after the medieval period, especially after the contributions of Maimonides. There is a surprising dearth of literature on the question of providence and science among Jewish scholarship from the modern period on. Second, while the Jewish tradition has never suffered the same sort of schisms that have riddled the Christian church, especially Protestantism, the modern period saw the development of three main branches of Judaism—Orthodox, Reform, and Conservative, each of which has had a very different take on the relationship between science and religion.

Orthodox Judaism has been influenced more by mysticism than rationalist philosophy. This is due to the influence not only of Maimonides, but also of Moses ben Naham, another medieval Jewish rabbinical scholar more commonly referred to as Nahmanides. Nahmanides is associated with Jewish mysticism more than philosophy. Indeed, his name does not appear in most philosophical encyclopedias.[27] He was a prominent representative of an esoteric movement known as *Kabbalah*, that arose largely in reaction to Maimonidean rationalism. While Maimonides accepted the basic tenets of Aristotelian physics, using his philosophical

27. See: *The Cambridge Dictionary of Philosophy*, *The Encyclopedia of Philosophy*, *The Stanford Encyclopedia of Philosophy*.

and rabbinical training to aid him in harmonizing the two, kabbalists were more reticent. On the issue of divine providence, in particular, Nahmanides altogether rejected the Aristotelian notion of immanent causes underlying the regularity of the natural world and argued instead that it is "divine providence that sustains the world through 'hidden miracles' (*nassim nistarim*)."[28] There has been much scholarly debate about meaning and significance of Nahmanides' use of "hidden miracles," and I will not pursue that debate here.[29] Suffice it to say, Orthodox Judaism has been more inclined to acknowledge the frequency of God's miraculous involvement in the world and less concerned with the regularity of the natural order, which is assumed in both ancient Greek philosophy and modern science.

Reform Judaism has not moved far beyond Maimonides on the issue of divine providence. This is ironic, given the fact that Reform Judaism developed in eighteenth-century Germany as a way of becoming more compatible with the Western Enlightenment tradition. The emphasis of this movement, however, was cultural and political, more so than scientific, focusing on conforming with modern ethical precepts, rather than with modern science itself. The chief intellectual movement responsible for this transition was known as the *Haskalah*, the Jewish enlightenment, which sought to bring Jews out of the margins of Eastern European society and into the center of cultural, political, and intellectual life.

On the question of the creation of the world and God's ongoing activity in it, it is telling that of the two most recognizable modern Jewish philosophers—Moses Mendelssohn and Baruch Spinoza—the former says nothing about this topic, despite having been introduced to Maimonides in his earliest studies;[30] while the latter creates a systematic and comprehensive philosophical system devoted to it, yet does so in such a way that so radically reformulates Jewish conceptions of God and the world that he was excommunicated by the synagogue of Amsterdam in 1656 at the age of twenty-three, after he was brought up on charges of heresy.[31] The irony, then, is that since the time of Maimonides, the Jewish tradition has not had a prominent representative who has sought to

---

28. Freudenthal, *Science in Medieval Jewish Cultures*, 496–97. Citation omitted.
29. See Berger, "Miracles and the Natural Order in Nahmanides," 107–28.
30. Tonelli, "Mendelssohn, Moses," 276.
31. Baird and Kaufmann, "Baruch Spinoza," 105. Spinoza was later exonerated by the new state of Israel in the twentieth century.

construct a distinctly Jewish understanding of God's special divine action in light of both the Torah and modern science. This is a significant lacuna.

The reality is that the modern, Newtonian description of the universe, as discussed at length in chapter 5, poses significant challenges for the God-world relationship as all three Abrahamic traditions have historically understood it; and those challenges are distinct from the ones posed by the ancient and medieval periods. Distinctions between matter and form as well as between being (*esse*) and existence, for example, no longer make sense in our contemporary context. The modern metaphysic is vastly different from that of the medieval period, and while many of the tenets of Newtonian physics are being challenged by recent discoveries (e.g., quantum physics, general and special relativity, chaos theory, and so on), many of the basic modern metaphysical commitments still hold sway—commitments to atomism, reductionism, and determinism. These commitments pose significant challenges to divine providence as historically conceived by all three Abrahamic traditions, and place a certain burden of proof on each, separately and together, to explain how God acts in light of these commitments.

Since the Abrahamic traditions share a vested interest in preserving similar notions of God's providence, it behooves us to work together. It is my contention that Christians, Jews, and Muslims stand to benefit from each other on this issue. Since we share a basic understanding of the same God and how that God works in the world, we are uniquely suited to aid one another in addressing this concern. In the medieval period, Christians benefited substantially from the work of Muslims and Jews. At this point, since the Christian tradition has directly addressed the crisis posed by modern science for special divine providence, the Islamic and Jewish traditions may now be in a position to learn from our history of progress and set-backs on this issue.

Conclusion

This chapter concludes our investigation into the three Abrahamic traditions. I have tried to show that the issue of special divine providence has posed challenges for all three in both the medieval and the modern periods, and that all three traditions have stood to benefit from each other in resolving their respective crises. During the medieval period, this has involved a protracted discussion among leading philosophical-theologians such as al-Ghazālī, Maimonides, and Thomas Aquinas, as they sought to explain scriptural understandings of God's acts of creation and providence in light of Neoplatonic conceptions of emanation. However, I have also tried to show that a similar challenge now faces all three traditions in light of modern metaphysical commitments. Assumptions taken for granted by modern science regarding naturalism, reductionism, determinism, and so on, have created a broader metaphysical worldview that has raised significant challenges for all three Abrahamic traditions regarding commitments to special divine providence. I believe that, together, we can aid each other in resolving this crisis, and that in doing so, we can model precisely the sort of mutual constructive engagement that I have been arguing for throughout this book.

Part III

Eastern Faiths in Mutual Constructive Engagement

Overview of Part III:
Eastern Faiths in Mutual Constructive Engagement

THE CAREFUL READER WILL note that focusing on the three Abrahamic traditions for the purposes of comparison in the context of this book is relatively unproblematic. Recall that I am proposing a form of deep pluralism that assumes that each tradition emerges from its own unique history of development, resulting in fundamentally different rational resources for describing God and the world. While this is certainly true of the Abrahamic traditions, their histories of development overlap in ways that make that comparison less problematic. As I have discussed at length in the preceding chapters, the Abrahamic traditions share much of the same intellectual history from the medieval period on, drawing on the same philosophical heritage from the ancient Greeks. However, because of the historical contingencies of these three traditions and their geographical proximity at various points, they also share quite a bit in common theologically.

The three Abrahamic traditions, then, are inheritors of similar theological and philosophical antecedents, creating something of a shared discourse of meaning. That is, they tend to use some of the same basic terminology for God, the world, sin, forgiveness, and so on, and they even seem to agree on the basic meanings of these terms. Where they diverge is over the theological interpretation and application of those key terms. Of course, the differences are significant, resulting in an array of divergent theological terminology, exegetical and extra-canonical sources, primary and secondary authoritative voices, and, in short, entirely disparate standards of rationality. Nevertheless, looking for points of commonality and intersection between these three traditions is relatively unproblematic, given how much they share in common historically, philosophically, and theologically.

The same is not true when considering the Eastern faith traditions, particularly Buddhism and Hinduism, relative to the Abrahamic traditions, in general, and the Christian tradition, in particular. The Eastern traditions have radically different histories of development, which share little or no overlap with the three Abrahamic traditions. They have entirely different conceptions of the divine (e.g., God, gods, the ultimate), as well as vastly different authoritative texts and voices, beliefs and practices, and so on. In fact, some might go as far as to say that the Eastern traditions are fundamentally *incommensurate* with the Abrahamic faiths. That is, the standards of rationality among these traditions are so different that they do not correspond in any meaningful way to allow for either agreement or disagreement. While I do not believe that this sort of incommensurability is insurmountable, it does raise the question of how to broach interreligious dialogue under these circumstances. It is the goal in this final part of the book to examine this possibility. As I have done so far, I will consider each tradition's relationship to questions of creation and providence, as well as what possibilities for mutual constructive engagement exist between Buddhism, Hinduism, and Christianity.

Of course, where this project becomes problematic is precisely in respect to notions of creation and providence. Whereas the Abrahamic traditions share a similar understanding of God, the world, and God's action in the world, this basic metaphysical structure is different for the Eastern traditions. The Buddhist tradition, in particular, rejects the notion of a single, creator-God, responsible for the creation and preservation of the universe. Instead, Buddhists hold that the universe itself is ultimate and eternal, and that all other beings—gods, humans, animals, and so on—are bound up in ongoing cosmological cycles known as *mahākalpas* and participate in the endless metaphysical cycle of *saṃsāra*, the process of death and rebirth. Hindus hold similar cosmological beliefs in the ultimacy and eternity of the universe, likewise maintaining that the universe undergoes endless cycles of renewal (*mahā-yugas*), and that individuals participate in the endless process of reincarnation (*saṃsāra*).

However, unlike Buddhists, Hindus do posit belief in a supreme deity, a God who is responsible for creating and sustaining the universe. Nevertheless, Hindu and Christian conceptions of God are not identical. As I will discuss in more detail in chapter 9, the creating and sustaining responsibilities attributed to God in the Hindu tradition are distributed among three deities, who make up a triumvirate—Brahmā, Vishnu, and Shiva—while ultimacy is attributed not to any of these three, but to brahman, the supreme deity described in the *Upaniṣads*. This means that the metaphysical picture of the God-world relationship in the Hindu tradition is still different from that of the Abrahamic traditions.

The question, then, is whether or not Buddhism and Hinduism are susceptible to the same epistemological crisis I have been considering throughout the book. If Buddhists reject the notion of a creating, sustaining God, then does modern science pose any threat to their fundamental metaphysical beliefs? Likewise, to what extent is Hinduism's conception of God and the ultimate vulnerable to the challenges of modern science and its underlying metaphysic? In this part of the book, I will argue that Buddhism and Hinduism *are* as vulnerable to the crisis posed by modern science as the Abrahamic traditions. While their respective conceptions of the ultimate are different from each other and from the other traditions considered so far, their traditions are, nonetheless, irreducibly metaphysical. Moreover, both depend on a form of revelation for their metaphysical beliefs and practices. Thus, the same problem that has plagued the other traditions faces Buddhism and Hinduism. If their respective forms of revelatory experiences are precluded in light of modern science, then their basic metaphysical beliefs and practices would also be called into question. In this sense, neither tradition escapes the possibility of the fundamental crisis that has been considered throughout this book.

Chapter 8

Buddhism, Metaphysics, and Science

If you will avoid all bigotry, go on. In every instance of this kind, whatever the instrument be, acknowledge the finger of God. And not only acknowledge, but rejoice in his work, and praise his name with thanksgiving. Encourage whomsoever God is pleased to employ, to give himself wholly up thereto. Speak well of him wheresoever you are; defend his character and his mission.[1]

—JOHN WESLEY

Introduction

THROUGHOUT THIS BOOK I have been attempting to show how various religious traditions can aid each other in resolving similar epistemological crises—crises that call into question a tradition's ability to make rational sense of the world. The three traditions considered so far share similar theological worldviews that make each susceptible to a similar type of crisis, namely, one related to the issue of special divine providence. Since each of the Abrahamic traditions relies on special revelation for its theological knowledge, any scientific worldview that precludes God's special divine action undermines the possibility of revelation, constituting an

---

1. Wesley, "Sermon 38," 491, sec. 4, par. 5.

epistemological crisis. When considering the Buddhist tradition, the problem, at first glance, does not seem to present itself. Buddhists, as I will discuss at length below, do not believe in a creator-God, a single supreme deity who is responsible for the creation and preservation of all things. On this count, it would appear that problems related to special divine action and modern science would never arise, thus never posing an epistemological crisis in the first place.

What I hope to show in this chapter, however, is that Buddhism, though holding no particular theory of divine action, nevertheless holds a very robust metaphysic, one that permeates the tradition's entire view of the universe, our place in it, and how individuals attain enlightenment (*nirvāṇa*). Buddhists depend on practices such as meditation that grant them access to the ultimate and provide revelatory knowledge of ultimate reality. In this sense, Buddhism is little different than Christianity or any of the other Abrahamic traditions; it depends on the intersection of the metaphysical and the physical for its epistemological beliefs and practices. If this intersection is called into question, their fundamental beliefs would also be called into question, constituting an epistemological crisis. This is precisely the challenge that Newtonian physics presents to *all* the religious traditions. For better or worse, the burden of proof has shifted to any religious tradition that would claim that its metaphysical view of the universe comports with the physical regularities of nature. This may entail challenging, amending, or altogether rejecting Newtonian physics, but the sheer success of the Newtonian tradition means that it cannot be ignored.

Toward this end, I will begin by providing a very brief overview of the origins of Buddhism and its general worldview. I will then consider the relationship between Buddhist metaphysics and modern science. Finally, I will consider some resources that the Christian tradition has developed in response to its own crisis pertaining to the issue of divine action and will consider their usefulness to the Buddhist tradition in addressing its own potential crisis.

Buddhist Origins and Worldview

In this section, I want to provide the barest of overviews for the origins of Buddhism. I have not provided this sort of overview for the other religious traditions for several reasons. First, it is the not in the purview of this book to provide an exhaustive account of each world religion. That is a task for another volume. Second, I assume that people in the West are more familiar with the origins and beliefs of Judaism and Islam, at least at a passing level. This is not the case with the Eastern traditions, with which Westerners are still largely unfamiliar. Moreover, the origins of Buddhism are directly connected to the metaphysical cosmology of the tradition. As we shall see, the basic Buddhist metaphysic is encapsulated in the Buddha's initial enlightenment and his first sermon.

Early origins

Buddhism began in the 500s BCE with the life of Siddhārtha Gautama. He was born in the foothills of the Himalayas in Nepal, India to an affluent family and was afforded a life of luxury and comfort throughout his childhood and early adulthood, living a sheltered life within the walls of his father's palaces (Keown, 13).[2] Buddhist tradition recounts how on four occasions Gautama was permitted to leave the confines of his palace life in order to visit the surrounding villages. While his father went to great lengths to protect his son from seeing the suffering of the common people, going as far as removing "all aged and infirm people" from the route (Keown, 22), Gautama wound up encountering a different form of suffering on each occasion—old age, illness, death, and stringent religious observance. These experiences were taken by Gautama to be "four signs" that eventually motivated him to leave his life of comfort and to pursue spiritual knowledge. Thus, at the age of twenty-nine, he left his wife and child and began his religious quest.

In his search, Gautama began by exploring various forms of meditation under the tutelage of several yoga masters. This was followed by a period of extreme asceticism, where Gautama deprived himself of basic necessities such as food and even breath, experimenting with breathing exercises that allowed him to hold his breath for longer and longer periods of time, and limiting his food intake to "minuscule" portions, such as "a spoonful of bean soup a day" (Keown, 13). These practices, however, brought him to the conclusion that extremes do not lead to spiritual enlightenment. Neither total self-indulgence, which he experienced in

---

2. I will be following very closely the historical accounts in Keown's *Buddhism: A Very Short Introduction* and Harvey's *An Introduction to Buddhism*. Going forward, I will cite both authors parenthetically.

his youth, nor extreme self-mortification, lead to spiritual fulfillment. Instead, the answer must be the "middle way" between these extremes. It was immediately following this realization that Gautama then spent a night in meditation under a Bodhi tree—a fig tree that came to be known as the "Awakening tree" (Harvey, 22)—where he is said to have achieved the state of enlightenment that he had been searching for.

After several weeks of meditation under the Bodhi tree, Gautama decided to return to his earlier yoga masters to share with them what he had experienced. He was greeted by five former companions, all of whom immediately noticed a change in him and began to greet him as an equal. Gautama, however, insisted that he was now a *Tathāgata*, "one-attuned-to-reality" (Harvey, 23) or "one who has attained what is really so" (Keown, 25). It is at this point that Gautama as the Buddha gave his first sermon (*dharma*).[3] In this sermon, the Buddha lays out the basic belief structure that would govern most Buddhist belief and practice from that point forward. In fact, the Buddha is often referred to as "one who has become *dharma*," the idea being either that the teachings are embodied in the Buddha or that the Buddha is embodied in the teachings (Harvey, 167). Either way, *dharma* and Buddha are inseparable.

The *dharma* of the Buddha focuses on the Four Noble Truths: (1) the truth of suffering (*dukkha*); (2) the truth of origin of suffering (*samudaya*); (3) the truth of the cessation of suffering (*nirodha*); and (4) the truth of the path out of suffering (*magga*). As noted above, the Buddha recognized that the path to enlightenment is the middle way between suffering and pleasure. This path begins with the acknowledgment that suffering is a reality, that it originates in human desire (*taṇhā*, lit. "thirst") and attachment, and that it can only end with letting go of these desires and attachments. Acceptance of the first three truths leads to the fourth truth, that there are practices that will allow one to experience liberation or freedom from their own personal attachment. This is the Noble Eightfold Path, which includes right view, right resolve, right speech, right conduct, right livelihood, right effort, right mindfulness, and right meditation. The goal of this path is *nirvāṇa*, the release from the endless

---

3. It should be noted that the term *Buddha* is not a name, but a title. In this sense, it is similar to the term *Christ*, which is not a surname for Jesus, but a title designating messiah or king (*lit.* anointed one). The title Buddha, then, designates one who has reached spiritual enlightenment. In this sense, Gautama is neither the first nor the last Buddha. He is the first in the present world cycle, but there are others who have held this title in other world cycles and still others who will hold it in future ones.

cycle of *karma* and rebirth. At this point, however, it is necessary to consider the basic cosmology of Buddhist thought in order to understand this cycle.

Basic Buddhist cosmology

The basic cosmology of Buddhism can be summarized by *saṃsāra*, literally "wandering on" (Harvey, 32). This is the process of *karma* and rebirth that was revealed to the Buddha in his awakening, where he is said to have remembered more than a hundred thousand lifetimes (Harvey, 32). This notion of reincarnation, which is not unique to Buddhism, but rather already present in Indian thought, is connected to a very specific cosmology.

In Buddhist cosmology, time is cyclical, not linear as we think of it in the West. It is cyclical, not in the sense that events repeat themselves, but rather in the sense that major epochal cycles repeat themselves. While the universe (*bhājana*) for Buddhists is eternal with no definitive origin or terminus, it is comprised of various "world systems" that undergo cycles of creation, development, and decline. These world systems are created from the primordial winds of the eternal universe, which whip together the five basic elements of earth, water, fire, air, and space into something comparable to a galaxy or a smaller universe. One entire cycle of a world system is known as a "great eon" (*mahākalpa*) and can last for billions of years. These cycles are sometimes subdivided into four lesser eons—(1) the eon of evolution (*vivartakalpa*), (2) the eon of duration (*vivartasthāyikalpa*); (3) the eon of dissolution (*saṃvartakalpa*); and (4) the eon of nothing (*saṃvartasthāyikalpa*), which lasts until the primordial winds begin to tie the five elements into another world system.

This spatial (horizontal) cosmology is connected through moral choice (*karma*) with a metaphysical (vertical) cosmology that is often referred to as the "wheel of life" (*bhavacakra*), or the six planes of existence and rebirth. These include the planes of the gods, titans, humans, ghosts, animals, and hells. The plane of the gods was later subdivided into twenty-six levels or "mansions" (*vimānavatthu*), making for a total of thirty-one planes of existence, which are categorized into three broad realms: (1) the realm of sense-desire (*kāmāvacara*), (2) the realm of pure form (*rūpāvacara*), and (3) the realm of formlessness (*arūpāvacara*).

Movement between these planes depends on one's *karma*, the moral choices that one makes in the course of one's life, and the merit one acquires as a result of those choices. This applies to humans and non-humans alike. Since the cycle of *saṃsāra* spans all planes of existence, one cannot prioritize *human* moral choice exclusively. Instead, all living things—gods and ghosts, humans and animals—are responsible for their own moral choices. Evaluation of those choices is based on both motive and action. Motives such as greed, hatred, and delusion, for example, are considered to be selfish and thus not productive of good *karma*; while non-attachment, benevolence, and understanding are considered selfless, and thus productive of good *karma*. Good motives, alone, however, are not enough. They must be accompanied by right action, which brings us back to the Noble Eightfold Path. Only when one performs the right practices with the right motivation is one able to merit good *karma*, which will increase the possibility of good consequences both in this life and the next.

Free will, then, plays a central role in determining one's existence, both in one's current plane and in future states of rebirth. Indeed, one of the reasons that Buddhists reject the notion of a single God responsible for the entire universe is that this would make God responsible for all evil and would remove the moral responsibility of individual agency. So *karma* is not a system of punishments and rewards dealt out by a divine judge. Rather, for Buddhists, *karma* is a natural law of the universe that applies equally and indiscriminately to all living things. Again, this law applies to all levels. Those in hell, for example, have the chance to improve their status in another life. For Buddhists, there is no eternal hell that is the final place of damnation. Rather, there are multiple hells, each of which serves as a place of temporary torment from which one is eventually released back into the cycle of *saṃsāra*. The gods, too, are susceptible to this karmic law, and in fact, it can be more challenging for them to live the Eightfold Path. Being in a state of bliss and harmony, it is easy for gods to "become complacent and lose sight of the need to strive for *nirvāṇa*" (Keown, 37). Thus, the realm of humans is considered to be the "middle way," for it presents a constant reminder to maintain the balance between pleasure and suffering.

Only those in the realm of formlessness, the top five planes ("Pure Abodes"), are known as "non-returners." These are "beings on the point of gaining enlightenment who will not be reborn again as human beings" (Keown, 37). The top-most two levels are known as the plane of "nothingness" and "neither perception nor non-perception," and they are "almost indescribably sublime state[s] beyond all shape and form in which beings exist as pure mental energy" (Keown, 39). The ultimate goal of *saṃsāra* is *nirvāṇa*, the total liberation from the endless cycle of rebirth. This ultimate state, however, is something closer to *non-being*, the utter cessation of existence. Otherwise, for Buddhists, there is no being—divine or otherwise—that is above the cycle of suffering, the cycle of *karma* and rebirth.

Buddhist Metaphysics and Science

At this point, I want to look at the intersection of Buddhist metaphysics and Western science. It should be noted at the outset, when considering this connection, that Buddhism is quite open to scientific enquiry and, in some respects, may be more compatible with the natural sciences, than the Abrahamic traditions.[4] There are several specific points on which Buddhism seems particularly open. First, because of the autonomy it grants to the physical universe, Buddhism tends to be more open to "the laws of nature," as understood in the classical Newtonian sense. Recall that the major source of the epistemological crisis for the Abrahamic traditions regarding the issue of divine providence centers on the balance they seek to maintain between God's total sovereignty, on the one hand, and the autonomy of creation, on the other. However, since Buddhists do not posit the need for a divine being who has ultimate control over all things, this tension does not arise in the first place. Consequently, there is no intrinsic threat to their basic metaphysical beliefs in assuming that the physical universe is subject to natural laws. Indeed, such a notion complements the metaphysical belief in *karma* as a natural law.

Second, since Buddhism holds to the development of world systems over billions of years, there is no fundamental conflict between their metaphysical beliefs and contemporary scientific theories of evolution. Insofar as the universe, as we understand it today, is taken to be its own world system, the Buddhist theory of the universe coming into being over billions of years before coming to a final destruction, comports with some current cosmological theories of the origins of the universe (Big

---

4. The current Dalai Lama has been quoted as saying, "If science proved some belief of Buddhism wrong, then Buddhism will have to change." See Impey, "What Buddhism and Science Can Teach Each Other."

Bang), its evolution over vast periods of time, and its ultimate collapse (Big Crunch). Buddhist theories can even be seen to be compatible with certain notions of a multiverse, where this process of origin, development, and collapse may happen multiple times, either in succession or simultaneously.

What I hope to have shown in the preceding section, however, is that Buddhism, while not holding to any notion of a single creator-God or to notions of providence, nevertheless has a robust metaphysical understanding of the universe, both in a horizontal and a vertical sense. Horizontally, they hold a specific cosmology of the universe as eternal with innumerable cycles of world systems that each last billions of years. Despite the similarities, just noted, between Buddhist notions of a "world cycle" and current cosmological models, these two systems cannot be conflated. They may be compatible and, thus, bear some family resemblance, but they are not identical. For example, in what sense does the Buddhist terminology of "universe" and "world system" correspond to modern scientific terminology? Some scholars compare the notion of "world system" to contemporary notions of "galaxies," but this is clearly not what Buddhists have in mind. For Buddhists, a world system is closer to what we think of as a universe, and whatever metaphysical realm that houses this universe constitutes the larger "universe" of Buddhist thought. It is in this sense that Buddhism bears more resemblance to contemporary notions of a multiverse, than to the classical distinction between galaxies and the cosmos. Nevertheless, notice that there is a metaphysical assumption about the larger context of the universe that cannot be verified by direct, empirical study.

Furthermore, Buddhists clearly hold a robust vertical metaphysic too. Notions of *karma*, reincarnation, planes of existence are all metaphysical in nature and have no immediate confirmation in the physical sciences. More importantly, the ability to access these metaphysical realities and describe them requires something like transcendental meditation, as seen in the life of the Buddha. Although the Buddhist tradition may not use this term, the truths of the Buddhist cosmology and the Noble Eightfold Path were *revealed* to the Buddha, not in the sense that the Abrahamic traditions believe, where a personal God deliberately chose to reveal something, but rather in the sense that through meditation the Buddha was able to experience something of the larger metaphysical reality. The interconnection between the physical and the metaphysical in Buddhism, then, is inseparable. Indeed, Buddhists even believe that world systems are directly affected by *karma*, such that a world system that is full of corruption may not endure as long as one that is not (Keown, 33).

Perry Schmidt-Leukel argues that there are basically two approaches to notions of the divine: "either as that which guarantees salvation, that is, as the *ultimate goal of everything*, or as the divine creator, that is the *ultimate source of everything*."[5] Christians affirm both, while Buddhists affirm only the first. The motivation for this, as noted earlier, is principally over concerns of theodicy. Buddhists argue that if there were a God responsible for creating everything, that God would also be responsible for the evil in the world and would remove the moral responsibility of created beings, which is central for their karmic system. Instead, Buddhism avoids these pitfalls by positing an ultimate reality that is unconditioned, meaning beyond causation. It is outside of time and thus can neither be caused by anything nor be the cause of anything. Nevertheless, "this unconditioned reality is . . . not entirely bereft of causal effectiveness."[6] Schmidt-Leukel contends that this causal interaction occurs in at least two senses:

> First, *nirvāṇa* can be the object of consciousness and hence a kind of causal condition for cognition. Second, as an object of cognition, it "causes an obstacle to the vices"—"as the stars are not visible when the sun shines." That is to say, the realization of *nirvāṇa* puts a lasting end to all the defilements, and is thus the cause of their final cessation.[7]

Schmidt-Leukel notes that this tension was present, to some extent, even for classical Buddhist thinkers. In one sense, they wanted to deny any causal efficacy on the part of the ultimate so as to preserve its status as timeless, changeless, and unconditioned; at the same time, however, they wanted to affirm transcendental reality as a basis for salvation and karmic causality. The result of this tension, then, is that eternity has now taken on a dual meaning of "firstly, the *eternal, immutable stillness* of the unconditioned, and secondly, the *eternal activity* of the Buddha in relation to the conditioned world."[8]

---

5. Schmidt-Leukel, "Bridging the Gulf," 143. His emphasis.
6. Schmidt-Leukel, "Bridging the Gulf," 155.
7. Schmidt-Leukel, "Bridging the Gulf," 156.
8. Schmidt-Leukel, "Bridging the Gulf," 160.

While Schmidt-Leukel focuses principally on the ways in which *nirvāṇa* impinges on reality and exhibits causal constraint, I would argue that there are actually several points at which Buddhist cosmology intersects with the physical universe in such a way as to raise empirical questions as to *how* this connection is possible. How, for example, is *karma* interconnected with the physical laws of the universe? Even if one could empirically verify that *karma* exists, how would one then go about establishing how this metaphysical notion is interwoven into the nature of the world? A similar set of questions can be raised for the planes of existence, the notion of human souls, and the movement of these souls between these various planes. Each of these are metaphysical notions that require an explanatory theory for what Austin Farrer calls the "causal joint," the point at which the divine or, in the case of Buddhism, the metaphysical, intersects with and influences the natural processes of the universe.[9]

To be clear, I am not challenging Buddhist belief. I am merely noting the ways in which empirical science has shifted the onus of responsibility to those making metaphysical claims, regardless of their tradition. In fact, science itself is not above this same critical examination. It was this same scrutiny that led Albert Einstein to raise questions about Newtonian notions of force. While concepts such as "gravity" and "force" were efficacious in explaining natural events and were calculable in mathematical terms, they left unanswered the larger metaphysical question of what force *is*. This led to Einstein's theory that space, itself, is bent by objects of large enough mass, making it possible for smaller objects to fall within the indented space, thus removing metaphysical notions of force. Prior to this point, however, the notion of force was no less metaphysical than *karma*, and required a similar explanatory theory.

It is precisely the problem of the causal joint that presents a potential epistemological crisis for Buddhism as much as for any other religious tradition. Any tradition that cannot explain its metaphysics in light of modern physical theories of the universe is in jeopardy of the epistemological crisis I have been considering. If modern science precludes the possibility of metaphysical revelation, of any variety, then it is also calls into question divinely revealed beliefs predicated on that revelation. It is at this point, I contend, that the Buddhist and Christian traditions have something to learn from each other.

---

9. Farrer, *Faith and Speculation*, 62.

Buddhism, Christianity, and Science

In this section, I want to consider some resources that the Christian tradition has developed that may prove beneficial to Buddhism in confronting a potential crisis. Since the Buddhist tradition has not yet encountered this crisis, it may benefit from the hard-won insights of the Christian tradition. I will begin by looking at process theology, which several theologians, John Cobb most notably, have proposed as a possible common ground between Buddhism, Christianity, and science. I will then consider the possibilities that have been created as a result of the work of the Divine Action Project with Robert J. Russell and the Center for Theology and the Natural Sciences.

Process theology

In *Beyond Dialogue*, John Cobb argues that process theology offers a common metaphysical ground for Buddhism and Christianity.[10] Some explanation of process thought is in order here. Process theology developed out of the philosophy of Alfred North Whitehead. Whitehead argues that the substance metaphysic that began with Descartes is no longer congruent with the post-Newtonian worldview.[11] Instead of conceiving the world as comprised of discrete bits of inert matter, Whitehead argues for a dynamic conception of reality in which the "final real things" of existence are "actual entities" or, more precisely, "occasions of experience." These are not enduring substances, but rather the process, itself, of coming into being and ceasing to be, a "cell-theory of actuality" (Whitehead, 219). Actual occasions result from *concrescence*, the process by which the multiplicity of all things converges and unites in the present to create one unified, novel moment, or occasion. Prior to concrescence, an entity may be real ("merely real"), but not yet actualized (Whitehead, 214). Whitehead contends that subjective experience characterizes all actual entities, which relate to one another by means of *prehension*, or feeling. This involves three stages: responsiveness, supplementation, and satisfaction, which, together, allow actual entities to synthesize aesthetic information, culminating in the moment of satisfaction, at which point all indeterministic options vanish, as does the actual occasion itself, thus

---

10. Cobb, *Beyond Dialogue*, 145.

11. Whitehead, *Process and Reality*, 18. Going forward, I will cite Whitehead parenthetically.

becoming the new starting point for a further process of concrescence. For Whitehead, everything from God to the "most trivial puff of existence" is an actual entity; there is nothing else (Whitehead, 18).

Philosopher Charles Hartshorne and theologians Schubert Ogden, John Cobb, and David Ray Griffin, among others, have sought, respectively, to construct a theology of process that avoids what they understand to be the failings of classical or neo-Thomistic theology. In *Philosophers Speak of God*, Hartshorne and William Reese argue that classical theology has limited conceptions of God and God's action by focusing on only one pole of divine attributes. That is, while more primitive theologies draw from an array of "ultimate contraries" such as "one and many, permanence and change, being and becoming,"[12] more sophisticated theologies, such as classical theism in the West and pantheism in the East, seek to resolve this problem by choosing from one side, or pole, of these contraries over the other. Classical theism ascribes to God oneness, permanence, being, necessity, self-sufficiency, and actuality, while pantheism ascribes the alternate pole—many, change, becoming, contingency, dependent (relative), potential.

Process theology resists this dichotomy, contending that "ultimate contraries are *correlatives*" so that God, or the ultimate, cannot be understood in light of only one pole over the other;[13] instead, God is *dipolar*. In *The Reality of God*, Ogden contends that the dipolar view allows God to be understood as (1) wholly relational—related to the life of the world in such a way that all aspects of the world, including ourselves and our actions, genuinely affect God's actual being; *and*, (2) relative to nothing—related to the world in such a way that nothing can make any difference to God's *existence*. Many process theologians argue that this dipolar view of God lends itself to a *panentheistic* model of the God-world relationship, wherein God is part of, but still more than, all that exists.

It is precisely at this point that process thought seems amenable to both Christian and Buddhist metaphysics. In seeking to preserve both poles of the divine—the relational and non-relational dimensions—process thought allows for both Christian and Buddhist notions to coexist as corollaries of the same experience of the ultimate. Furthermore, since process thought views God as one more actual entity among others, and thus unable to will the world to be one way or another, process presents

---

12. Hartshorne and Reese, *Philosophers Speak of God*, 1–2. Hartshorne, along with Whitehead, is credited for the formulation of process philosophy.

13. Hartshorne and Reese, *Philosophers Speak of God*, 2. My emphasis.

a notion of God that is not radically different from the impersonal ultimate of Buddhism. As Cobb argues, one should never ask "why God caused *that* world to be," but rather "why, given that world, God seeks to persuade it in the way he does."[14] In this way, God can be viewed in the Buddhist sense as a being that is not above the cycle of *saṃsāra*, but rather as one more entity among others.

Unfortunately, the greatest strength of Whitehead's proposal is also its greatest liability. His metaphysic is an ambitious attempt to correct the reductive, mechanistic metaphysic of the modern worldview that has contributed to the present crisis. Nevertheless, it is still a metaphysic and, thus, raises similar questions to the ones posed above regarding *karma*, force, and gravity. It is unclear what it would mean to *confirm* or *apply* Whitehead's metaphysic. The genius of Kepler, Galileo, Boyle, Newton, and Einstein lies in the fact that they were able to assign concrete mathematical meanings to terms such as "mass," "force," "resistance," "velocity," "acceleration," and "relativity," which had no precise significance prior to their physical theories.[15] These terms could then be applied with methodological precision in calculating natural phenomena. It is not clear how Whitehead's metaphysical language of actual entities, concrescence, or prehension would lend itself to a similar methodological application, or how it would be confirmed empirically. Thus, it only pushes the problem back to another stage—metaphysics upon metaphysics!

Furthermore, from a Christian perspective, Whitehead's metaphysic does as much to constrain God's action as the modern scientific worldview, perhaps more so. In Whitehead's system, God is not above the created order, responsible for its creation and preservation, but rather bound to it as one more actual entity among others. The classical notion of *creatio ex nihilo* would have to be rejected, along with notions of preservation, governance, special providence, and certainly any notion of God's extraordinary acts (miracles). Much of traditional theology would have to be abandoned or radically reformulated, which would only serve to entrench the very epistemological crisis that the Christian tradition is trying to resolve.

---

14. Cobb, *God and the World*, 92. My emphasis.
15. Burtt, *The Metaphysical Foundations of Science*, 92.

Divine Action Project

Perhaps the most thoroughgoing attempt on the part of the Christian tradition in the recent past to locate an adequate theory of divine action is the Divine Action Project (DAP),[16] a consortium of scientists, philosophers, and theologians concerned, principally, with finding areas of ontological openness and possibilities for divine action. Three major areas of consideration were proposed by this consortium: top-down causation, chaos theory, and quantum mechanics. In chapter 5, I discussed one particular approach that the DAP took to resolving this issue: Russell's non-interventionist, objective, divine action (NIODA), looking specifically at the possibilities that quantum physics provides for this approach. This was the most promising proposal for those in the Christian tradition seeking to preserve classical notions of God's sovereignty and special divine providence.

However, quantum physics and NIODA were far from the only options considered by the DAP. Indeed, the success of the project lay in the fact that the members of this consortium were able to secure a range of possibilities for special divine action in a modern scientific context. In fact, the primary goal of the DAP was to find points of intrinsic openness in the physical universe that would allow for a variety of approaches to divine action and metaphysics. Along these lines, perhaps the greatest contribution of the DAP was the fact that the classical Newtonian model, with its underlying metaphysical assumptions, is waning. The picture of the closed cosmological model discussed in chapter 5 is giving way not only because of advances in specific areas of science such as quantum theory, chaos theory, and relativity, but because the classical commitments to atomism, reductionism, and determinism that gave rise to this picture in the first place are being called into question.

On this count, there have been three recent developments that are of particular note: emergence, top-down causation, and decoupling.[17] Emergence (or emergent order) is the discovery that higher levels of complex systems exhibit new causal powers, which are irreducible to "the combined effects of lower-level causal powers."[18] As such, many complex

---

16. This appellation was first used by Wildman in "The Divine Action Project, 1988–2003."

17. Murphy, *Anglo-American Postmodernity*, 20.

18. Murphy, "Reductionism," 27. See also: Stephan, "Emergence—A Systematic View on Its Historical Facets," 25–48.

systems *cannot* be explained by reducing them to their constituent parts, but are explainable *only* at the higher-levels. The concept of emergence has been available—in one form or another—since the nineteenth century, when J. S. Mill was groping for language to describe "'effects' that were resultant of intersecting laws" and George Lewes supplied the term "emergent."[19] In the recent past, Terrence Deacon has been helpful in clarifying this term, maintaining that "we do not need a 'new physics' to deal with emergent phenomena, nor to appeal to strange features of quantum physics, nor abandon standard notions of physical reduction. *What we need is to trace ways that nature can tangle causal chains into complex knots.*"[20] The emphasis, then, is on the manifestation of new complex forms of *causation*. When certain types of systems reach a certain level of complexity their higher-order configurations begin to display novel causal powers that were not there at the lower-levels and cannot be reduced to those levels.

Similarly, top-down causation refers to those instances where higher-level causal powers strictly govern the micro-level and not vice versa. This is also known as whole-part constraint, where larger environmental factors exhibit causal influence on the components, the way an ecosystem, for example, effects the organisms living in it. A simple illustration of top-down causation is the behavior of a paper airplane. The lower-level properties of the plane—cellulose and other basic particles—do little but offer mass and rigidity.[21] The relevant governing factors are all *top-down*—(1) the shape of the plane, a holistic property, and (2) the environmental factors such as the person that throws it and the air current surrounding it. Once again, reductionism does not account for the behavior of the plane. What is required is more holistic analysis. The same is true for the third discovery, *decoupling*, which refers to instances where there is strict autonomy between lower- and higher-level systems.[22] Again, in such cases systems can only be explained in terms of their own respective levels and *not* by reducing one level to another. Taken together, these three discoveries considerably challenge strict reductionism and with it, the philosophical theories of atomism and causal

---

19. Murphy, *Anglo-American Postmodernity*, 25.
20. Deacon, "Three Levels of Emergent Phenomena," 94. His emphasis.
21. Murphy, *Bodies and Souls, or Spirited Bodies?* 77.
22. Murphy, *Anglo-American Postmodernity*, 20.

determinism. They suggest that the universe is not causally-closed, but rather exhibits a significant degree of openness.

It is discoveries such as these that have led to an array of possibilities for divine action and metaphysics that were previously unavailable in the modern scientific worldview. To name a few, Arthur Peacocke has posited that God's influence in the world works through whole-part constraint, whereby God serves as the larger environment of the universe as a whole;[23] John Polkinghorne has proposed that chaos theory can serve as a potential area for divine providence, where small changes in the initial conditions of dynamic systems are capable of producing cumulative and unpredictable changes later in the system;[24] and, as discussed in chapter 5, Nancey Murphy maintains that God is able to work through the intrinsic irregularity at the quantum level. What this suggests is an array of possibilities for talking about the influence of the divine in the natural world. Moreover, these same resources are also available for the Buddhist tradition and may provide a similar array of possibilities in accounting for their metaphysical beliefs and practices.

Conclusion

In many ways the argument of this chapter has been a simple one: to show that Buddhism, despite its differences with the Christian tradition, nevertheless, potentially shares the same problem, namely how to the align its metaphysical beliefs with modern science and, more importantly, how to *justify* its metaphysical claims in light of that scientific worldview. Recall that the crux of the epistemological crisis under consideration in this book pertains not only to the question of divine action in light of modern science, but the fact that if divine action is precluded, then so too is special revelation and, with it, reliable religious knowledge. In this chapter, I have tried to show that Buddhism is also susceptible to this challenge.

As I have argued, while Buddhism holds no beliefs in particular divine providence, it nevertheless holds a robust metaphysic, one that is taken to be intertwined in the universe in such a way that it has bearings on the lives of individuals, both in the this plane of existence and in others. This sort of metaphysic is as open to scientific scrutiny as Christian claims of special divine providence and, more importantly, would equally

23. Peacocke, "God's Interaction with the World."
24. Polkinghorne, *Science and Creation*.

undermine the reliability of Buddhist belief and practice if they were called into question by modern science, creating an epistemological crisis not unlike the one experienced by the Christian tradition during the modern period. Nevertheless, insofar as both traditions are confronted with the same problem, I contend that they can benefit from the same solution—or *solutions*. In this chapter, I hope to have presented some of the resources that the Christian tradition has developed for resolving its crisis, possibilities that may benefit Buddhist views of metaphysics as well. In doing so, I hope I have also modeled one way in which Christianity and Buddhism can engage in mutual constructive engagement.

In the next chapter, I will consider one final tradition—Hinduism—and attempt to make a similar argument.

Chapter 9:

Hinduism, Metaphysics, and Science

Whosoever feels the love of God and man shed abroad in his heart, feels an ardent and uninterrupted thirst after the happiness of all his fellow-creatures. His soul melts away with the very fervent desire which he hath continually to promote it; and out of the abundance of the heart his mouth speaketh. In his tongue is the law of kindness. The same is impressed on all his actions. The flame within is continually working itself away, and spreading abroad more and more, in every instance of good-will to all with whom he hath to do. So that whether he thinks or speaks, or whatever he does, it all points to the same end, the advancing, by every possible way, the happiness of all his fellow-creatures. Deceive not, therefore, your own souls: He who is not thus kind, hath not love.[1]

—JOHN WESLEY

Introduction

OF ALL THE TRADITIONS considered so far, Hinduism may be the most challenging in the sense that it resists the simple identification of a single tradition. By all accounts, Hinduism is not a unified tradition in the sense

---

1. Wesley, "Sermon 139," 492, sec. 2, par. 7.

that we have come to consider the other major world religions, but rather a collection of traditions that were loosely grouped together by European colonialists under the title "Hinduism." As Kim Knott states:

> The term "Hinduism" implies a unified religious system, and indeed many Hindus and non-Hindus describe it in this way. Others, however, say there are many Hindu traditions, even many "hinduisms:" they are related to one another, but remain different in important ways.[2]

While, in a certain sense, this is true of each of the religious traditions considered so far, each having its own distinct sects and denominations, Hinduism seems unique in that its contemporary unity was superimposed on it by the Western colonizers. As Sue Hamilton notes: "Hinduism is a label that was attached in the 19th century to a highly complex and multiple collection of systems of thought by . . . Westerners who did not appreciate that complexity."[3] Thus, while I will continue to use the term "Hinduism" in the conventional sense, I recognize that in doing so I may be flattening important distinctions. Nevertheless, I will endeavor to focus on those aspects of Hinduism that are generally reflective of the tradition as a whole.

In another sense, however, Hinduism presents less of a challenge than Buddhism when it comes to identifying a potential crisis concerning the issue divine action. Whereas Buddhism denies the existence of a creator-God that both transcends the physical universe and is immanent in it, responsible for its creation and preservation, Hinduism does not. Belief in a single God as well as a plurality of divine manifestations of that God is a central part of the Hindu tradition. Consequently, the epistemological crisis concerning the issue of divine action in light of modern science is a much more obvious possibility for Hindus.

In this chapter, then, I want to address several major concerns. In the first section, I will discuss the extent to which Hinduism is a religious tradition in the MacIntyrean sense of the term, considering its status both as a religion and as a tradition. In the second and third sections, I will consider some of the central metaphysical beliefs of the Hindu tradition and show how they are dependent on divine revelation. In so doing, I will argue that the Hindu tradition, no less than any of the other traditions considered so far, is subject to the epistemological crisis under

---

2. Knott, *Hinduism*, 1. See also: Killingley, "Hinduism," 13.
3. Hamilton, *Indian Philosophy*, 8.

consideration. That is, if the possibility of divine revelation is precluded by modern science, then so are the epistemological beliefs and practices derived from such revelation. In the final section, I will consider some of the strengths of the Hindu tradition in addressing this potential crisis and the possibilities that exist for mutual constructive engagement between Christianity and Hinduism.

Hinduism as a Religious Tradition

The first question to consider is the extent to which Hinduism is a *religious tradition*. To be clear, its status both as a *religion* and as a *tradition* are under consideration here. Many scholars have debated the extent to which Hinduism constitutes a "religion" in the Western sense of the term. Some have argued that Hinduism grew more out of "this-worldly concerns" such as the acquisition of love, wealth, and power than out of concern for the divine or the transcendent.[4] The early brahmins, for example, practiced certain sacrificial rites not only for worship and devotion, but also for the purposes of maintaining cosmic order and bringing about desired ends, both in terms of natural events, such as rain, sun, and crops, and in terms of abstract affairs such as contracts and agreements (Hamilton, 19). Also, some of the early texts of the *Vedas*, such as the *Brāhmaṇas*, were not religious, *per se*, but rather served as ritual manuals to instruct brahmins in how to perform their rites properly to bring about these desired ends. This is not to take away from the undoubtedly religious elements of the tradition that were present from the beginning, only to highlight aspects that colonizing Westerners overlooked or purposefully ignored in their initial encounter with Hinduism.

Others have argued that the term "religion" is a Western concept that was superimposed on non-Western traditions, such as Hinduism, in a way that does not accurately reflect their own self-identity. The early Christian missionaries to India in the eighteenth and nineteenth centuries, for example, tended to view Hinduism through the lens of their own preconceived notions about religion, focusing on those aspects that comported with their own experience of Christianity and disregarding or altogether rejecting other aspects. Likewise, they tended to focus on those passages of Hindu texts that appeared more "religious," such as the

---

4. See Hamilton, *Indian Philosophy*, 19–20 and Knott, *Hinduism*, 8–9. Going forward, I will cite both authors parenthetically.

Ṛg Veda and the *Bhagavad gītā*. Indeed, these early Christian missionaries believed that Hinduism would be a "better religion" if they removed the worldly components and emphasized the "theistic, philosophical, and spiritual elements" (Knott, 8). The fundamental concern, then, is that this Western portrayal of Hinduism has led to a somewhat skewed interpretation of the tradition as a religion when it may not always see itself exclusively through that lens.

The question about the status of Hinduism as a religion is compounded further by the question of whether or not it is *a tradition*. Most scholars agree that Hinduism originated as a loose collection of smaller traditions, rather than as a single, unified one. While professing Hindus hold the core beliefs of their tradition to be timeless, having existed eternally before the creation of the world, the term "Hindu" originated as a Persian term in the 500s BCE to designate the people of a certain geographical region. It referred to all the inhabitants living in and around the Indus Valley and, thus, was a geographical term, not a religious designation, much less an attempt to describe a monolithic set of beliefs and practices. It was not until the nineteenth century that the word *Hinduism* was coined by European colonizers, particularly missionaries, as a way of referring to the religions of India, and then only as a means of distinguishing them from Christianity. In so doing, Westerners lumped together a range of ritualistic practices that were not necessarily viewed as one cohesive tradition previously.

Today, there is wide disagreement among both scholars and practitioners as to what constitutes *the* Hindu tradition. Several potential defining characteristics have been proposed, such as the caste system, the authority of the *Vedas*, the concept of *dharma*, and so on; however, many have also challenged the hegemony of any one of these traits (Knott, 105). The most that can be said is that these pluriform traditions bear a family resemblance. As I noted at the outset, some argue that it is better to talk in terms of Hindu *traditions*, rather than a single tradition, while others, even professing Hindus, disagree with this assessment.

In this brief chapter, I could not hope to resolve these longstanding debates. However, in some sense, the question of whether or not Hinduism is a single religious tradition is inconsequential for our present purposes. First, in terms of Hinduism's standing as a religion, what is under consideration presently is the extent to which any metaphysical tradition—religious or otherwise—can account for its metaphysical beliefs and practices in light of modern science. Each of the major sub-traditions within Hinduism holds robust metaphysical beliefs regarding God, reincarnation, *karma*, and so on. More importantly, as I will discuss in more detail below, all Hindus maintain that their sacred texts, principally the *Vedas*, are of divine origin. Thus, the rationality of each sub-tradition, despite any other substantive differences that may or may not exist, still hinges on their ability to account for divine revelation in order to make sense of its overall rationality—its beliefs and practices in all their variegated forms. Whether or not those beliefs and practices can be categorized as "religious" is secondary.

The question of whether or not Hinduism is a single tradition or a cluster of loosely connected traditions, is also somewhat unimportant for our purposes insofar as the issue under consideration, namely the ability of any metaphysical tradition to account for its epistemological claims in light of modern science, applies to each sub-tradition. While there may or may not be a single, unifying characteristic that binds each of these sub-traditions together, each holds basic metaphysical beliefs that are susceptible to the epistemological crisis we have been considering throughout the book. Furthermore, the plurality of Hindu sub-traditions takes nothing away from the application of MacIntyre's definition of a tradition. In fact, it supports it. Recall that a central component of MacIntyre's definition of a tradition is *debate*. Insofar as communities remain in debate over the interpretation and application of common standards of rationality and common authoritative texts and voices, they constitute the same ongoing tradition of enquiry. The same is true for sub-traditions, communities that tend to share some of the same formative texts and voices as the overall tradition (or other sub-traditions), but remain in debate with those other sub-traditions over the application and interpretation of the primary sources.

I suggest that something similar may be happening with the Hindu tradition. For the purposes of this chapter, however, all that needs to be shown is that Hinduism, in general, as well as in all its diversity, is irreducibly metaphysical and that its metaphysical beliefs and practices are dependent upon divinely revealed sources. In what follows, then, I will consider, first, the central metaphysical beliefs and practices of most Hindus; second, I will show how those beliefs and practices are connected to the divinely revealed status of their authoritative texts and voices and how those sources also serve to support their various forms of rationality.

Hindu Metaphysics

Hindu metaphysics and cosmology bear a strong family resemblance to those of Buddhism. Buddhism and Hinduism, as we know them today, have their historical origins in the Brahmanism of ancient India.[5] The fifteenth to the fifth century BCE (1500–500) is known as the Vedic period, and played a significant role in shaping Brahmanism. During this time, the Vedas (*lit.* "knowledge"), were preserved by a class of priests known as the brahmins, who were the custodians of the Vedic knowledge and ritual-based sacrificial system, which was passed down orally and collected over a period of nearly a thousand years. Thus, many of the same cosmological and metaphysical assumptions prevalent in Brahmanism carried over into the Buddhist and Hindu traditions.

Hindus, like Buddhists, hold a cosmological view of the world where the universe is eternal, having no definite beginning or end. Similarly, the Hindu tradition also holds that there is an infinite number of smaller universes within the larger, eternal universe that undergo cycles of creation and destruction many times in an infinite span of time. The duration of each individual cosmos is known as a "great eon," or a *mahā-yuga*, that lasts 4.32 billion years, or one *kalpa*, the day of Brahmā. Every *mahā-yuga* is sub-divided into four *yugas*, or lesser eons. *Mahā-yuga's* inherently devolve over time, such that each *yuga* is worse than the one before it. The first eon, *Satya yuga*, is a period of socio-religious order (*dharma*), where human desires are kept in check and the order of *brahman* is preserved. This is often referred to as the golden age and is the longest of the four *yugas*. This moral order, however, declines through the course of the ensuing *yugas* (the *Treta* and *Dvapara yugas*) until the final age, the *Kali yuga*, which is characterized by an erosion of morality, governed by greed, deceit, and licentiousness. The *Kali yuga* is the shortest of the four epochs and is the period that many Hindus believe we are currently inhabiting.

Once the four cycles (*mahā-yuga*) have run their course, the cosmos is absorbed back into its primordial (*prakritik*) source, where individual souls remain in a state of "suspended animation" until the cycle begins again and a new *satya* age emanates from Brahmā, the creator-God of Hindu belief. However, following a span of one hundred Brahmā-*years*,

---

5. Killingley, "Hinduism," 14. It should be emphasized that practicing Hindus generally do not talk in terms of their historical origins, but rather maintain that Hinduism is timeless, having no definitive beginning or end.

even Brahmā, who presides over all of these *yuga*-cycles, is absorbed back into the absolute, where "there is creational quiescence for an equally long period. Then the productive cycle begins again. And the process continues indefinitely."[6]

Furthermore, for the Hindu tradition as much as for the Buddhist, this cosmology is intersected with an ethical metaphysic that applies to individual creatures and their moral place in the universe. The individual is a part of the cycle of *saṃsāra*, the endless cycle of death and rebirth, commonly known as reincarnation. The ultimate goal of this process is *mokṣa*—liberation from the cycle of rebirth. One's moral standing within that cycle is determined by several interrelated concepts—*dharma, karma*, and rational choice (free will). First, as already indicated, *dharma* is the moral order of the universe, and it applies at both the universal and the individual level. At the universal level, *dharma* is the cosmic law underlying all moral and social order in the universe. As I noted above, it is the inherent structure of the first *yuga*, providing order to all things. However, *dharma* is also the moral obligation of every individual. At this level, the term implies law, duty, obligation, and virtue. It pertains to "the right way of living" or the social and religious moral code of conduct. The cosmic and individual levels are connected in that living in accordance with *dharma* enables one to live in compliance with the moral order of the universe.

Karma, in the original Sanskrit, simply means action, and it pertains to the moral actions one takes in order to live in accordance with *dharma*. However, *karma* also has both cosmic and personal applications. On the one hand, *karma* is merely the moment-to-moment actions that individuals take and the natural consequences that follow from those actions. On the other hand, *karma* also pertains to the totality of one's choices over the course of their entire cycle of *saṃsāra*, and the consequences of those choices for subsequent lifetimes in that cycle. In this sense, *karma* carries the connotation of the law of merit. It is a form of cosmic justice, connected to *dharma*, that determines the consequences for an individual in the present life and the next. As discussed in the previous chapter, *karma* is not a system of punishment and reward meted out by a supreme deity. Instead, it is connected to *dharma*, the intrinsic law of the eternal universe that applies impartially to all living beings and is predicated strictly on the moral choices of those beings.

---

6. Lipner, *Hindus*, 207–8.

Dharma and *karma*, then, are connected. One's *karma* is determined in part by how well one has lived in accordance with *dharma*; while, by the same token, *dharma* is also affected by the collective *karma* of each eon (*yuga*). Recall that *dharma* tends to decline over the course of the four *yugas*. Julius Lipner contends that even though this seems to be an intrinsic aspect of the universe, this does not have to be the case. Rather it is predicated on the assumption that individuals have "baser instincts," which have a tendency to "go wrong," resulting in the degeneration of the cosmos over time. However, it does not have to be this way. It is the state of the collective *karma* of each eon that contributes to this degeneration. This is where *rational choice* is important. Individuals have the capacity to exercise their reason and free will to live in accordance with *dharma* or not. This capacity for rational choice is further dependent on another key metaphysical belief in Hinduism, that of *ātman*, the "divine ground within persons—their true Self or Soul."[7] The *ātman* is the "empowering agent" that allows for consciousness, perception, speech, thought, and so on.[8] Thus, there is real contingency—the possibility of either decline or progress within the universe. In this way, *dharma*, *karma*, and *ātman* are all interconnected and, together, play a vital role in shaping the course of individual and communal affairs, including the course of the entire cosmos.

Finally, a word should be said about Hindu belief in God. Hindus have a robust understanding of the divine, though it has been widely misunderstood in the West. To begin with, very few Hindus are polytheistic. Most believe in one God, though it is believed that God is revealed in pluriform ways. Hinduism embraces both the One and the many, viewing all things to be connected and interrelated. Hindus tend to believe that the many are a manifestation of the One. Broadly speaking, it is believed that the divine is manifested in five general ways: (1) in the ultimate transcendent form, (2) in its pluriform emanations or *avatars* (*avatāra*), (3) in the heart of each individual, (4) as the one in charge of operations of the universe, and (5) as the divine presence in the various icons (*murtis*) (Knott, 50). God, then, is taken to be both transcendent and immanent, supreme and accessible.

---

7. Baird and Heimbeck, "Vedic Origins," 5.

8. Baird and Heimbeck, "Vedic Origins," 5. It should be noted that certain Hindu texts, such as the *Mundaka Upaniṣad* (Part III.1) indicate that the individual has two souls, one being the individual ego, the other the *ātman*, or the true self.

Here a distinction needs to be made between *brahman* and Brahmā. These are two distinct realities in Hindu thought with similar characteristics, at least for Westerners accustomed to these distinctive qualities being attributed to one divine being. For Hindus, *brahman* is the impersonal creative power initially found in the Vedic hymns, which came to be identified with "the impersonal cosmic principle or absolute reality" (Knott, 16). It is neither created nor destroyed, having existed eternally before all things. It is all-pervasive, imbuing all things with life. Indeed, some contend that each individual soul (*ātman*) is a fragment of the One ultimate *brahman*. It is also sometimes equated with absolute truth. Brahmā, by contrast, is the proper name of the personal creator-God, who is responsible for creating all living things and their destinies. He is said to live in the separate world of *Satyaloka* with his wife or consort Saraswati and their son Narada.

Some view Brahmā as a part of a triumvirate of gods who are responsible for the creation, preservation, and ultimate destruction of the world. Brahmā, as we have seen, is the one responsible for creation, while Vishnu is understood to be the one responsible for the world's preservation and Shiva its destruction. Others recognize the canonical gods of Vishnu, Shiva, Ganesha, Surya, and Devi. The pantheon of gods and goddesses in Hinduism is numerous (some speculate thirty-three million in all); but for most Hindus these gods are the manifestation of the One ultimate God, and the choice of which god(s) or goddess(es) an individual or community worships depends greatly on family tradition and personal experience. This is known as the *ishtadeva,* or chosen deity, the god venerated by the particular community in question.

Divine Revelation of Hindu Belief and Practice

Hopefully, the foregoing is enough to show that the Hindu tradition is irreducibly metaphysical. That is, while there may be great variance among the various sub-traditions in terms of which gods (*ishtadeva*) are venerated or which philosophical and theological perspectives are emphasized, there is little deviation from the fundamental metaphysical outlook. Indeed, to remove Hindu metaphysics would be to make Hinduism something other than what it is. Moreover, these metaphysical beliefs and practices are dependent on divine revelation such that if special divine revelation were challenged by modern science, the tradition's epistemic knowledge would also be called into question, resulting in the very epistemic crisis we have been considering. At this point, then, I want to show that the beliefs and practices of the Hindu tradition are predicated on this sort of divine revelation. Specifically, I want to consider the divinely revealed status of the Hindu authoritative texts and voices and, in turn, how the various forms of rationality for the tradition are dependent on those divinely revealed sources.

Authoritative texts

There are a number of texts taken to be central for Hindu belief and practice: (1) the *Vedas*, (2) the *Upaniṣads*, (3) the *Rāmāyaṇa*, (4) the *Mahābhārata*, which contains the *Bhagavad gītā*, (4) the *Puranas* (myths), (5) the Epics, and (6) the *sutras*, to name but a few. The first two texts are considered to be *shruti*, or divinely revealed, while the others are taken to be *smriti*, or "handed down" (Knott, 12–3). The *smriti* texts were written later and were designed to transmit the essence of the *shruti* texts in a way that is more accessible for practicing Hindus. Thus, while they are not divinely revealed, themselves, they are dependent on the revealed status of the *shruti*.

The term *shruti* literally means "that which is heard," referring to those texts that were received directly from the divine source as a form of explicit revelation. The *Vedas*, in particular, are the most sacred texts of the Hindu tradition. They are thought to be eternal and to contain "the essential knowledge of life," which has "existed eternally in the form of vibrations throughout the universe."[9] *Shruti* texts, then, are recognized by Hindus to be authoritative in every sense, with some viewing them to be "the defining aspect of Hinduism" (Knott, 15). They are the principle source of rational belief and practice, precisely because of their status as revealed texts, "the manifestation of the divine in the world" (Knott, 12). Again, if the possibility of revelation were ruled out on the grounds of modern science, it would present a fundamental epistemological crisis, calling into question not only the particular metaphysics of the tradition, but also the rationality of the tradition predicated on that metaphysics.

---

9. Baird and Heimbeck, "Vedic Origins," 3.

HINDUISM, METAPHYSICS, AND SCIENCE 171

Authoritative voices

While Hinduism has no central figure responsible for its inception in the way that Buddhism, Judaism, Christianity, and Islam do with the Buddha, Abraham, Jesus, and Muḥammad, this does not mean that it does not have authoritative voices. Hindus look to *brahmins*, *gurus*, and *sages*, among others, as those who are responsible for the transmission of ritual, ethical, practical, and spiritual knowledge. Of course, there is disagreement as to *who* is recognized as an authoritative brahmin, guru, or sage; but the *institutions* themselves have been a staple of the tradition since its inception.

Brahmins, to begin with, have held a special place in the Hindu tradition from the beginning, performing a number of ritualistic functions, both spiritual and practical. Their origin is rooted in the Purusha hymn (*sūkta*) of the *Ṛg Veda* (10.90). The *sūkta* tells of a cosmic being, a primordial human named Purusha, whose body was offered in a primeval self-sacrifice, from which all life was created. Most notably, from this sacrifice, each of the four castes (*varṇa*) of Hindu society was created, each one associated with a major part of Purusha's body—servants (*shudra*) with the feet, the commoners (*vaishya*) with the thighs, the warriors (*kshatriya*) with the arms, and the brahmin (*brahmana*), the highest of the classes, with the mouth. Thus, brahmins—as Purusha's mouth—were forever associated with "language and communication, with the recitation of the Vedic hymns and formulas (*mantra*), and, ultimately, with the sacred power inherent in them" (Knott, 16). From an early age, brahmin boys memorized the texts of the *Vedas*, originally transmitted orally, learning to recite them "through imitation of their elders" (Knott, 16).

Brahmins, then, were viewed as the transmitters of spiritual and ritual knowledge, specifically by maintaining and transmitting the *Vedas*. In doing so, brahmins were able to preserve the eternal revelation and maintain a relationship between humans and the divine (Knott, 17). Their ritual practices were also connected to *dharma*. As discussed above, *dharma* is tied to the Hindu tradition's larger metaphysical beliefs about *brahman*, *karma*, and *saṃsāra*, in the sense that when one lives in accordance with *dharma*, one also ensures certain *karmic* ends, not only for oneself as an individual, but also for the cosmos as a whole. Thus, in reciting the *Vedas* and in practicing certain rites, the brahmins were seeking to preserve *dharma*—harmony at both the personal and universal level (*brahman*). Consequently, these rites canvased a wide range of matters from the seemingly mundane—marriage, childbirth, and death—to the explicitly religious. Nevertheless, all these practices were inescapably spiritual and metaphysical, with the primary goal of connecting others to the "knowledge of the ultimate truth, or *brahman* . . . ."[10]

In addition to brahmins, the Hindu tradition has also recognized gurus as authoritative voices. Like brahmin, gurus are also considered to be transmitters of religious knowledge. They are considered to be "spiritual masters" and teachers, and their function is considered to be one of the most important and most prestigious roles in Hinduism.[11] Gurus are believed to be wise, using homiletic stories to guide and advise others; they are held in reverence and believed to be pure and beyond temptation, sometimes even viewed as god-men and the focus of devotion (Knott, 98). They manifest unique spiritual gifts as a result of their ascetic practices, such as fasting, prayer, and meditation, and, as a result, are able to intercede with God; and their primary function is to "enlighten others and . . . help them cross the ocean of repeated death and rebirth (*saṃsāra*) to gain liberation (*mokṣa*)" (Knott, 19). In doing so, gurus also play a central role in passing down oral tradition, usually through the lineage of students in a community, a *sampradaya*, or small tradition. There are numerous *sampradayas*, the most prominent dating back to the eighth-century teacher Shankara, but they are all centered around a guru and the spiritual and ritual knowledge they pass on to their pupils (Knott, 11). The heads of these communities were known as *Shankara-acharyas*, religious leaders or masters, and they can be brahmins or gurus, who have themselves received the training in the *Vedas*.

Finally, sages (*rishis*), like brahmins and gurus, are mystics or spiritual teachers. They are considered to be divinely inspired philosophers with direct knowledge of universal truth. Historically, they were responsible for receiving the revealed truth (*shruti*) and incorporating it in the form of scriptures. Again, there is great variance among sages, and they by no means always agree with each other, sometimes even presenting philosophies that are opposed to one another.[12] Nevertheless, there is general agreement within Hinduism over the *role* of the sage, itself, as an authoritative voice connected to divine revelation.

---

10. Killingly, "Hinduism," 16.
11. Knut, "*Gurus* and *Ācāryas*," online.
12. Herman, *A Brief Introduction to Hinduism*, 1.

The foregoing authoritative texts (*shruti* and *smriti*) and voices (brahmins, gurus, and sages) confirm, in part, the basic premise of this section, that religious knowledge for the various Hindu traditions relies on divine revelation. The *shruti* texts are, by definition, divinely revealed from God, while the *smriti* texts, are dependent on them. Likewise, the brahmins, gurus, and sages are each considered to be saints who seek revelation directly from the divine and then transmit that knowledge to others. Thus, if the possibility of revelation were precluded in light of modern science, it would undermine the major epistemological resources of the Hindu tradition. What needs to be shown now is that Hindu practices are also dependent upon these divinely revealed sources, and that to call into question the revealed status of the sources, is to call into question the practices as well.

Modes of rationality

It is important to remember, here, that MacIntyre's definition of rationality is broad, encompassing all of the meaning-making structures unique to a given tradition, including not only ratiocination, the proposition-based reasoning prioritized by the West, but also art and architecture, morality and jurisprudence, names and modes of naming, customs and rituals, stories and myths, and so on. Thus, when looking for Hindu forms of rationality, we are considering not merely their beliefs, but also their wide range of practices, customs, and cultural expressions. In this section, I will briefly highlight a few: the Hindu caste system, the epics, and traditional dance.

The caste system is perhaps the most prominent example of a practice that is inescapably metaphysical and derivative of *shruti*, the divinely revealed sources. As is widely known, Hindu countries such as India have historically implemented a caste system as a way of structuring their society. Traditionally, there have been two distinct, though related, means of doing this—the *varṇa* (class) and the *jāti* (caste). The *varṇa*, as noted above, is connected to the Purusha hymn of the Vedas, according to which the four classes originated from the primordial self-sacrifice of Purusha's body. This class system is highly structured and is viewed as the primary form of social structuring in Hindu society. It is centered around the concept of *dharma*, the fact that every person has certain duties and moral obligations associated with their "particular social class and stage of life" (Knott, 17). It is also associated with ritual purity and ritual status,[13] so that, for example, the brahmin, by virtue of fulfilling *dharma* to the highest extent in their moral responsibilities, are considered to be the most ritually pure and, thus, the highest caste. The untouchables, by contrast, are considered the lowest caste of Hindu society, predicated on similar notions of ritual purity.

The term *jāti* literally means "birth," and refers to the particular social stratum to which one is born.[14] *Jāti* is defined by local tradition and, thus, tends to place greater constrictions on social behavior, governing everything from marriage and birthright customs, to governance and economic mobility. There are hundreds of *jātis* compared to the four distinct *varṇa*. However, there is overlap since one can be a part of a *varṇa* and a local *jāti*. For example, there are numerous *jāti* for the one brahmin *varṇa*. While the *jāti* is not as consistent or uniform as *varṇa*, it is, nevertheless, hierarchical, pertaining to "the membership of a group and the status within it."[15]

There are two important things to note about these two overlapping caste systems. The first is that, together, they serve to govern rational behavior within the society in all its various forms—religious, social, economic, and so on. This is a clear example of the sorts of rational resources MacIntyre identifies—the rational modes of ordering the world and making rational choices in it. They are the meaning-making structures of life. The second thing to note is that these two caste systems are, themselves, predicated on divinely revealed sources (*shruti*) (Knott, 18).[16] Indeed, the entire caste system is, itself, irreducibly metaphysical, predicated on notions of *saṃsāra*, *dharma*, and *karma*, where one's socio-religious standing in this life (*varṇa*, *jāti*) is determined by the choices made in a previous one. The caste system, then, is a reflection of an individual's place in this larger metaphysical ordering. Moreover, however, this entire complex of metaphysical notions—*saṃsāra*, *dharma*, *karma*, *varṇa*, and *jāti*—derive from *shruti*, the divinely revealed sources. Thus, if the possibility of revelation were undermined, then so too would these very rational modes of behavior.

---

13. Thapar, *Early India*, 62.
14. Lipner, *Hindus*, 112.
15. Thapar, *Early India*, 64.
16. See also Robinson, *Religions of the World*, 92 and Thapar, *Early India*, 64.

The caste system, of course, is only one example of Hindu rationality. Another prominent example is the use of epics—poetry and story—in Hinduism. Unfortunately, this brief chapter on Hinduism is not enough to capture the vast array of epic stories in Hinduism and the central role they play in the epistemology of the tradition. Sabrina D. MisirHiralall, a practicing Hindu and Hindu scholar, argues that the "complexity of Hindu epics is beyond the neat categories of history or mythology, fact or fiction, philosophy or religion," and that Westerners have undermined "the religious epistemological framework" of the Hindu tradition by attempting to recontextualize these epics to meet Western preconceptions.[17] While many of the epics are *smriti*, or handed down, their function is to illuminate the revealed texts (*shruti*) in a way that makes them more accessible to the average person.[18] The *Ramayana*, for example, is an epic that has been told and retold for over two and a half millennia, recited by gurus and storytellers and captured in modern day adaptations for television and film (Knott, 38–39).[19] The epistemological significance of these epics, however, would be substantially undermined if the divinely revealed status of the *shruti* literature were called into question.

The same is true of another interesting form of rationality in Hindu society, that of traditional dance. Again, MisirHiralall discusses at length the role of dance in guiding oneself and others toward the path of *mokṣa*. Dance is one way of telling the epics and displaying, visually, the importance of these stories for Hindu belief and practice. Dance also connects humans to specific deities, such as Shiva and Krishna, who are associated with dancing. Dance, like the epic stories, is a way of making these divine realities accessible to everyone. It is an ancient form or rational expression that has been a part of the tradition from the beginning.

These are only a few examples of Hindu forms of rationality. Others have been noted above regarding the ritual practices of the brahmin and the function they play in religious, practical, and socio-ethical contexts. The important thing to emphasize through these examples is the extent to which they are vital to the rationality of the tradition and the extent to which they are dependent on divine revelation. The practices of the brahmin in their various forms are directly connected to the *Vedas*; the caste system is embedded in the metaphysical notion of *samsāra* and all

---

17. MisirHiralall, *Confronting Orientalism*, 143.

18. MisirHiralall, *Confronting Orientalism*, 144.

19. Knott recounts how 80 million Indians tuned in to watch a televised version of the *Ramayana* every Sunday morning at 9:30 in 1987.

its attendant metaphysical beliefs, which, in turn, are dependent on the divinely revealed texts. It is all of a piece, and if the possibility of special revelation were ruled out on the grounds of modern science, these fundamental beliefs and practices would also be called into question, constituting the very epistemological crisis we have been considering.

Hinduism and Its Potential Crisis

The preceding sections should suffice to show that the Hindu tradition is as susceptible to the crisis regarding the issue of divine action in light of modern science as any other tradition considered so far. In this final section, then, I want to consider the resources available to the Hindu tradition that might help it resolve such a crisis or avoid it altogether. I will begin by looking at several resources inherent to the Hindu tradition, itself, which may prove beneficial to them and others, the Christian tradition included. Second, I will offer some considerations that the Christian tradition has learned from its own encounter with this crisis. In so doing, I also hope to model a way in which these two traditions can engage in mutual constructive engagement.

The resources of the Hindu traditions

There are several resources that the Hindu tradition possesses that may benefit it and other religious traditions in responding to a potential crisis concerning divine action. First, the pluralistic nature of Hinduism, itself, can be viewed as an asset. The Hindu tradition tends to be more amenable to various ideas and practices, seeking to integrate knowledge in a way that ensures "pluralistic coexistence."[20] This general attitude is encapsulated in the principle of *ahiṃsā*, or non-violence. This is the highest virtue of the Hindu tradition and refers specifically to non-injury toward living beings. However, it includes a broader understanding of "'respect for difference,' 'coexistence,' 'peaceful resolution of conflicts,' 'multi-dimensional perspectives,' 'learning from each others' experiences,' 'humility,' or 'ecological harmony of all life forms'" (Menon, 9). As the highest virtue of Hindu thought, it is one of the greatest resources that the Hindu tradition offers to the discussion of religion and science as

---

20. Menon, "Hinduism and Science," 8. Going forward, I will cite Menon parenthetically.

well as to inter-religious dialogue. It allows for everything from respectful approaches to nature, including ecological concerns, to respect for other perspectives, scientific or otherwise. Theologically, it is also close in principle to Christian notions of non-violence, and comports with the argument that Nancey Murphy makes based on anabaptist commitments that God never coercively controls outcomes, even at the sub-atomic level (see chap. 5).

This regard for diversity and difference, however, does not negate the fundamental commitment of the Hindu tradition to truth, or *satya*. Again, the concept of *satya* is broad, encompassing moral, epistemological, metaphysical, and spiritual dimensions. It is an integrated notion of truth that seeks coherence across disciplines. For example, from the Vedic period on, Hindus incorporated mathematics and science as a part of their larger socio-religious experience of the world. Science was not a separate, objective enterprise, as it is today in the West. Instead, for Hindus, pursuit of science was a "blend of personal and social engagement, ecological awareness, and advanced mathematics," resulting in the development not only of mathematics and astronomy but also linguistics and metaphysics (Menon, 10). In turn, all of these disciplines served as a means of aiding ritual practices, which helped them "harness forces of nature in their favour to gain victory in battle, to receive timely rain, for healthy children, for more cattle, for a good harvest, and for a place in heaven after death" (Menon, 10). When the principle of *satya* is coupled with the notion of *ahiṃsā*, the result is a tradition that "encourages consensus building based on principles of honesty and non-violence" (Menon, 10). These are virtues that all religious traditions would benefit from incorporating, and they are the virtues at the very heart of this book, namely: How can we show respect toward those who hold different religious commitments, while, at the same time, pursuing honest discussions of truth?

Perhaps one of the greatest epistemological resources that the Hindu tradition possesses, however, especially for the present discussion of divine action, is the idea of *parabrahman* or *purushottama*. The later *Upaniṣads* made a distinction between two aspects of reality, the world of the spirit (*para*) and the world of matter (*apara*). This presented a problem not unlike the one in the West of integrating the spiritual and the material, a problem that has plagued not only Western discussions of divine action, but also discussions of the relationship between mind and body. The central question, at least in the West, has been: How does an immaterial substance interact with the material? The later *Upaniṣads* and the *Bhagavad gītā* resolved this tension by positing the notion of *parabrahman*, or *purushottama*, a higher reality "that transcends and includes the duality of matter and spirit, *prakrti* and *purusha*" (Menon, 11). The various schools of Hindu thought each maintain the same basic idea with varying metaphysical explanations. As Sangeetha Menon states:

> The thread that runs through all forms of Hindu metaphysics and belief systems is the idea that God, ultimate reality, permeates all material manifestations, and hence that there is no fundamental antagonism between matter and spirit, world and God. Hindu enlightenment is seeing God in every bit of the world and experiencing the harmony of dualities. (Menon, 11)

While in some ways the concept of *parabrahman* seems to evade the problem of divine action—how an immaterial God can bring about changes in a physical universe—the fact is, it only side-steps it. The concept of *parabrahman* falls into a similar category as process theology discussed in chapter 8. Like process thought, it is a metaphysical response to a metaphysical problem. In some sense, this is unavoidable. Even the modern scientific worldview is a metaphysic, where notions of gravity, force, reductionism, atomism, determinism, and so on, are all metaphysical in nature. Where natural science has succeeded is in providing concrete, calculable meanings to these terms and concepts such that they have practical applicability. Where most metaphysical systems falter relative to modern science is their inability to do the same. Moreover, by virtue of postulating a larger metaphysical category to explain the interaction of spiritual and physical, Hinduism, no less than process theology, has only pushed the problem back a step. Now the question arises: How do we confirm the existence of *that* metaphysical reality?

Some resources of the Christian tradition

At this point, I want to offer some general considerations that the Christian tradition has reached as a result of its own encounter with the crisis concerning the issue of divine action. In earlier chapters I have discussed at length the resources that the Christian tradition has developed as a means of resolving this crisis (see chaps. 5 and 8). In the previous chapter, in particular, I discussed the Divine Action Project (DAP) and the wide-ranging possibilities that were secured by that consortium. I do not intend to recount those resources here. However, suffice it to say, the resources discussed in those earlier chapters are as available to the Hindu tradition as they are to any others. At this point, I simply want to provide some general considerations for any metaphysical tradition faced with the challenges of modern science.

In attempting to deal with modern science, there seem to be only a few options. One is to ignore modern science altogether or attempt to refute it outright and press forward in spite of it. The danger in this approach is twofold. First, the modern scientific tradition has demonstrated time and again its ability to explain and anticipate a wide range of phenomena. Its staying power is incontestable, at least for the present. Second, though closely related, the world has become so dependent on the technological advances of modern science that we wind up relying on the scientific tradition and seeking to integrate it in various ways, even if our basic metaphysical beliefs are not always in accord with it. The scientific tradition is an inescapable part of modern life at this point. We have to deal with it in one way or another. The second option is to attempt to fortify one's basic religious beliefs with a more sophisticated metaphysical explanation. I have already discussed how the Christian tradition has attempted to do this with process theology and how the Hindu tradition has attempted to do this with the concept of *parabrahman*. The problem with this approach, as I have already noted, is that it merely pushes the metaphysical questions back to another stage. We are still left with the question of how to account for some metaphysic in light of modern science.

The third option is twofold: first, to identify the ways in which modern science *is* its own metaphysic and to show how some of those metaphysical assumptions are inadequate on the basis of scientific enquiry itself. Examples of this were discussed in chapters 5 and 8, where I noted that quantum physics, emergence, decoupling, and whole-part causation, separately and together, call into question atomist-reductionism and determinist assumptions of modern science. In doing so, we may find that the underlying assumptions of science are not as problematic for religious, metaphysical belief as previously thought. This is very MacIntyrean, by the way, identifying inherent problems within a tradition, not by means of applying outside criteria, but rather by applying criteria internal to the tradition in question, in this case the scientific tradition.

The second part of this approach is to accept those elements of the scientific tradition that are not inherently threatening to one's religious tradition and to consider how those points of intersection can augment our respective understandings of the world. This is in keeping with the argument of *this* book, looking for points of mutual constructive engagement between traditions, in this case between one's religious tradition and the scientific tradition. It is this third approach that Robert J. Russell and other members of the DAP have sought to take and, in so doing, have provided a wide range of resources for the tradition to resolve its crisis. I suggest that each of the religious traditions considered in this book would benefit from this same two-fold approach. It allows for mutual constructive engagement not only among religious traditions, but between each individual religious tradition and the scientific tradition itself.

Conclusion

In this chapter, I hope to have shown that Hinduism is no different than the other major religious traditions in the sense that its beliefs and practices are predicated, at least in part, on divine revelation, and that if such revelation is precluded as the result of modern science, then many of its beliefs and practices would also be called into question, constituting an epistemological crisis. However, insofar as the Hindu tradition is susceptible to the same crisis as the other traditions, it also stands to benefit from the same solution(s). It is for this reason that all of the traditions considered so far have an incentive to remain in mutual constructive engagement, so that they can aid one another in developing resources to avoid potential crises and, hopefully, to help each other toward a shared understanding of the nature of reality.

Conclusion
Honesty, Truth, and Humility

> *We should be rigorous in judging ourselves*
> *and gracious in judging others.*[1]
> —JOHN WESLEY

IN THESE PAGES I have tried to propose a *via media* for interfaith dialogue, a middle way between two extremes. On the one hand, I hold that interreligious dialogue must avoid *antipathy* toward religious others, that is, any attitude that disregards the authenticity of other people's religious experiences, making it easier to view them as mere objects to be dismissed, converted, or worse, harmed and maltreated. On the other hand, I hold that interreligious dialogue must also avoid *relativism*, the belief that all religious traditions are essentially saying the same thing, or near enough as to make any differences inconsequential. In its own way, relativism, as much as antipathy, objectifies religious others by flattening any real difference or distinctiveness among religious traditions and claiming that they are essentially the same. Moreover, it removes one of the primary reasons for interfaith dialogue in the first place, a desire to learn from one another in such a way that helps us move toward clearer (truer) descriptions of God and the world.

    I have argued, then, that interreligious dialogue should take place at the level of descriptive language about our religious experiences, not at the level of the religious experiences, themselves. That is, we should take it as given that others have had authentic religious experiences, but

---

1. Wesley, attributed.

recognize that our descriptions of those experiences are always subject to revision. This approach allows us to avoid the two extremes noted above, permitting us to honor the authenticity of the spiritual experiences that other religious traditions have had while, at the same time, allowing us to recognize that not all descriptions of those experiences are the same or equally true. Stated positively, this proposal allows us to retain respect for religious others, including their beliefs and practices, while also preserving the notion of truth, the possibility that we can help each other describe God and the world more accurately.

Here it may be helpful to make a distinction between *honesty* and *truth*. Honesty speaks to the sincerity of belief; truth to its correctness. One can be honest in holding a belief, but mistaken in its correctness. The same cannot be said of truth—either something is true, regardless of opinion, or it is not. In this book, then, I have been assuming several things: first, that people of other faith traditions are being honest in their descriptions of their religious experiences; that is, that they are sincerely describing their experiences with no attempt to beguile or deceive. Second, I am assuming that people of other faith traditions are being truthful in that they have actually had these experiences of the divine. That is, they are not deceived, themselves, in their experiences of God and the ultimate. They have truthfully had religious experiences that they are then attempting to describe as honestly as possible. What I am proposing, however, is that it is always possible that we may be wrong in our *description* of those experiences. The experiences may be true and honest, but the descriptions may be in error.

It is this possibility that opens the door for genuine dialogue, for only when there is the possibility of error do we stand to benefit from religious others. This is where *humility* is of utmost importance in interreligious dialogue. Only when we are humble enough to admit where we may have *mis*described our own experiences might we then also be humble enough to learn from those of another religious tradition. Epistemological crises make this possible. Individuals, communities, and traditions are always capable of encountering problems that their epistemological resources— their meaning-making structures—are not equipped to resolve. When this happens, it will raise questions for the members of that tradition about the reliability of the descriptions of their own experiences of reality, religious or otherwise.

In this book, I have tried to show how this model might work in a practical way. I began in Part I by outlining my proposal for deep pluralism and the very possibility of epistemological crises in the first place. There, I argued that all traditions develop within the context of their own unique historical contexts and that these unique histories of development shape the rationality of each tradition—from its language and conceptual schemes to its art and architecture, ethics and jurisprudence, science and metaphysics, and so on. It is rationality in this broadest sense—in all its various modes—that helps the members of each tradition make sense of the world around them, including their understanding of God and the divine. However, since this rationality is always being constructed reciprocally with the tradition's engagement of the world, and since that engagement is never a God's-eye perspective, it is always subject to error.

This possibility of error manifests itself most prominently in the form of epistemological crises, circumstances in which our rational resources have so misled us that we find ourselves compelled to reexamine them either in part or in whole. It is at this point, so I have argued, that individuals and communities become humble enough to listen to the experience of others who have either (a) avoided the problem altogether or (b) encountered the same problem but found a successful resolution to it. This, I believe, is where interreligious dialogue is most promising, because it allows for enough vulnerability (humility) on the part of the members of a tradition to be open to learning something genuinely novel from those of another tradition. It is this posture of humility that allows interreligious dialogue to avoid the extremes of antipathy and relativism. On the one hand, humility allows us to view the religious other as a genuine other, not an object, but rather a person or a community honestly struggling to understand the nature of the divine and the world around us. An epistemological crisis helps us see our own limitations and humbles us enough to relinquish any presumption of superiority; it places us in a position to see religious others as equals, fellow sojourners striving to make sense of God and the world.

On the other hand, this sort of humility also allows us to avoid relativism by permitting us to face real differences head on. Antipathy and relativism both have a certain fear of difference. Antipathy, because we do not want our beliefs to be shown wrong; relativism because we do not want to accuse others of being wrong. Both positions presume a certain degree of arrogance, assuming either "we cannot be wrong" or "no one can be wrong." But humility recognizes that to err is human; all traditions tend to err in their description of reality. This is not a liability to be avoided in interreligious dialogue, but an asset. In fact, as I have been arguing, it is the only true starting place for genuine dialogue. Only when we recognize that we may be in error in our own beliefs do we become open to learning from others who see things differently. Until this point, we are usually too confident in our own beliefs to hear others in any way that might move us to change. Humility, then, allows for the possibility of genuine dialogue, whereby we are truly willing to reexamine some of our closely held beliefs.

In the second and third parts of this book, I applied the model of deep pluralism outlined in Part I, first, to the three Abrahamic traditions—Judaism, Christianity, and Islam—and, then, to the two major Eastern traditions, Buddhism and Hinduism. There, I considered an epistemological crisis that each tradition has either encountered or exhibits the potential for encountering and the ways in which those traditions have stood to learn from one another. The specific epistemological crisis under consideration has been one concerning the issue of divine action. My basic argument has been that insofar as any religious or metaphysical tradition is dependent on some form of special divine revelation for its basic beliefs and practices—its rationality in the broadest possible sense—it is subject to this sort of crisis. For if modern science precludes revelation, in any form, then, by extension, it also calls into question any beliefs and practices predicated on such revelation.

In Part II, I argued that the three Abrahamic traditions encountered this sort of crisis initially during the medieval period, where the problem centered around the integration of ancient Greek philosophy. While ancient philosophy offered much in terms of science, cosmology, and metaphysics, it also challenged the simple God-world metaphysic found in the Torah, the Qur'ān, and the Christian scriptures. Adopting this alien metaphysic created conceptual problems for each tradition in its understanding of how God works in the world. Specifically, the Neoplatonic model of emanation restricted God's action in two ways. First, it implied that any act of creation must be *necessitated* by God's very existence, thus removing divine choice in the creation of the world. Second, emanation implied that God's direct action would be restricted to the next immediate sphere, and no other. Therefore, God would not be able to act directly in the world of human affairs. Together, these two implications undermined notions of both general and special divine action common to the three Abrahamic traditions. Moreover, such a model ruled out the possibility of special revelation and, with it, the justification for any theological beliefs and practices predicated on it.

Resolving this crisis required the work of theologians and philosophers from each tradition—al-Ghazālī, Maimonides, and Aquinas, to name the most prominent. More importantly, and more to the point of this book, many of these philosophers relied on each other's work across religious traditions to help them formulate an adequate resolution to the crisis. The Islamic tradition led the way, having been the first of the three traditions to re-encounter ancient Greek philosophy, and having undergone an extensive process of translating these texts and integrating them into their tradition. It was al-Ghazālī, in particular, who offered a solution to this crisis for the Islamic tradition, first arguing on philosophical grounds that there is no necessary connection between causes and effects and on theological grounds that all such connections are the result of God's reliable habit; then arguing that something in the mind of God can be possible without being actualized, thus preserving the theological belief that creation is not a necessary product of God's existence, but a genuine possibility that God could chose to enact or not.

Maimonides goes on to argue from the Jewish tradition that even if there is a necessary connection between causes and effects, such a connection does not necessarily apply to creation as a whole. Since the creation of the world is a unique event, it follows no set pattern, having no precedent. Thus, there is no grounds for arguing that the world must issue necessarily from God's existence, even if this is the pattern for all subsequent causes and effects. Finally, Aquinas, drawing explicitly on the work of Avicenna and Maimonides, argues that even if there is a necessary connection between God and the world, this does not have to diminish the ontological priority of the former over the latter. That is, the world can still be said to be metaphysically dependent on God, even if there is no temporal distinction between the two. Furthermore, remaining in dialogue with Ibn Gabirol, Maimonides, and Avicenna, Aquinas argues that God's interaction in the world is principally through existence (*esse*). Since God's *esse* is connected to that of all things, God's providence is available to all things precisely through their *esse*.

Here we have a clear example of three traditions remaining in a form of protracted mutual constructive engagement, each one drawing on the advances and liabilities of the others in an attempt to resolve a common crisis and, hopefully, arrive at a clearer description of reality. The same possibility presents itself now as all three traditions encounter a similar crisis with the rise of Newtonian science in the modern period. The metaphysical worldview that developed during this time, not unlike that of the medieval period, was also the result, at least in part, of adopting ancient Greek notions, in this case, atomism and Pythagoreanism. Once these Greek notions were supplemented with the additional notions of reductionism, determinism, and laws of nature, the picture that began to develop was one of a sophisticated clock that runs on its own internal processes and does not require any outside assistance. If all things happen as a result of strict causal laws that are determined by the motions of the smallest bits of matter, then what room is there for God's action?

While neither the Jewish nor the Islamic traditions have encountered the crisis in the modern period in quite the same way that the Christian tradition has, I contend that all three are vulnerable to it. Thus, in Part II I also examined some of the resources that the Christian tradition has developed in response to this crisis that may benefit those of the other two traditions. In particular, I considered the work of the Divine Action Project (DAP), focusing specifically on the contributions of Robert J. Russell and Nancey Murphy. Russell argues that the Newtonian picture of the world that developed during the modern period has shifted in light of recent scientific developments such as general and special relativity and quantum physics, and that there is now reason to believe that the universe offers genuine openness, points at which God can act directly in the world in objective ways that are also non-interventionist (NIODA). Murphy looks specifically at the domain of quantum physics, arguing that since the behavior of electrons at this level is intrinsically indeterminate, there is sufficient openness for NIODA, God's non-interventionist, objective, divine action. Such a model, I have suggested, may also benefit the Jewish and Islamic traditions as well.

In Part III, I argued that the two primary Eastern traditions—Buddhism and Hinduism—are as susceptible to the crisis raised by modern science as the Abrahamic traditions are. The Buddhist tradition, I noted, seems, at first glance, to avoid the crisis as it does not posit belief in a supreme creator-God who both transcends the world and acts immanently in it. However, I made the case that insofar as Buddhism holds central certain metaphysical beliefs and practices that are predicated on some form of revelation, they remain as vulnerable to the crisis concerning the issue of divine action as any other tradition. For if modern science rules out the possibility of any form of special revelation, religious or metaphysical, it also challenges any beliefs and practices predicated on such revelation. Along these lines, I argued that the Buddhist tradition's commitment to *saṃsāra* and *karma* are metaphysical in nature and are predicated directly on the revelation received by the Buddha under the Bodhi tree. If this sort of revelation were precluded by modern science, then so too would be the fundamental metaphysical beliefs and practices of the Buddhist tradition.

The Hindu tradition, by contrast, does posit belief in a supreme creator-God as well as a plurality of manifestations of that God and, thus, stands closer to the Abrahamic traditions in the potential for this crisis. However, what was said about the Buddhist tradition is relevant for all the traditions considered so far. Insofar as any religious tradition maintains beliefs and practices that are predicated on some form of divine revelation—religious or metaphysical—it is subject to the same sort of epistemological crisis. Hinduism, I argued, is irreducibly metaphysical, from its cosmological and ethical commitments reflected in *dharma*, *karma*, and *saṃsāra* to its various forms of rational practice—the caste system, epics and poetry, traditional dance, and brahminic practices. Moreover, these various forms of rationality are directly dependent on divine revelation, both in the form of spiritual leaders such as brahmins, gurus, and sages, who receive spiritual insight directly from the divine and transmit it to the rest of the tradition, and in the form of sacred texts, both those that are divinely revealed (*shruti*) and those that are passed down from revelation (*smriti*). Again, insofar as modern science challenges the possibility of any such revelation, it also challenges any beliefs and practices predicated on such revelation, constituting an epistemological crisis.

Remember, the purpose in identifying these vulnerabilities is not to raise criticisms of these traditions, but rather to identify a common problem and to initiate dialogue that can lead toward shared solutions to that problem. Throughout, I have tried to highlight resources that each tradition possesses that could aid it and the other traditions in responding to this crisis. The Buddhist tradition, for example, incorporates elements that make it more amenable to modern science, in the first place, such as the Buddhist belief in the autonomy of the physical universe, which comports with modern notions of physical laws of nature, and Buddhist cosmological beliefs, which comport with modern notions of evolution at both the biological and cosmological level. Similarly, the Hindu tradition's dual commitment to *ahiṃsā* and *satya*, suggests a concern for both cooperation and truth, virtues that are at the heart of the argument of this book—specifically, how can we preserve enough humility to cooperate with others while not abandoning sincere discussion of truth. In highlighting these and other resources, I hope to have modeled one way in which the various religious traditions can enter into mutual constructive engagement over a shared crisis and, in so doing, help each other toward a clearer understanding of the world.

There is an old story of two villages that lived on opposite sides of a road. Every day a traveler would pass between the two villages wearing a two-toned hat. One half was blue, the other red, so that the villagers on either side of the road each believed that the traveler only wore either a blue or a red hat, depending on their vantage point. The moral of the story, of course, usually has to do with the limitedness of human perception and knowledge—we think ourselves so sure of our beliefs when, in fact, those beliefs are based on limited knowledge of the whole. There may be some truth to this, but is there no resolution to it? What if the villagers of each opposing community crossed the road and began to discuss their experiences in earnest? What if they took each other's experiences seriously, taking them to be honest and sincere descriptions of reality as the different villagers encountered it? And what if they remained humble enough to hold their own beliefs open to revision so that they could genuinely learn from those of the other village? Might they then be able to aid one another to a shared explanation of why the traveler appears to wear both a blue and a red hat? And if they were able to come to some sort of consensus about their observations, wouldn't that serve as some sort of confirmation that they were closer to the truth than each had been previously, independent of each other?

This is what I am suggesting in this model of interreligious dialogue. Mutual constructive engagement allows religious traditions to work together toward a more common description of reality and, in doing so, can serve as further confirmation of the truth of our beliefs.

Works Cited

Adeney, Miriam. "When the Elephant Dances, the Mouse May Die (Unintended Consequences of Short-Term Missions)." *Short-Term Missions Today.* Inaugural edition, 2000. Abridged version accessed April 29, 2020. http://www.kidzatheart.org/2014/10/when-the-elephant-dances-the-mouse-may-die/.

Al-Ghazālī. *The Incoherence of the Philosophers: A Parallel English-Arabic Text.* Translated and annotated by Michael E. Marmura. Provo, UT: Brigham Young University Press, 2000.

Aquinas, Thomas. "On Being and Essence." In *Medieval Philosophy Vol II: Philosophic Classics,* edited by Forrest E. Baird and Walter Kaufmann, 420–36. 4th ed. Upper Saddle River, NJ: Prentice Hall, 2003.

———. *On Being and Essence.* 2nd rev. ed. Translated by Armand Maurer, CSB. Toronto: The Pontifical Institute of Medieval Studies, 1968.

———. *On the Eternity of the World* (*De Aeternitate Mundi*). Translated by Robert T. Miller. Online, 1991, 1997. Accessed September 6, 2020. https://d2y1pz2y630308.cloudfront.net/15471/documents/2016/10/St.%20Thomas%20Aquinas-On%20the%20Eternity%20of%20the%20World.pdf.

———. "The Principles of Nature." In *Medieval Philosophy Vol II: Philosophic Classics,* edited by Forrest E. Baird and Walter Kaufmann, 410–19. 4th ed. Upper Saddle River, NJ: Prentice Hall, 2003.

———. "Summa Theologica (in part)." In *Medieval Philosophy Vol. II: Philosophic Classics,* edited by Forrest E. Baird and Walter Kaufmann, 335–410. Vol. II. 4th ed. Upper Saddle River, NJ: Prentice Hall, 2003.

Aristotle. "De Interpretatione." In *The Complete Works of Aristotle: The Revised Oxford Edition,* edited by Jonathan Barnes, vol. 1. Princeton, NJ: Princeton University Press, 1984.

Atwood, Kathryn J. *Women Heroes of World War II: 26 Stories of Espionage, Sabotage, Resistance, and Rescue.* Chicago: Chicago Review, 2011.

Avicenna. "Metaphysics." Excerpted from *The Salvation.* Reprinted in "Ibn Sīnā." In *Classical Arabic Philosophy: An Anthology of Sources,* edited and translated by Jon McGinnis and David C. Reisman, 209–18. Indianapolis, IN: Hackett, 2007.

Baird, Forrest E., and Walter Kaufmann. "Baruch Spinoza." In *Philosophic Classics Vol. III: Modern Philosophy,* edited by Baird and Kaufmann, 105–7. 2nd ed. Upper Saddle River, NJ: Prentice Hall, 1997.

———. "Islamic and Jewish Philosophy in the Middle Ages." In *Philosophic Classics Vol. II: Medieval Philosophy, Vol. II,* edited by Baird and Kaufmann, 217–18. 4th ed. Upper Saddle River, NJ: Prentice Hall, 2003.

———. "Moses Maimonides." In *Philosophic Classics Vol. II: Medieval Philosophy, Vol. II*, edited by Baird and Kaufmann, 261–62. 4th ed. Upper Saddle River, NJ: Prentice Hall, 2003.
Baird, Forrest E., and Raeburne S. Heimbeck. "Orthodox Perspectives." In *Philosophic Classics, Vol. VI: Asian Philosophy*, edited by Baird and Heimbeck, 135–49. Upper Saddle River, NJ: Prentice Hall, 2006.
———. "Vedic Origins." In *Philosophic Classics, Vol. VI: Asian Philosophy*, edited by Baird and Heimbeck, 3–8. Upper Saddle River, NJ: Prentice Hall, 2006.
Bakar, Osman. *The History and Philosophy of Islamic Science*. Cambridge: Islamic Texts Society, 1999.
Berger, David. "Miracles and the Natural Order in Nahmanides." In *Rabbi Moses Naḥmanides (Ramban) Explorations in His Religious and Literary Virtuosity*, edited by Isadore Twersky, 107–28. Cambridge: Harvard University Press, 1983.
Black, Deborah L. "Al-Fārābī." In *Routledge History of World Philosophies, Vol. 1: History of Islamic Philosophy*, edited by Seyyed Hossein Nasr and Oliver Leaman, 334–71. London: Routledge, 1996.
Brewer, David J. "Mutual Constructive Engagement: A MacIntyrean Approach to Theology of Religions—Christianity and Islam in Conversation." PhD diss., Fuller Theological Seminary, 2017.
———. "Rationality and Religious Traditions: An Epistemological Approach to Theology of Religions." *Journal of Ecumenical Studies* 50.3 (2015) 471–93.
Brooke, John Hedley. *Science and Religion: Some Historical Perspectives*. Cambridge: Cambridge University Press, 1991.
Brueggemann, Walter. *The Prophetic Imagination*. 2nd ed. Minneapolis, MN: Fortress, 2001.
Bultmann, Rudolph. "Jesus and the Word." In *Jesus and the Word and Other Essays*, edited by C. K. Barrett, 213–24. Eugene, OR: Scribner, 1995.
Burrell, David B. "Aquinas and Islamic and Jewish Thinkers." In *The Cambridge Companion to Aquinas*, edited by Norman Kretzmann and Eleonore Stump, 60–84. Cambridge: Cambridge University Press, 1993.
———. *Faith and Freedom: An Interfaith Perspective*. Malden, MA: Blackwell, 2004.
———. *Knowing the Unknowable God: Ibn-Sina, Maimonides, Aquinas*. Notre Dame, IN: University of Notre Dame Press, 2001.
———. *Towards a Jewish-Christian-Muslim Theology*. Malden, MA: Wiley-Blackwell, 2011.
Burtt, E. A. *The Metaphysical Foundations of Modern Science*. Mineola, NY: Dover, 2003.
Campanini, Massimo. "Al-Ghazālī." In *Routledge History of World Philosophies Vol. 1: History of Islamic Philosophy*, edited by Seyyed Hossein Nasr and Oliver Leaman, 258–75. London: Routledge, 1996.
Chung, Judy. "Leading a Bible Study on Incarnational Mission for the 21st Century." DMin. dissertation, Wesley Theological Seminary, 2015.
Cobb, John. *Beyond Dialogue: Toward a Mutual Transformation of Christianity and Buddhism*. Philadelphia: Fortress, 1982.
———. *God and the World*. Eugene, OR: Wipf & Stock, 2000.
Cohen, Mark R. *Under Crescent and Cross: The Jewish Middle Ages*. Princeton, NJ: Princeton University Press, 1994.
Cornwell, John. "MacIntyre on Money." Prospect. https://www.prospectmagazine.co.uk/magazine/alasdair-macintyre-on-money.

Culpepper, R. Alan. "The Gospel of Luke: Introduction, Commentary, and Reflections." In *The New Interpreter's Bible: A Commentary in Twelve Volumes, Vol. IX*, edited by Leander E. Keck et al., 3–490. Nashville, TN: Abingdon, 1998.

Dahlstrom, Daniel O. "Moses Mendelssohn." *Stanford Encyclopedia of Philosophy*. Edited by Edward N. Zalta. Accessed May 28, 2020. https://plato.stanford.edu/entries/mendelssohn/.

Davies, Noel, and Martin Conway. "Witness among the People of Other Living Faiths: Section of the 1989 World Conference on Mission and Evangelism of the WCC." In *World Christianity in the Twentieth Century: A Reader*, edited by Noel and Conway, 274. London: SCM, 2008.

Deacon, Terrence. "Three Levels of Emergent Phenomena." In *Evolution & Emergence: Systems, Organisms, Persons*, edited by Nancey Murphy and William R. Stoeger, SJ., 88–110. Oxford: Oxford University Press, 2007.

Dempsey, Carol J. "Alien, Foreigner, Stranger, Orphan, Widow." In *The Westminster Theological Wordbook of the Bible*, edited by Donald E. Gowan, 6–8. Louisville, KY: Westminster John Knox, 2003.

Dharmaraj Glory E., and Jacob S. Dharmaraj. *A Theology of Mutuality: A Paradigm for Mission in the Twenty-First Century*. New York: United Methodist Women, 2014.

Druart, Thérèse-Anne. "Al-Fārābī and Emanationism." In *Studies in Medieval Philosophy*, edited by John F. Wippel, 23–44. Washington, DC: The Catholic University of America Press, 1987.

Easwaran, Eknath, trans. "The Bhagavad Gita." In *Philosophic Classics, Vol. VI: Asian Philosophy*, edited by Forest Baird, 150–87. Upper Saddle River, NJ: Prentice Hall, 2006.

———. "The Chandogya Upanishads." In *The Upanishads: A Classic of Indian Spirituality*, edited and translated by Easwaran, 119–52. Tomales, CA: The Blue Mountain Center of Meditation, 2007.

el Omari, Racha. "Muʻtazilah." *The Oxford Encyclopedia of the Islamic World*. Oxford Islamic Studies Online. Accessed April 29, 2020. http://www.oxfordislamicstudies.com/article/opr/t236/e1073.

Emon, Anver M. *Religious Pluralism and Islamic Law: Dhimmis and Others in the Empire of Law*. Oxford: Oxford University Press, 2012.

Falk, Randall M., and Walter J. Harrelson. *Jews and Christians: A Troubled Family*. Nashville, TN: Abingdon, 1990.

———. *Jews and Christians in Pursuit of Social Justice*. Nashville, TN: Abingdon, 1996.

Farrer, Austin. *Faith and Speculation: An Essay in Philosophical Theology*. London: Adam & Charles Black, 1967.

Feiner, Shmuel. *The Jewish Enlightenment* Translated by Chaya Naor. Philadelphia: University of Pennsylvania Press, 2002.

Franco, Aaron, and Morgan Radford. "Ex-KKK member denounces hate groups one year after rallying in Charlottesville." *NBC News*. Accessed April 29, 2019. https://www.nbcnews.com/news/us-news/ex-kkk-member-denounces-hate-groups-one-year-after-rallying-n899326.

Frank, Richard MacDonough. *Beings and Their Attributes: The Teaching of the Basrian School of the Muʻtazila in the Classical Period*. Albany, NY: State University of New York Press, 1978.

———. *Creation and the Cosmic System: Al-Ghazālī & Avicenna*. Heidelberg, DE: Universitatsverlag, 1992.

———. "The Structure of Created Causality according to al-Ashʿarī: An Analysis of Kitāb al-Lumaʿ." In *Early Islamic Theology: The Muʿtazilites and al-Ashʿarī: Texts and Studies on the Development and History of Kalām*, Vol. II, edited by Dimitri Gutas, 13–75. Aldershot, UK: Ashgate, 2007.

Freudenthal, Gad. "Arabic and Latin Cultures as Resources for the Hebrew Translation Movement: Comparative Considerations, Both Quantitative and Qualitative." In *Science in Medieval Jewish Cultures*, edited by Gad Freudenthal, 74–105. Cambridge: Cambridge University Press, 2011.

———. "The Assimilation of Greco-Arabic Learning by Medieval Jewish Cultures: A Brief Bibliographic Introduction." In *Science in Medieval Jewish Cultures*, edited by Gad Freudenthal, 13–16. Cambridge: Cambridge University Press, 2011.

Gabirol, Solomon ben Judah ibn. *The Fountain of Life (Fons Vitae)*. Translated by Alfred B. Jacob, revised by Leonard Levin. New York: The Jewish Theological Seminary, 2005.

Galilee, Galileo. "Excerpts from The Assayer." *Discoveries and Opinions of Galileo: including The Starry Messenger (1610), Letter to the Grand Duchess Christina (1615), and Excerpts from Letters on Sunspots (1613), The Assayer (1623)*. Translated by Stillman Drake, 229–80. New York: Anchor, 1990.

General Board of Global Ministries. "Guiding Principles for Missionary Service." A policy articulating the common understanding of the values of missionary service set forth by the Missionary Services Unit of the General Board of Global Ministries. New York: October 2012.

Gilkey, Langdon B. "Cosmology, Ontology, and the Travail of Biblical Language." *The Journal of Religion* 41.3 (1961) 194–205.

Gimaret, Daniel. "Muʿtazila." *The Encyclopaedia of Islam, Vol. VII*, edited by C. E. Bosworth, E. Van Donzel, W. P. Heinrichs, and C. Pellat, 783–93. New York: Brill, 1993.

Goodal, Norman, ed. *The Uppsala Report 1968: Official Report of the Fourth Assembly of the World Council of Churches. Uppsala July 4–10, 1968*. Geneva: World Council of Churches, 1968.

Green, Joel B. *The Gospel of Luke*. The New International Commentary on the New Testament. Grand Rapids: Eerdmans, 1997.

———. *The Wesley Study Bible*. NRSV. Nashville, TN: Abingdon, 2009.

Grenz, Stanley J. *Theology for the Community of God*. Grand Rapids: Eerdmans, 1994.

Griffel, Frank. *Al-Ghazālī's Philosophical Theology*. Oxford: Oxford University Press, 2009.

Guder, Darrell L. *The Incarnation and the Churches Witness*. Harrisburg, PA: Trinity International, 1999.

Gutas, Demitri. "Islam and Science: A False Statement of the Problem." *Islam and Science* 1.2 (2003) 215–20.

Hamilton, Adam. "The Britt Lecture." First Honolulu United Methodist Church, 2011.

———. *Christianity and the World Religions: Questions We Ask about Other Faiths*. Rev. ed. Nashville, TN: Abingdon, 2018.

Hamilton, Sue. *Indian Philosophy: A Very Short Introduction*. Oxford: Oxford University Press, 2001.

Hartshorne, Charles, and William L. Reese. *Philosophers Speak of God*. Amherst, NY: Humanity, 2000.

Harvey, Peter. *An Introduction to Buddhism: Teachings, History, and Practices*. 2nd ed. Cambridge: Cambridge University Press, 2013.
Hebblethwaite, Brian. "Introduction." In *Divine Action: Studies Inspired by the Philosophical Theology of Austin Farrer*, edited by Brian Hebblethwaite and Edward Henderson, 1–20. Edinburgh: T. & T. Clark, 1990.
Heilman, Samuel. *Defenders of the Faith: Inside Ultra-Orthodox Jewry*. Berkley, CA: University of California Press, 2000.
Herman, A. L. *A Brief Introduction to Hinduism: Religion, Philosophy, and Ways of Liberation*. London: Routledge, 2018.
Hick, John. *An Interpretation of Religion: Human Responses to the Transcendent*. New Haven, CT: Yale University Press, 1989.
Hooykaas, Reijer. *Religion and the Rise of Modern Science*. Vancouver, BC: Regent College, 1972.
Hyman, Arthur. "Jewish Philosophy in the Islamic World." In *History of Islamic Philosophy Part II. Routledge History of World Philosophies, Vol. 1*, edited by Seyyed Hossain Nasr and Oliver Leaman, 677–95. London: Routledge, 1996.
Impey, Chris. "What Buddhism and Science Can Teach Each Other—and Us—about the Universe." The conversation.com. Accessed June 22, 2020. https://theconversation.com/what-buddhism-and-science-can-teach-each-other-and-us-about-the-universe-134322.
Iqbal, Muzaffar. *Islam and Science*. Burlington, VT: Ashgate, 2002.
Jefferson, Thomas. *The Jefferson Bible: The Life and Morals of Jesus of Nazareth Extracted Textually from the Gospels Together with a Comparison of his Doctrines with Those of Others*. Chicago: N. D. Thompson, 1902.
Jenkins, Philip. *The Next Christendom: The Coming of Global Christianity*. Oxford: Oxford University Press, 2002.
Kärkkäinen, Veli-Matti. *Creation and Humanity: A Constructive Christian Theology for The Pluralistic World, Vol. 3*. Grand Rapids: Eerdmans, 2015.
———. *An Introduction to the Theology of Religions: Biblical, Historical, and Contemporary Perspectives*. Downers Grove, IL: InterVarsity, 2003.
———. *Trinity and Revelation: A Constructive Christian Theology for the Pluralistic World, Vol. 2*. Grand Rapids: Eerdmans, 2015.
Keown, Damien. *Buddhism: A Very Short Introduction*. Oxford: Oxford University Press, 2013.
Kerr, Gaven. "Aquinas: Metaphysics." *Internet Encyclopedia of Philosophy*. https://iep.utm.edu/aq-meta/#H2. Accessed August 30, 2020.
Kierkegaard, Søren. *Philosophical Fragments*. Translated by David F. Swenson. Vancouver, BC: Vintage Kierkegaard, 2007.
Killingley, Dermot. "Hinduism," In *Major World Religions: From Their Origins to the Present*, edited by Lloyd Ridgeon, 8–58. London: Routledge, 2003.
King, L. W., ed. *Enuma Elish: The Epic of Creation: The Seven Tablets of Creation Volume One and Two*. London: Luzac, 1902.
Klaaren, Eugene M. *Religious Origins of Modern Science: Belief in Creation in Seventeenth-Century Thought*. Grand Rapids: Eerdmans, 1977.
Klausner, Joseph. "The Philosophy of the *Fons Vitae*: Jewish Pantheism." In *The Fountain of Life (Fons Vitae)*, translated by Leonard Levin, v–xviii. New York: The Jewish Theological Seminary, 2005.
Knitter, Paul. *Introducing Theologies of Religions*. Maryknoll, NY: Orbis, 2002.

Knott, Kim. *Hinduism: A Very Short Introduction.* Oxford: Oxford University Press, 2016.
Knut, Axel Jacobsen, "*Gurus* and *Ācāryas.*" *Brill's Encyclopedia of Hinduism. Online.* https://referenceworks.brillonline.com/entries/brill-s-encyclopedia-of-hinduism/guru-s-and-acarya-COM_9000000033?s.num=7&s.f.s2_parent=s.f.book.brill-s-encyclopedia-of-hinduism&s.q=guru. Accessed June 21, 2020.
Kraemer, Joel L. *Maimonides: The Life and Work of One of Civilization's Greatest Minds.* New York: Doubleday, 2008.
Kuhn, Thomas S. *The Structure of Scientific Revolutions.* 3rd ed. Chicago: University of Chicago Press, 1996.
Leaman, Oliver. "Ash'arī, Abū Al-Ḥasan ʿAlī." *The Oxford Encyclopedia of the Islamic World* online, Vol. 1, by John L. Esposito, 221. Oxford: Oxford University Press, 2009. Online: http://www.oxfordislamicstudies.com/article/opr/t236/e0994/.
———. *Moses Maimonides.* London: Curzon, 1997.
Levine, Amy-Jill. "What Is the Difference between the Old Testament, the Tanakh, and the Hebrew Bible?" https://www.bibleodyssey.org/en/tools/bible-basics/what-is-the-difference-between-the-old-testament-the-tanakh-and-the-hebrew-bible. Accessed July 11, 2020.
Lipner, Julius. *Hindus: Their Religious Beliefs and Practices.* London: Routledge, 1998.
MacIntyre, Alasdair. "Epistemological Crises, Dramatic Narratives, and the Philosophy of Science." In *Paradigms and Revolutions: Appraisals and Applications of Thomas Kuhn's Philosophy of Science*, edited by Gary Gutting, 54–74. Notre Dame, IN: University of Notre Dame Press, 1980.
———. *Whose Justice? Which Rationality?* Notre Dame, IN: University of Notre Dame Press, 1988.
Maimonides, Moses. *The Guide for the Perplexed.* 2nd ed. Trans. M. Friedländer. New York: Dover, 1956.
Masih, Y. *A Comparative Study of Religions.* Delhi: Motilals Banarsidass, 2000.
Matson, Wallace. *A New History of Philosophy: From Thales to Ockham, Vol. 1.* 2nd ed. San Diego: Harcourt College Publishers, 2000.
McClendon, James, and James Smith. *Convictions: Defusing Religious Relativism.* Eugene, OR: Wipf & Stock, 1994.
Menon, Sangeetha. "Hinduism and Science." In *The Oxford Handbook of Religion and Science*, edited by Philip Clayton and Zachary Simpson, 7–23. Oxford: Oxford University Press, 2006.
MisirHiralall, Sabrina D. *Confronting Orientalism: A Self-Study of Educating through Hindu Dance.* Rotterdam, NL: Sense, 2017.
Murphy, Nancey. *Anglo-American Postmodernity: Philosophical Perspectives on Science, Religion, and Ethics.* Boulder, CO: Westview, 1997.
———. *Bodies and Souls, or Spirited Bodies?* Cambridge: Cambridge University Press, 2006.
———. "Divine Action in the Natural Order: Buridan's Ass and Schrödinger's Cat." In *Chaos and Complexity: Scientific Perspectives on Divine Action*, edited by Robert J. Russell, Nancey Murphy, and Arthur Peacocke, 325–57. Berkeley, CA: The Center for Theology and the Natural Sciences, 1995.
———. "Emergence, Downward Causation and Divine Action." In *Scientific Perspectives on Divine Action: Twenty Years of Challenge and Progress*, edited

by Robert J. Russell, Nancey Murphy, and William Stoeger, SJ, 111–31. Oxford: Oxford University Press, 2007.
———. *A Philosophy of The Christian Religion for the Twentieth Century*. London: SPCK, 2018.
———. *Reasoning and Rhetoric in Religion*. Eugene, OR: Wipf and Stock, 2001.
———. "Reductionism: How Did We Fall into It and Can We Emerge from It?" In *Evolution and Emergence: Systems, Organisms, Persons*, edited by Nancey Murphy and William R. Stoeger, SJ, 19–39. Oxford: Oxford University Press, 2007.
Murphy, Nancey, and Warren S. Brown. *Did My Neurons Make Me Do It? Philosophical and Neurobiological Perspectives on Moral Responsibility and Free Will*. Oxford: Oxford University Press, 2007.
Nasr, Seyyed Hossein. *An Introduction to Islamic Cosmological Doctrines: Conceptions of Nature and Methods Used for Its Study by the Ikwān, Al-Safā, Al-Bīrūnī, and Ibn Sīnā*. Albany, NY: State University of New York Press, 1993.
———. *Knowledge and the Sacred*. New York: The Crossroad, 1981.
———. *The Need for a Sacred Science*. Albany, NY: State University of New York Press, 1993.
———. *Religion and the Order of Nature: The 1994 Cadbury Lectures at the University of Birmingham*. Oxford: Oxford University Press, 1996.
———. *Science and Civilization in Islam*. Cambridge: Harvard University Press, 1968.
Neely, Alan. "Incarnational Mission." *Evangelical Dictionary of World Missions*, edited by A. Scott Moreau, Harold A. Netland, Charles Edward van Engen, and David Burnett, 474–75. Grand Rapids: Baker, 2000.
Olson, Dennis T. "The Book of Judges: Introduction, Commentary, and Reflections." In *The New Interpreter's Bible: A Commentary in Twelve Volumes, Vol. II*, edited by Leander E. Keck et al., 723–946. Nashville, TN: Abingdon, 1998.
Orchard, Ronald. *Missions in a Time of Testing*. Philadelphia: Westminster, 1964.
Peacocke, Arthur R. "God's Interaction with the World: The Implications of Deterministic 'Chaos' and of Interconnected and Interdependent Complexity." In *Chaos and Complexity: Scientific Perspectives on Divine Action*, edited by Robert J. Russell, Nancey Murphy, Peacocke, 263–87. Berkeley, CA: The Center for Theology and the Natural Sciences, 2000.
Perl, Eric D. *Thinking Being: Introduction to Metaphysics in the Classical Tradition*. Leiden: Brill, 2014.
Pessin, Sarah. *Ibn Gabirol's Theology of Desire: Matter and Method in Jewish Medieval Neoplatonism*. Cambridge: Cambridge University Press, 2013.
———. "The Influence of Islamic Thought on Maimonides." In *Stanford Encyclopedia of Philosophy*, edited by Edward N. Zalta. Accessed May 5, 2020. https://plato.stanford.edu/entries/maimonides-islamic/.
———. "Solomon Ibn Gabirol [Avicebron]." In *Stanford Encyclopedia of Philosophy*, edited by Edward N. Zalta. Accessed May 5, 2020. https://plato.stanford.edu/entries/ibn-gabirol/.
Peters, F. E. *Aristotle and the Arabs: The Aristotelian Tradition in Islam*. New York: New York University Press, 1968.
Placher, William. *Unapologetic Theology: A Christian Voice in a Pluralistic Conversation*. Louisville, KY: Westminster/John Knox, 1989.

Pocock, Michael, Gailyn Van Rheenen, and Douglas McConnell. *The Changing Face of World Missions: Engaging Contemporary Issues and Trends.* Grand Rapids: Baker Academic, 2005.

Polkinghorne, John. *Science and Creation: The Search for Understanding.* Philadelphia: Templeton Foundation, 2006.

Race, Alan. *Christians and Religious Pluralism: Patterns in the Christian Theology of Religions.* Maryknoll, NY: Orbis, 1982.

Roberts, Dana. "Rethinking Missionaries from 1910 to Today." Presented at the "Rethink Mission" Conference, Nashville, TN, October 14–17, 2010.

Robinson, James B. *Religions of the World: Hinduism.* Philadelphia: Chelsea House, 2004.

Rudderman, David B. *Jewish Thought and Scientific Discovery in Early Modern Europe.* New Haven, CT: Yale University Press, 1995.

Russell, Robert J. *Cosmology, Evolution, and Resurrection Hope: Theology and Science in Creative Mutual Interaction.* London: Pandora, 2006.

———. *Cosmology: From Alpha to Omega—The Creative Mutual Interaction of Theology and Science.* Minneapolis, MN: Fortress, 2008.

Russell, Robert J., Nancey Murphy, William Stoeger, SJ. *Scientific Perspectives on Divine Action: Twenty Years of Challenge and Progress.* Berkeley, CA: The Center for Theology and the Natural Sciences, 2008.

Russell, Robert John, Philip Clayton, Kirk Wegter-McNelly, John Polkinghorne, eds. *Quantum Mechanics: Scientific Perspectives on Divine Action.* Berkeley, CA: The Center for Theology and the Natural Sciences, 2001.

Schindler, D. C. *The Catholicity of Reason.* Grand Rapids: Eerdmans, 2013.

Schlieter, Jens. "Did the Buddha Emerge from a Brahmanic Environment? The Early Buddhist Evaluation of 'Noble Brahmins' and the 'Ideological System' of Brahmanism." In *Dynamics in the History of Religions between Asia and Europe: Encounters, Notions, and Comparative Perspectives,* edited by Volkhard Krech and Marion Steiniche, 137–48. Boston: Brill, 2012.

Schmidt-Leukel, Perry. "Bridging the Gulf." In *Buddhism, Christianity and the Question of Creation: Karmic or Divine?* edited by Schmidt-Leukel, 143–76. Burlington, VT: Ashgate, 2006.

Seeskin, Kenneth. "Maimonides." In *Stanford Encyclopedia of Philosophy,* edited by Edward N. Zalta. Accessed May 5, 2020. https://plato.stanford.edu/entries/maimonides/.

Sela, Shlomo. *Abraham Ibn Ezra and the Rise of Medieval Hebrew Science.* Boston: Brill, 2003.

Sonn, Tamara "Tawḥīd." In *The Oxford Encyclopedia of the Islamic World, Vol. 5,* edited by John L. Esposito, 144–60. Oxford: Oxford University Press, 2009.

Stephan, Achim. "Emergence—A Systematic View on Its Historical Facets." In *Emergence or Reduction? Essays on the Prospects of Nonreductive Physicalism,* edited by Ansagar Beckermann, Hans Flohr, and Jaegwon Kim, 25–48. New York: de Gruyter, 1992.

Stromberg, Jean. *Mission and Evangelism: An Ecumenical Affirmation.* Geneva: World Council of Churches, 1983.

Swinburne, Richard. *The Concept of Miracle.* London: MacMillan, 1970.

Ten Boom, Corrie, Elizabeth and John Sherrill. *The Hiding Place.* 35th anniversary ed. Grand Rapids: Chosen, 2006.

Thapar, Romila. *Early India: From Origins to AD 1300*. Berkeley, CA: University of California Press, 2002.

Tonelli, Giorgio. "Mendelssohn, Moses." In *The Encyclopedia of Philosophy*, Vol. 5, edited by Paul Edwards, 276–77. New York: MacMillan, 1967.

Trible, Phyllis. *Texts of Terror: Literary-Feminist Readings of Biblical Narratives*. Philadelphia: Fortress, 1984.

Vatican II Council. *Nostra Aetate (Declaration on the Relation of the Church to Non-Christian Religions)*. Accessed April 29, 2020. https://www.vatican.va/archive/hist_councils/ii_vatican_council/documents/vat-ii_decl_19651028_nostra-aetate_en.html.

Verkuyl, Johannes. *Contemporary Missiology: An Introduction*. Grand Rapids: Eerdmans, 1978.

Wall, Robert W. "The Acts of the Apostles: Introduction, Commentary, and Reflections." *New Interpreter's Bible: A Commentary in Twelve Volumes, Vol. X: Acts, Introduction to Epistolary Literature, Romans, 1 Corinthians*. Nashville, TN: Abingdon, 2002.

Watt, W. Montgomery. *Islamic Philosophy and Theology: An Extended Survey*. Edinburgh: Edinburgh University Press, 1985.

Werpehowski, William. "Ad Hoc Apologetics." *Journal of Religion* 66 (1986) 282–301.

Wesley, John. "Notes on the Gospel according to St. Luke." In *Explanatory Notes upon the New Testament, Vol. I*, edited by Thomas Cordeux, 167–257. London: Thomas Cordeux, 1813.

———. "Sermon 36: The Law Established through Faith: Discourse 2." In *The Works of John Wesley: Complete and Unabridged*, Vol. V. *Sermons on Several Occasions, Vol. I*, 458–66. 3rd ed. Grand Rapids: Baker, 1984.

———. "Sermon 37: The Nature of Enthusiasm." In *The Works of John Wesley: Complete and Unabridged*, Vol. V. *Sermons on Several Occasions, Vol. I*, 467–78. 3rd ed. Grand Rapids: Baker, 1984.

———. "Sermon 38: The Nature of Enthusiasm." In *The Works of John Wesley: Complete and Unabridged*, Vol. V. *Sermons on Several Occasions, Vol. I*, , 479–92. 3rd ed. Grand Rapids: Baker, 1984.

———. "Sermon 67: On Divine Providence." In *The Works of John Wesley: Complete and Unabridged*, Vol. VI. *Sermons on Several Occasions, Vol. II*, 313–25. 3rd ed. Grand Rapids: Baker, 1984.

———. "Sermon 139: On Love." In *The Works of John Wesley: Complete and Unabridged*, Vol. VII. *Sermons on Several Occasions, Vol. III*, 492–99. 3rd ed. Peabody, MA: Hendrickson, 1984.

Whitehead, Alfred North. *Process and Reality: An Essay in Cosmology*. Corrected ed. Edited by David Ray Griffin and Donald W. Sherburne. New York: Free, 1978.

Wildman, Wesley. "The Divine Action Project, 1988–2003." *Theology and Science* 2.1 (2004) 31–75.

Wilson, Frederick R., ed. *The San Antonio Report: Your Will Be Done: Mission in Christ's Way*. Geneva: WCC, 1989.

World Council of Churches. "Mission and Evangelism in Unity Today." Conference on World Mission and Evangelism. Athens, Greece, 12–19 May 2005. Accessed April 29, 2020. http://www.wcc-coe.org/wcc/what/mission/m-e-in-unity.pdf.

Index

A

ātman, 168–69
Abraham, 15, 19
Abrahamic. *See* tradition(s), Abrahamic
ad hoc apologetic approach, 48, 49, 54, 61
'adl, 105–6
ahiṃsā, 176–77, 187
al-Ash'arī, 105–8
al-Fārābī, 55, 108–9, 111, 128–29, 134
al-Ghazālī, 55–56, 103–4, 110–14, 116–18, 120, 128, 134, 138, 185
alien, 8, 16–19, 25, 27
    foreigner, 15–22, 25–27, 47, 75
    stranger, 17, 25–6
al-Juwaynī, 111
al-Kindī, 55
Allah, 102
Almohad, 128, 132–33
Aquinas, 33, 35, 55–57, 111, 115–17, 123, 128, 131–34, 138, 185
Arabic, 103, 117, 122, 124, 128, 132, 133
Aristotelian, Aristotelianism, 42, 55, 57, 68, 91, 103, 109, 111, 113, 114, 117–18, 124, 135–36
Aristotle, 34, 37, 42, 55–56, 90, 103, 109, 113–15, 118, 128–29, 132, 134

Ash'arite. *See* tradition(s), Ash'arite
Asymmetry, 54, 81
ātman, 168–69
atomism, 91–2, 106–7, 137, 157–58, 178, 186
Augustine, 3, 33, 35, 55, 84
Augustinian. *See* tradition(s), Augustinian
Avatars, *avatāra*, 168
Averroës, 55–56, 112, 115–17
Avicebron, 124–25
Avicenna, 55–56, 108, 111, 113–14, 116–17, 126, 129, 131, 133–34, 185

B

Barth, Karl, 35
Berkley, George, 93
Bhagavad gītā, 164, 170, 178
Bodhi tree, 147, 187
Bohr, Niels, 97
Boyle, Robert, 93–94, 156
Brāhmaṇas, 163
Brahmā, 143, 166–67, 169
brahman, 169, 171, 172, 178
Brahmanism, 166
brahmins, 163, 166, 171–73, 187, 196
Buddha, 6, 33, 146–48, 151–52, 187
Buddhism, 10, 142–43, 144–60, 162, 166, 171, 184, 186
Burrell, David, 134

C

Caliphate, 124
Calvin, John, 33, 35–36
caste system, 33, 164, 173–75, 187
Catholic, 3–6, 40, 67, 68n7
causal joint, 153
causation, 32, 84, 92, 97, 104, 108–10, 114, 120, 152, 157–58
Christ, 1–7, 9, 10, 13, 24, 29n2, 33, 64, 66–73, 78, 88
Christianity. *See* tradition(s), Christian
Christocentrism, 3
church fathers, 3, 29, 36
Cobb, John, 154–56
Coke, Thomas, 36
Comte, Auguste, 33
conceptual categories, schemes, resources, 32–3, 37–38, 40–41, 55, 58, 117, 184
conversation. *See* dialogue, interreligious
conversion, 3, 7–9, 13–14, 21, 25, 27–28, 34, 63–65, 67–68, 78
convert, 1, 3, 7, 65, 67, 70, 132, 181
conviction, ix, x, 1–2, 6
Copernicus, 34, 42, 90–91
cosmological
    argument, 129–30
    model (theories), 90, 120, 150–51, 157, 166, 187
    system, 103, 142
cosmology, 42, 50, 91, 120, 146, 148, 151, 153, 166–67, 184
covenant, 15–20, 65–66
creatio continua, 87–8
creatio ex nihilo, 123–24
creation, 84, 86–9, 93–4, 99–100, 104, 107–9, 111, 114, 116, 120, 126–27, 129–31, 136, 138, 142, 145, 148, 150, 156, 162, 164, 166, 169, 184–85
creator. *See* God, Creator
crisis. *See* epistemological crisis

D

Darwin, 34, 119
Deacon, Terrence, 158
decoupling, 157–58
deism, 85, 87, 101
deity. *See,* God, deity
Democritus, 34, 91
Descartes, René, 30–31, 91, 154
determinism, 92, 95, 137–38, 157, 159, 178, 186
dharma, 147, 164, 166–68, 171, 173–74, 187
dhimmī, 132
dialogue, interreligious, ix–x, xi, 1–4, 6–15, 21, 26–27, 28–30, 37, 39, 40, 43–45, 46–61, 62–63, 68, 78, 81–83, 116, 118, 120, 133–34, 142, 177, 181–88
dipolar, 155
divine action, 9, 85–90, 95–100, 101–11, 115–16, 121, 126, 131–32, 134, 135, 144–45, 152, 154–56, 157–60, 162, 177–78, 184, 186
    extraordinary acts, 88–89, 99, 156
    general, 84, 86, 88–90, 99, 102, 109–11, 115, 121, 123, 137, 184
    immanentism, 88, 93, 95–96, 100
    interventionism, 92–93, 95–96
    providence, 9–10, 81–2, 84, 85–89, 92–5, 99–100, 101–4, 115, 117, 119–21, 122–23, 129, 131–38, 142, 144, 150–51, 156, 157, 159, 185
    mighty acts of God, 88–89
    miracles, 85, 88–89, 92, 104, 111–12, 136, 156
    revelation, 5–6, 9–10, 37, 66–67, 71n17, 82, 84, 85, 88–90, 100, 112, 118, 123, 143–44, 153, 159, 162–63, 165, 169–76, 180, 184, 186–87

special, 9–10, 81–82, 85, 88, 89, 90, 92–96, 100, 102, 104, 110–12, 115, 120–21, 123, 131, 137–38, 144–45, 156, 157, 159, 169, 176, 184
Divine Action Project, 154, 157–59, 186

E

ecclesiocentrism, 3, 6
ecumenical, 4
Egypt, 16–17, 20, 25, 89, 128
Einstein, 34, 37, 153, 156
electrons, 96–97, 186
Ellis, George, 96
emanation, 9, 103–4, 108–11, 119–20, 122–27, 129–31, 133–34, 138, 168, 184
emergence, 157–58, 179
empathy, 47, 54, 56–57, 61, 64, 82, 111
Epicurus, 34, 91
epistemological crisis, 9–10, 40–45, 51–58, 61, 81–83, 85–86, 90, 93–94, 98, 100, 102–3, 104, 108–17, 121, 123, 126, 134, 137–38, 143–45, 150, 153, 154, 156, 159–60, 162–63, 165, 170, 176, 178, 180, 182–88
epistemology, 37, 68, 175
esse, 134, 137, 185
evangelism, 4, 10, 14, 69, 73
exclusivism, 3, 5
extraordinary acts. *See* divine action

F

Faiths. *See* tradition(s), faith traditions
Falk, Randall M., 48–49, 56
Farrer, Austin, 153
Fletcher, John William, 36
Fons Vitae, 124
foreigner, 15–22, 25–27, 47, 75
Four Noble Truths, 147
four signs, 146

G

Galileo, 34, 42, 90, 156
Gaon, Saadia, 124, 133
Gassendi, Pierre, 91
Gautama, Siddhārtha, 146–47
General Board of Global Ministries (GBGM), 74
Gentiles, 22, 24, 65–6
God, gods, 6, 15, 17, 20–21, 25–27, 35, 41, 55, 66–67, 105–6, 118, 148–49, 152, 155–56, 168–69
  action of. *See* divine action
  creator, 86, 93–94, 108, 119, 130, 142, 145, 151, 152, 162, 166, 169, 186, 187
  deity, 143, 145, 167, 169
  descriptions of, conceptions of, xi, 7, 9–10, 29–30, 33, 37–40, 44–5, 51, 59, 61, 62–3, 65, 141–43, 181–87
  the divine, 6, 36, 37, 44, 50, 59, 119, 142, 150, 152, 153, 171, 173, 183
  experiences of, 9, 32, 36,
  kingdom of, 21, 24, 26, 33, 49, 71, 77, 87–88
  mission of. *See missio dei*
  presence of, 3, 4–5, 16, 63–5, 70–71, 73, 119
  prevenient, 64–65, 68–69, 73
  revelation of. *See* divine action, revelation
  salvation, 2, 52, 29n2, 65, 68, 74, 152
  Trinity, triune, 4, 73, 88
grace, 2, 7, 21, 27, 33, 55, 64, 65, 68, 73
Greek philosophy, 9, 55, 103, 106, 108, 111, 114, 115–17, 118, 121, 128, 133, 136, 184–85
Griffin, David Ray, 155
gurus, 171–73, 175, 187

H

Hamilton, Adam, 60

Hamilton, Sue, 162–63
Harrelson, Walter J., 48–49, 56
Hartshorne, Charles, 155
Haskalah, 136
Hick, John, 5–6
Hinduism. *See* tradition(s), Hindu
Hooykaas, Reijer, 93
hospitality, ix–x, xi, 7–8, 13–15, 18–21, 25–27, 58–61, 76
humility, ix–x, xi, 8, 30, 40, 44–45, 46–47, 51–53, 56, 61, 62, 64, 71, 73–74, 78, 176, 182–84, 187

I

Ibn Gabirol, 123–28, 132–34, 185
Ibn Sīnā. *See* Avicenna
immanentism. *See* divine action
incarnation, 64–65, 70–71, 78
incarnational mission, 65, 69–73, 78
inclusivism, 5
incommensurate, incommensurability, 39, 142
interventionism. *See* divine action
Iqbal, Muzaffar, 118
Irāda, 124, 126–27
ishtadeva, 169
Islam. *See* tradition(s), Islamic
Islamic Golden Age. *See* science, Islamic Golden Age of
Israel, Israelites, 15–20, 22, 25, 66, 89, 136n31

J

jāti, 173–74
Jenkins, Philip, 74
Jesus. *See* Christ
Judaism. *See* tradition(s), Jewish
justification, 14, 85, 91, 184

K

Kabbalah, 135
kalpas, 142, 148, 166
karma, 32–33, 39, 148–53, 156, 165, 167–68, 171, 174, 186–87

Khan, Deeyah, 23
Kierkegaard, Søren, 72
kingdom of God, 21, 24, 26, 33, 71, 77, 87–88
Klausner, Joseph, 127
Knott, Kim, 162–64, 168–75
Kuhn, Thomas, 38

L

laws of nature, 37, 92–94, 97, 120, 150, 153, 158, 186–87
Leucippus, 91
Levite, 14, 18–21, 26
liberation,
  theology, 53
  from cycle of rebirth, 150, 167, 172
Lipner, Julius, 168
Luther, Martin, 33, 36, 42

M

MacIntyre, Alasdair, 30–31, 34–36, 41, 52, 57, 67, 82, 165, 173–74
MacIntyrean, 117, 162
mahākalpa. *See* kalpas
mahā-yuga. *See* yugas
Malebranche, Nicolas, 93
Marcion, Marcionism, 15
Maurice, Frederick D., 69
medieval period, 9–10, 42, 55–6, 82, 89, 100, 102–4, 110, 115–16, 121–23, 124, 129, 133–37, 141, 184, 186
meditation, 145, 147, 151, 172
Mendelssohn, Moses, 136
Messiah, 36, 147n3
metaphysics, 90, 106, 109, 114, 120, 133, 150, 156, 159, 160, 166–67, 170, 177–78, 183–84
Middle Ages, 86, 89, 90, 102n3, 104n7, 117
mighty acts. *See* divine action
Mill, John Stuart, 33
miracles. *See* divine action
MisirHiralall, Sabrina D., xii, 175

missio dei, 4, 69, 74–75
missions, xii, 4, 9–10, 61, 62–78, 100, 103, 110, 113, 115, 118, 120, 121, 135, 160, 185–86
modern period, 42, 57, 85–86, 88–89, 92–94
mokṣa, 32-3, 167, 172, 175
Muḥammad, 33, 35, 89, 171
Murphy, Nancey, xii, 55, 96–98, 159, 177, 186
Muʿtazila, Muʿtazilites, 105–8, 129
mutual constructive engagement, xi, 10, 45, 50, 54, 56, 58, 61, 63, 64, 78, 79–83, 102, 115, 121, 135, 138, 139–43, 160, 163, 176, 180, 185, 188

N

Naḥmanides, 135–36
Nasr, Seyyed Hossein, 57–58, 102, 118–20
Neely, Alan, 69
Neoplatonism, 9, 91, 104n7
Newton, 34, 37, 42, 90, 156,
Newtonian physics. *See* science, Newtonian
NIODA, 95, 98–99, 157, 186
nirvāna, 32–33, 145, 147, 149, 150, 152, 153
Noble Eightfold Path, 149
Nostra Aetate, 4

O

occasionalism, 85, 87, 98, 101, 107, 108
Ogden, Schubert, 155
ontology, ontological, 37, 91, 185

P

panentheism, 155
Pannenberg, Wolfhart, 35
parabrahman, 177–79
paradigm, 30, 38, 64
Paul, Apostle, 63–64, 77
Peacocke, Arthur, 159

Perry Schmidt-Leukel, 152
Peter, Apostle, 64–65
Placher, William, 48
pluralism, ix, 5–6, 30, 141
    identist, 6
    deep, 6, 30, 36, 37, 38, 44–45, 49, 78, 141, 182, 184
Pocock, Michael, 71
Polkinghorne, John, 159
prevenient. *See* God, previence
process thought
    philosophy, 154–55
    theology, 117, 154–55, 178–79
proselytization, 2, 8, 29, 46, 64
Protestantism, 74, 135
providence. *See* divine action
Ptolemy, 34, 37, 42
Purusha, 171, 173, 178

Q

quantum physics, 37, 50, 96–99, 137, 157–59, 179, 186
qudra, 104, 106–8, 117
Qurʾān, 33, 35, 55, 105, 109, 112, 118, 120, 123, 184

R

rational resources, 30, 32, 33–38, 40–45, 49, 51–52, 54, 81, 94, 117, 174
rationality, 31, 36, 43–44, 165, 183, 184
    standards of, 34–35, 43, 54, 141, 142
    forms of, 170, 173, 175, 187
Rawls, John, 33
reality-centrism, 6
rebirth. *See* reincarnation
reductionism, 92, 120, 137–38, 157–58, 178–79, 186
reincarnation, 32, 142, 148–49, 151, 165, 167, 172
relativism, 30, 43, 45, 51, 61, 181, 183
religions, *See* tradition(s), faith traditions

revelation. *See* divine action, revelation
Russell, Robert J., 95–96, 154, 157, 180, 186

S

sages, 171–73, 187
salvation, 2–3, 5, 29n2, 65, 68, 74, 152
saṃsāra, 32–3, 142, 148–50, 156, 167, 171, 172, 174–75, 186–87
Samaritan, 15, 21–24, 26, 76
sampradaya, 172
satya, 177, 187
Schleiermacher, Friedrich, 35
science, 38, 62
    Buddhism and, 150, 154–60
    Hinduism and, 161–65, 170, 173
    Islam and, 145, 150, 176–80
    Islamic Golden Age of, 55–56, 102, 122, 132
    Islamization of, 117
    Judaism and, 124, 127, 128, 133, 135–38
    laws of, 37, 92–94, 97, 120, 150, 153, 158, 186–87
    medieval, 103
    modern, 9–10, 42, 82, 86, 90–97, 102, 118, 123, 135–38, 143, 145, 154–60, 161–65, 170, 173, 176–80, 184, 186–87
    Newtonian, 9, 96, 118, 137, 145, 150, 154, 157, 185
    paradigms in, 38
    philosophy of, 57
    reductionism in. *See* reductionism
    Western, 57, 85, 115, 118–21, 150
scientia sacra, 118
Second Vatican Council, 3
Seeskin, Kenneth, 130
Shankara-acharayas, 172
Shiva, 143, 169, 175
shruti, 170, 172–75, 187
smriti, 170, 173, 175, 187

Spinoza, 136
superposition, 96–97

T

Tathāgata, 147
tawḥīd, 102, 109, 111, 114
ten Booms, 7–8, 60
theodicy, 87, 152
Tillich, Paul, 35
top-down causation, 120, 157–58
Torah, 21, 33, 123, 125, 128, 131, 132, 137, 184
Tracy, Thomas, 96
tradition(s), 8–10, 28–61, 62–64, 70, 70n17, 78, 82, 100, 135, 180, 183
    Abrahamic, 9, 10, 49, 78, 81, 89, 100, 137–38, 141–45, 150, 151, 184, 186–87
    Aristotelian, 42, 55, 57, 68, 91, 103, 109, 111, 113–14, 117, 118, 124, 135–36
    Ash'arite, 105–6, 108–9, 111–12, 114
    Augustinian, 55–57, 117
    Buddhist, x, 32, 142, 143, 144–60, 166–67, 186–87
    Christian, 2–5, 7, 9, 10, 13, 14, 23, 32, 33, 35–36, 40, 42–43, 48–49, 53, 55, 57, 61, 63–66, 68–71, 73–74, 76–78, 81–82, 84–100, 103–4, 115–18, 120–23, 132–35, 137, 142, 145, 152–60, 163–64, 171, 176–79, 184, 186
    Eastern, 10, 139–43, 146, 184, 186
    Enlightenment, 30, 33, 64, 70, 75, 78, 133, 136, 146, 162, 163, 164, 169, 175, 177
    faith traditions, religious, religions, ix–xi, 2–10, 13, 14, 27, 28–39, 43–47, 49, 58–62, 64, 65, 68, 73, 78, 89, 132, 135, 142, 145, 153, 162, 164, 174, 180–88

Greek, 9, 55, 82, 91, 103, 106–8, 111, 114, 115, 117, 118, 121, 126, 128, 136, 141, 184–86
Hindu, 10, 32, 142, 143, 160, 161–80, 184, 186–87
Islamic, 55–7, 60, 82, 89, 101–21, 122–24, 129, 132, 137, 185–86
Jewish, 49, 55, 71n17, 82, 89, 102, 116, 121, 122–38, 185–86
Newtonian. *See* science, Newtonian
scientific, 34, 37–38, 42, 50, 57, 81–82, 85, 89, 90, 95–96, 102, 115, 118–19, 132, 144, 150, 156, 157, 159, 177–80, 186
sub-, 35–36, 82, 165, 169
Thomistic, 68, 114, 155
Western. *See* tradition(s), Enlightenment
transcendent, 151–52, 163, 168
truth, ix, 5, 28–29, 41–44, 49–43, 56, 62–63, 71, 85, 112–13, 116–17, 126, 135, 147, 151, 169, 172, 177, 182, 188

U

Ultimate reality, 6, 10, 29, 30, 32, 39, 86, 125, 142, 143, 145, 178, 182
Umayyad, 104
Upaniṣads, 143, 170, 177, 178

V

Vedas, 33, 163–66, 170–73, 175
  Ṛg Veda, 164, 171
Vedic, 166, 168–71
Verkuyl, Johannes, 70
Vishnu, 143, 169

W

Werpehowski, William, 48
Wesley, John, 33, 36, 64, 68, 73
Whitehead, Alfred North, 154–56
World Council of Churches, WCC, 4, 64, 68–69, 73, 78

Y

YHWH, 15–17, 19–20, 25, 65
yugas, 142, 166–68